Not Like Other Nations

Toward An Ideal State

†

†

Mirror Of Justice Society

Not Like Other Nations

Toward An Ideal State

Non fecit táliter omni natióni, et judícia sua non manifestávit eis.

He hath not done in like manner to every nation, and his judgments he hath not made manifest to them.

Ps. 147:9 (146:20)

Mirror Of Justice Society © 2025

†

Copyright 2025 by Mirror Of Justice Society – R. Michael McGowan (editor); Peter E. Chojnowski, Ph.D.; John O'Neill Green, J.D.; Hendrik A. Mills, M.S.; and others.

All rights reserved. Except for purposes of review or commentary, no part of this book may be reproduced or transmitted in any form or by any means, electronic or mechanical, including photocopying, recording, or by any information storage or retrieval systems, nor may its contents be altered in any way, without written permission from the publisher. The authoritative text of this book is that found in the hardcover print edition.

First edition, first printing — December 8, 2025

Contact the Mirror Of Justice Society at *MOJS@keemail.me*

Mirror Of Justice Society : *Not Like Other Nations: Toward An Ideal State*

ISBN: 979-8-9925791-1-6 (paperback)

Cover by Nicholas F. Ries

All other graphics, design and production, are by the editor.

†

Hiláro Bélloco ac Gilbérto Cestratónae,
expositóribus bellatoribúsque exímiis
pro doctrína sociále cathólica tempóribus
modérnis, hic liber est dedicátus, cum grátiis
máximis.
Jesus Christus, Rex Omnium Natiónum atque
illórum, et María, eorúndem Regína,
praemium idóneum illis útinam déderint
sempitérnum.

†

TABLE OF CONTENTS

General Introduction.. p. i – iii

Chapter 1 : God And Man.. p. 1
Chapter 2 : Man And Man.. p. 7
Chapter 3 : Man And The State... p. 27
Chapter 4 : The Church And The State...................................... p. 35
Chapter 5 : Forms Of State Government................................... p. 55
Chapter 6 : Matrimony And The State....................................... p. 85
Chapter 7 : Gender Equality And Inequality............................. p. 97
Preparatory Note For Following Chapters.................................. p. 114
Chapter 8 : Private Property And The State............................. p. 115
Chapter 9 : Economic Equality And Inequality........................ p. 125

Appendix 1: On Ranking The Value Of Human Goods............ p. 139
Appendix 2 : On Civil Obedience, Disobedience, Rebellion..... p. 145
Appendix 3 : On Moral Hazard And The Welfare State........... p. 153
Glossary.. p. 157
Index... p. 167

GENERAL INTRODUCTION

The Purpose

This is a guide to Christian governance, meant primarily to help a devout Catholic believer who finds himself in a position of political power, whether modest or great, to do justice to the people of his jurisdiction. He will find here a condensed source of doctrine on the most important matters concerning social life, and at intervals, principles of action, derived from that doctrine, that can be applied to those matters. Those who are in a position of supreme political power in a nation will be able to implement justice more fully than those who exercise some limited authority within a system hostile or indifferent to our Creator: the one, true God. But whatever degree of influence a person may have, the ideas and principles herein will act as a line of streetlights in the darkness, enabling him to do what he can to truly serve the material and spiritual well-being of his brothers and sisters over whom he exercises authority.

It may sometimes happen that a person of good will attains influence and political authority without having a chance or even an intention of thinking through a consistent plan of governance. Such a person has an opportunity to make decisions which will be either a blessing on thousands or even millions of fellow human beings – or a curse on them. For such a ruler, the well-thought-out principles in this book can lead him in blessing his town, city, county, province, state, or nation with wise rule based on the infinite wisdom of God. These principles are derived from divine revelation as recorded in the Sacred Scriptures, developed and elucidated over the course of two millennia by the doctors, popes, saints, political rulers and thinkers of the Catholic Church, and confirmed by reason and the lessons of history.

A person who soberly considers the proper way to govern before attaining any political power will also greatly improve the wisdom of his future decisions by studying and assimilating the principles presented herein. Of course, in the actual implementation of these principles, a person in power must prudently take into account the specific conditions which prevail in his nation and in his jurisdiction. A full actualization of these ideas is hardly possible unless the bulk of the nation is already convinced of the truth of the Gospel of Jesus Christ, along with the orthodox Catholic interpretation of it, and is trying to live according to its precepts.

All those in authority, however limited or vast the authority may be, should remember that there is a greater Authority to whom they must give an account of their actions at the end of their lives. They should recall to mind, every day, that each order that they issue, together with the intention behind each order, will one day be reviewed by a Supreme Judge who cannot be deceived.

What simple idea must the ruler adopt to prepare for this inevitable Judgment? The words of Our Lord Jesus Christ reveal the heart of this matter: "'Thou shalt love the Lord thy God, with thy whole heart, and with thy whole soul, and with thy whole mind, and with thy whole strength.' That is the First Commandment. And the second is like to it: 'Thou shalt love thy neighbor as thyself.' There is no other commandment greater than these."

This work aims to point out to the wielder of power how this love of God and of neighbor may be effected in practice. It is applicable to every continent, to every race, and to every culture found in the various places on God's earth. Because this Guide is based on *eternal* principles, the contents herein are applicable also to every historical era, even far into the future.

The Plan

We endeavor to work from the ground up; to proceed from the deepest realities to the more superficial or less important. We may say we are trying to build a house; one that will hold together solidly and endure as long as possible; a house able to contain the entire human family, and provide for them a congenial life, not indeed devoid of suffering and sacrifice – for what worthy person wishes to live a life vacant of the noble deeds that these require? – but one in which such suffering is tempered in good part by the commiseration of like-thinking and like-feeling brothers and sisters.

Our house will be solid in the measure that it will be built in incrementally strong and well-placed layers. Firstly we need to find a good building site – an elevated area that no flood can touch, under the soil of which we can find monolithic bedrock upon which to place our foundation. This bedrock is the Natural Law, which must be hardened by the additional cementitious bonds of the ancient and immutable Catholic Faith.

On this bedrock we must set our foundation: a foundation made of high-strength concrete, with rebar reinforcement to hold it all together, to prevent cracks and resist earthquakes. This is the Political System.

On this foundation, we can build the house proper: well-framed, mutually supportive walls, sustaining a solid roof. This will be the Economic System.

Finally, we will want to install doors, windows, plumbing, climate controls, furniture, and even suitable decorations and art. This would be the various institutions of culture: medical, military, educational, artistic, and all the rest.

We will therefore view the study of human society under the following heads, in order of importance:

1. Religion

2. Politics

3. Economics

4. Culture

This present book covers the first two headings. We are working on additional volume(s) that will treat of the third and fourth headings.

Of the most basic concepts and elements of society, with which the present book deals, some of these are specific to a Catholic society, but many are also of the Natural Law, and essential to any human society whatever. When the latter is true we will for the most part point this out explicitly. As we will see, the principles of religion and politics are closely interlaced, and so we will treat of both together.

Now here it seems apropos to state a consoling fact:

Life can indeed be wonderfully complicated, but it has a way of wonderfully *un*complicating itself when one keeps the most essential things in the foreground.

The old philosophical axiom is true: *A small mistake in first principles leads to big mistakes in the end*. But it has a corollary: *No mistakes in first principles means no big mistakes in the end.*

From ancient times up through the high middle ages there was hardly any science of, for example, economics or culture. In the high middle ages, outstanding economy and culture just *happened*. It was the natural and inevitable result of living, because life was driven by the moral principles of the true religion. In the measure that these principles were acted out, a functional politics, and life in general, just took care of itself.

As Pius XI has said so wisely:

> Indeed, all the institutions for the establishment of peace and the promotion of mutual help among men, however perfect these may seem, have the principal foundation of their stability in the mutual bond of minds and hearts whereby the members are united with one another. If this bond is lacking, the best of regulations come to naught, as we have learned by too frequent experience.[1]

Or better, as Wisdom Himself said:
"Seek ye first the kingdom of God, and His justice, and all these things shall be added unto you."

This book contains many actionable Principles, but that Principle of principles, from the King of kings, contains them all.

Finally, we must inform the reader that this work has been a collaboration of a number of individuals, some of whom wish to remain anonymous for various reasons.[2] It must be taken for granted that, due to the fallibility of human nature, we cannot possibly pretend that the authors and contributors to this work have agreed in every detail of its assertions. The contributors have come from a wide variety of backgrounds, and they were chosen for that very reason; so that the widest possible view of things might be obtained. Every single Principle that we propose has been thoroughly discussed. These discussions have at times been quite...animated (read *stressful*). Nevertheless, all the contributors have striven to place Truth before their own personal opinions. As may be imagined, it was not easy to do this (for original sin is the most persistent of enemies). After discussion, the Principles were voted on. Recognizing – *of course* – that Truth is not a function of majority vote, it is perhaps interesting to note that, in the end, we can say that the great majority of our Principles received unanimous approval.

---

1 Encyclical *Quadragésimo Anno*, §137
2 We are aware that some will say that anonymity is necessarily a sign of cowardice, or lack of conviction. This is a simplistic view. There are *many* reasons why someone may choose to remain anonymous. We will say more: in controversial matters, anonymity can be a very valuable means of achieving *objectivity*; the interlocutors have no rational basis for excusing themselves from that objectivity, for if no one knows who you are, your precious *person* cannot be attacked, but only the *ideas* that you propose for discussion. This at least potentially leaves one free from the influence of a love of self which tends to end in hating truth.

CHAPTER 1

GOD AND MAN
(Man's Relationship To God)

God

GOD AS "I AM WHO AM"

1.1 – It is not insignificant that when Moses went onto the holy mountain and saw the burning bush he should ask God for His Name. The meaning of God's response to that request is not well appreciated, however. Rather than giving Moses a specific name like all of the gods of the ancient world, He spoke not a name but expressed the very essence of His Being. He was I AM WHO AM: Existence Itself. In this regard it is very important to recognize that the God who gives His Name as I AM calls upon Moses himself by name: "Moses, Moses." This event, testified to in the Book of Exodus, is very important for understanding man's relationship to God. With God revealing Himself as the fullness of Existence, containing within Himself every perfection that will later be shared with His Creation, man should be the Great Cosmic Zero, for what being can stand in the face of Being Itself? But man exists. He has being to a certain limited extent as opposed to God Who is Being Itself. Man, and indeed all of Creation, has this status in the face of God.

> **PRINCIPLE 1: God exists as a personal being, *ipsum esse per se subsistens* (being itself subsisting through itself), and He has created all other things, and sustains them in being. Therefore, creatures belong to God, and exist in order to do His will.**

DIVINE PROVIDENCE AND CREATION

1.2 – When we hear that God is Existence Itself, self-subsistent existence, we are made aware of the fact that reality does not have Nothingness as its foundation and the source from which everything came. Rather, the foundation of all of reality is an Infinite Being, who possesses the fullness of what it means to be. This Being, who is Existence, is also a spiritual being who is utterly distinct from anything that He has created. The infinite power over all of existence and the intelligence by which He fashioned all things and directed them toward their ends, means that there is no existence outside His Will. After creating all things out of Nothing, He directs them toward an end or goal that will fulfill their nature and directs rational and intellectual creatures toward happiness. This direction of all things toward a state in which their natures would be fulfilled is a clear manifestation of God's Goodness. God is Goodness Itself, Truth Itself, and Beauty Itself, just as He is Being Itself. It is because God has all of these perfections and possesses them to their fullness that all creatures coming forth from the creative hand of God are good, true, and beautiful insofar as they exist. We call the Eternal Plan by which God directs all things to their own proper end, to their own happiness and fulfillment, the Eternal Law. The Eternal

Law, being the foundation of all subsequent Law that regulates all creatures and is written internally in the heart of all men as the Natural Law, is instantiated in the Divine Logos, or as Revelation has revealed Him to us, the Eternal Son of God. The Eternal Son, the Verbum, is the Uncreated of the Father, and is God, "through Whom all things were made". The Eternal Father and Eternal Son's love for each other as co-equal Divine Persons, spirates the Third Divine Person in all eternity, the Holy Ghost. The Holy Ghost is a co-equal divine person who, together with the Father and the Son, constitute the One Divine Being of the Most Holy Trinity.

The Creative Freedom Of God

1.3 – The question must arise as to why a Being who has the fullness of being and happiness within Himself would choose to create that which is not Himself. Here we can only grasp at that which can never fully be understood by man. It can only be because God does not envy, and because of His overflowing infinite goodness in which He decided from all eternity to share His happiness and goodness with all that He would create. It is significant that St. Athanasius, when arguing against Arianism at the Council of Nicea, said that the perfection of the Creation in its form and order, points to the divinity of the Logos, the Word, through Whom the universe was made. Christ's divinity is manifested through the intelligence and providential intention that runs through all of Creation.

> **PRINCIPLE 2: God's Eternal Law is His Plan and Will to bring all things to their state of fulfillment and happiness.**

Man

MAN AS CREATURE

1.4 – It was on the Sixth Day that God created Man. It has been written by the Fathers that it was on the first day of Creation, when God separated the Light from the Darkness, that the Angelic Realm of Pure Intellectual Substances was created. These Angels were very Similitudes of God and received their knowledge directly from God. They were designated to maintain the order of the universe that God had created, and they continually worship God Himself. Man, as opposed to the Angels, is not wholly spiritual in nature, but was created as a being both spiritual and material. All of material creation had been structured during the days of Creation to culminate in the creation of Man. All of material creation was made specifically to be crowned by the person of Man.

Man As Spiritual And Material, And Yet One

1.5 – The Man that was created by God was created as having a material body and spiritual soul animating that body. This meant that man straddled the spiritual and material realms and was therefore a material creature who was meant for a non-material end. In his created being, man is a microcosm of the entire Universe of Creation; he embodies the realms of materiality (vegetative life, brute animality), along with possessing the intelligence shared by the Angelic Order. Indeed, man's greatest power, his intellect, which allows him to be the only material creature in the universe to be able to reflect upon itself – one that does not only gaze outward, but also inward – is dependent upon his body and its five senses in order to understand.

> **PRINCIPLE 3: Man was created to be a microcosm of the created order; a unified spiritual/material being.**

Man's Knowledge Begins With Sensation

1.6 – It is through the five senses that man has an awareness of the world around him; according to St. Thomas Aquinas, sight is the most intellectual of the senses, giving the mind a full purview of the world around, with the sense of touch being the sense which infallibly registers and affirms the existence of things in the world. If I can kick it, it exists!

> **PRINCIPLE 4: Man as an animal (material) being, depends on his five (material) senses to know the world.**

Man As Rational Being And Master Of The Created Order

1.7 – Man, unlike the brutes, is not relegated to merely reacting to the stimuli of the external material world. The power of intellect, which can both engage in an abstractive process, disengaging the essence of things from their images, along with penetrating those same essences themselves, allows man to understand things and, consequently, to master them. Here we see the significance of Genesis' account of man as being the one who names the creatures which God has created in the Garden. By naming things, he classifies them and attains mastery. He is meant to exercise this mastery as his part in the hierarchical order of the universe, under God and the Angels.

> **PRINCIPLE 5: Man as a rational (spiritual) being is able to abstract from sense data the essences (natures) of things, therefore is able to perceive the relations between things, such as the relation of cause to effect or means to an end. Man is able therefore not merely to know things, but understand *what*, and *why* they are. He is also able to reflect upon and understand himself; what and why he is.**

Man As Obediential Potency

1.8 – Man's ability to know the true, and will the good, is characterized by an orientation to universal truth and universal goodness. This is the root of his freedom. If man was confronted with Goodness Itself, he could not choose otherwise. However, to guarantee man's unique status and freedom, God has willed that even He be presented to man as a "limited" good.

Having before himself, therefore, a range of limited goods, man can choose one or the other depending upon his free choice and his weighing of the goods. Even though man has the freedom to choose among those goods which he understands to be limited or understands in a limited way – as in the Good of the Infinite God – he is still oriented to the good and the true and therefore, ultimately, to Infinite

Goodness and Infinite Truth. This openness to, and even orientation toward, Infinite Truth and Infinite Goodness, is a manifestation of the obediential potency which is man's unique capacity to receive God's life in the Beatific Vision. He is not capable of attaining the Beatific Vision of God's own life through his own efforts; rather, through the elevation of sanctifying grace, man is such a being that he can share in the very life of God Himself. Ultimately, since man has this orientation toward Universal Truth and Goodness, it is only in God that man's longing for happiness can be fulfilled. This stands even though the attainment of various natural ends can satisfy and fulfill man to a certain limited extent.

> **PRINCIPLE 6: Being able to know essences means being able to know universals; that is, natures and attributes of beings that are common to a potentially infinite multitude of other beings. This in turn means being able to form a concept of infinitude itself, which subsequently forms in the will a desire to actually know and possess Infinite Truth and Good, which is found only in God.**
>
> **PRINCIPLE 7: While man through his natural power can attain a limited satisfaction in the limited truth and good found in finite nature, his true and full happiness can be found only in the possession of the supernatural vision of God, for which he has only an obediential power. This vision is given by God only through grace and the light of glory, and only when man obeys the conditions laid down by God.**

Man As Fallen

1.9 – Man, however, from the Garden of Eden itself, because of his pride, and envy of the divine prerogatives, lost the divine grace which had elevated him to be both an Image and a Likeness of God. Since man's Fall, instigated by the plotting of Lucifer, the arch-enemy of God and man, he has lost the grace and the preternatural gifts which guaranteed him perfect integrity in the natural and supernatural orders.

> **PRINCIPLE 8: Man is born with a tendency to evil, which we call original sin. Hence man's nature is weakened. Although man can in fact do some natural moral good and attain some natural happiness on earth merely by his natural powers, he cannot attain all that is available, nor maintain it, without God's grace.[3]**

---

3   See the condemned propositions in H. Denzinger, *Enchiridion Symbolorum (The Sources of Catholic Dogma)*, §1027 & 1389, 30th ed., trans. Roy J. Deferrari, Marian House, Powers Lake, ND. In our work, Denzinger will be cited as *Dz*. See also St. Thomas Aquinas, *Summa Theologiae*, I-II, Q.109, a2. All citations of the *Summa* used in this book are from the Marietti edition of 1948.

Christ, The God-Man : Conqueror Of Sin And Death

1.10 – The reconciliation between God and man, restoring the adopted sonship of man, is brought about by the death of Our Lord Jesus Christ, Incarnate Second Person of the Holy Trinity, on the Cross. Here Christ becomes King over the human world and over all humankind, both by His nature as Omnipotent God and by right of conquest by His vitiation of all things of man's world that separate man from the presence of his Creator: the Devil, sin, evil, and the fallen flesh. "All power in Heaven and earth is given to Me by My Father", explained Our Lord Jesus Christ after His Resurrection and before His glorious Ascension into heaven. In Christ the King is summarized all of man's capacities, all of his hopes, all of the Laws which govern human life, all of the truth by which his life is to be determined. As Our Lord Jesus Christ Himself said when asked by Pilate if He were a king, "I am a King; that is why I have come into the world, to testify to the truth."

> **PRINCIPLE 9:** Jesus Christ's incarnation and death provide man the means by which his fallen nature can be healed. Even in order to attain merely natural satisfaction, man must avail himself of the helps provided by Christ. However, the most essential help, sanctifying grace, of its nature orients man ultimately toward possession of the supernatural end which is God. Hence if any man wants any kind of happiness he must in fact strive for supernatural happiness, through Jesus Christ.

> **PRINCIPLE 10:** The Eternal Law exists inherently in Christ, the Son of God, True God and True Man. In Christ is summarized all man's capacities, hopes, and all truth and laws governing human life.

CHAPTER 2

MAN AND MAN
(Man's Relationship to Man)

Introduction

As said in Chapter 1 (1.2), God has an Eternal Plan for Creation. This plan includes man, as well as all other creatures, from mere empty space to Angels. These creatures of course have a direct relationship to God, but they also have relations with each other. Since this book concerns the social order of man, we will focus on the relations of individual men with each other, and *how* they ought to be ordered, keeping in mind that, since the Divine Plan encompasses all creatures, an individual cannot have a right relation with God without right relations to his fellow creatures. More than that, as we will see, social life among men is essential to a man's happiness, and his happiness increases in proportion to the perfection of his social life.

The Eternal Plan And The Eternal Law

2.1 – We have said in Chapter 1 (1.2) that God's Eternal (or Divine) Plan is also called The Eternal Law.

How can the Eternal Plan and the Eternal Law be considered the same thing?

A plan is an intentional (that is, purposeful) arrangement of things.[4]

Law then must in some way be synonymous with Plan. How therefore is Law an intentional arrangement of things? To find out, we will have to investigate the nature of law.

Josephus Gredt gives definitions of law in *Eleménta Philosophíae Aristotélico-Thomísticae*, §§ 934ff, & 854:

In the widest sense, *law is the rule and measure of any act* (e.g. laws of physics, laws of nature).

Example: The law of gravity is the rule and measure of the attraction that objects possessed of mass have for each other.

2.2 – Every rule and measure is determined by the end in view. If a thing has no end toward which to tend, there is no conceivable reason why it should act in any given manner or degree. All Creation has for its end the consummation of the Eternal Plan; that is, the consummation of the Purposeful Arrangement of Things. As St. Thomas says: "The reason itself for the government of things, existing in God as the Prince of the universe, has the meaning of law." (*Summa Theol.* I-II Q.91, a1) In

---

[4] This is the essential, philosophical definition of the term. Reference to a good dictionary will show that all the various definitions of 'plan' are within the comprehension of this essential definition. St. Augustine defines order in a way that conveys essentially the same idea: *Ordo est párium disparíumque rerum sua cuíque loca tríbuens dispositío.* (Order is a disposition of things equal and unequal, giving to each one its own place). (*Cívitas Dei*, XIX, 13, from Migne's *Patrológia Latína*, V. XLI, 1845)

other words, the *purpose or intention* behind the *arrangement* of things has the meaning of law. This then is how God's Eternal Plan and Eternal Law are identical. The Plan and the Law differ only in this: that while 'Plan' signifies merely the Order/Arrangement Of Things as such, the term 'Law' refers to the Plan, Order or Arrangement as *intended* to be fulfilled, or as *rules* for its own realization.

Every type of law then implies an end (or goal) which someone intends to be realized, and the correctness/goodness or incorrectness/badness of an act will be judged by how well it serves the goal for which the law exists.

In sum: *Every plan is made because of some intended good, or goal, to be achieved. Every law is a rule of action made to help bring about that intended goal.*

The Eternal Law then is the *rules* for the fulfillment of the Divine Plan. It can be defined as follows:

> ***The Eternal Law is the rules and measure for the actions of all the beings which God has created or will create, by which He intends those beings to fulfill the Eternal (Divine) Plan.***

The Eternal Plan For Man : Happiness

NATURAL LAW

2.3 – St. Thomas says: "All things participate in some way in the Eternal Law; that is, so far as from His impression they have inclinations toward their proper acts and ends." (*Summa Theol.* I-II Q.91, a2, resp.)

This plan and imposition of inclinations is a subset of the Eternal Law, called Natural Law:

> ***Natural Law is the natural (created) inclinations in creatures to do certain things and tend toward certain ends.***

This means that – at least within the natural order alone – all that creatures need to do in order to fulfill the Divine Plan is to be and act according to their nature as He created it. In the measure that they do so they will fulfill *themselves* as well; they will satisfy their natural inclinations; they will do and be and have the *good* that is proper to the particular kind of being that they are.

> ***The good for a being is that which perfects and thus satisfies its nature.***[5]

Natural Happiness

2.4 – When a being perfects and satisfies its nature, the result is happiness – in a more or less strict sense of the term depending on the type of being it is.

---

[5] "The word 'good' expresses suitability to an appetite." (Josephus Gredt, *Eleménta Philosophíae Aristotélico-Thomísticae*, 9th ed., § 622). "The good is what all things desire." (*Summa Theol.* I Q.5, a1, resp.; cf. I-II Q.8, a1, resp.) Here we are speaking of good in respect of final cause, or fulfillment of the *purpose* of a thing's existence or being, not of good in the deepest sense; that being itself is good, and the ground of all other good.

Happiness is to be, do, and possess, all the good that one is designed to be, do, and possess.[6]

The lower creatures tend toward their good and perfection, and consequently their own limited kind of happiness, without any attention or intention on their part. For instance, the elements, and the mineral objects compounded of them, obey the laws of chemistry and physics; plants obey these also, plus the vital forces that cause them to grow, to respond to stimuli, and to reproduce; animals do the same, with their more complex behaviors being governed by instinct. In following Natural Law in this way, they tend toward what is good, both for themselves and the universe. Plants and (more so) animals can be said to be "happy" (still in a non-strict sense) when they have what they need to blindly follow the laws of nature that govern them.

2.5 – On the other hand, creatures of an intellectual nature, such as Angels and men, have been given the ability to act with a great deal of freedom of choice. For they can know what they are, what their purposes are, and how to act to achieve them (cf. 1.7). For this reason they must intentionally apply themselves to making their actions conform to their nature and purpose, as God Himself intended.[7] If they do, then, just as the lower creatures, they will attain the natural happiness available in this world.

2.6 – God does not leave us intellectual creatures in the dark concerning the Natural Law. The basic rules of this law are knowable by observing the creation around us. For example, living creatures naturally operate with a hierarchy of rules in order to achieve the goods they are designed to achieve. In the broadest outline, these are, from lower to higher importance: individual thriving, individual surviving; the thriving, then the surviving, of the species; the thriving, then surviving, of the universe; the external glorification of the Creator. These goals are not mutually rivalrous; the individual seeks them in the order of their excellence. A normal creature, by physical laws, by instinct, or by intellect, will naturally find its *own* best good in promoting the good of something(s) more excellent. If necessary, it will sacrifice its own thriving for that of its species, or of the universe; it will even sacrifice its own life for the survival of its species, or of the universe, or for the glorification of the Creator.[8] This is all in accordance with the wisdom and uncompromising love of the Divine Plan, which orders creation for the sake of the perfection of the whole, and yet at the same time provides that individuals find their own best good in serving that whole, and, in the case of intellectual creatures, of ultimately possessing God Himself, the Source of the whole.

St. Thomas says it very well in the *Summa Theol.* I-II, Q.109, a3:

---

[6] *Summa Theol.* I Q.6, a3, resp. This article treats of perfection, but since the perfection of a being *results* in its happiness, perfection and happiness, in the context of our discussion, are equivalent.

[7] St. Thomas, *Summa Contra Gentiles*, Bk. III, c.109, 5ff.

[8] This is seen among human beings, even among those who know nothing of God or even Natural Law. There is a sort of instinctive loyalty to a greater good operating even in morally deformed persons. For instance, this is why Leftists celebrate Earth Day, or make such great sacrifices to achieve "social justice". It is also why Libertarians on the Right, while famous for their individualism, so often support "patriotic" causes, or even risk their lives for their country in voluntary military service.

To love God above all things is something connatural to man, and also to any creature, not only rational but irrational, and even inanimate, according to the mode of love which is competent to each. The reason of this is that to every creature it is natural to tend toward and love something according as it has been born to be apt (Aristotle, *II Physic.*). But it is manifest that the good of a part is on account of the good of a whole, whence also, by a natural appetite or love, each particular thing loves its own good on account of the common good of the whole universe, which is God.

SUPERNATURAL LAW[9]

Supernatural Happiness

2.7 – As stated (1.8), man's destiny is not limited to the natural happiness available in this world. His true goal is supernatural happiness. Just as Natural Law is the rule and measure which directs creatures to natural happiness, Supernatural Law directs us to supernatural happiness, which is the perfect happiness of man, who, by the Eternal Divine Plan, is called to the possession of God.

> ***Perfect happiness for man is the vision of the Divine Essence, which is the possession of all the good that man wants, and includes the knowledge that he possesses it and that he can never lose it.***[10]

As may be seen, this definition is entirely compatible with the general definition of happiness given in 2.4 above. It only takes into account certain specifying facts: that man is intellectual by nature, that the good of the intellect is knowledge, and that God has ordained that man's intellect should be satisfied not only with knowledge of the created beings around him, but also of the Creator Himself. It also recognizes that if someone knows that he is happy, but thinks it may be possible to lose that happiness, the fear itself of its future possible loss would detract from its perfection.

---

9   'Supernatural' literally means *above nature*. But since all nature (in the sense of the environment and the universe) is created, all things called 'natural' are created. Conversely therefore, only that which is not created is supernatural. But only God Himself, and things or actions directly connected to Him, are uncreated, and hence supernatural. For example, actual grace is a supernatural action (since it comes directly from God), and sanctifying grace is a supernatural quality in the soul (since it is a participation in God's own being).
    This footnote was thought necessary because it is *very* common today to speak of, for instance, Angels or ghosts as "supernatural" beings. This is incorrect. These are created beings, and thus are part of nature. To distinguish them and their action from the immediately obvious *materially* sensible nature of the rest of creation, however, theologians have used the term 'preternatural'. Literally this means *beside nature,* and is appropriate given that Angels, though natural beings in themselves, are outside *our* natural means of knowing, which is through the material senses. We should state also that, in saying God is the Author of supernature, we do not mean that God is the Author of Himself; He did not create Himself, but simply always was, is and will be. We mean that He is the Author of actual grace, sanctifying grace, and other *communications* of His supernatural Self.

10 Among the sources for this definition: *Summa Theol.* I-II Q.3, a8; I-II Q.5, a4, resp.; *Summa Contra Gentiles* Bk. III, cc.3 & 62.

Divine Law

2.8 – Therefore, the ultimate rule and measure of man's acts is that which directs him toward this supernatural end. Foremost in this kind of law is Divine Law.

> *Divine Law is that which has been infallibly revealed through Scripture or Tradition.*

For example, the Ten Commandments are Divine Law.

Since God is the Author of nature, and since He *is* Supernature, He is the source of both Natural Law and Divine Law, between which there can therefore be no contradiction; both are included in the Eternal Law; and the Divine Plan, coming from the Infinitely Perfect Intellect, is perfectly consistent. That part of Natural Law which governs man's acts, the most important part of which is included in the Ten Commandments, is simply the foundational part of Divine Law, because *grátia natúram pérficit* (grace perfects nature).

The first three Commandments directly concern duties to God, but since the existence of God can be known by the natural reason, even these are part of the Natural Law, and even the Third Commandment (to keep holy the Sabbath) also holds for those who do not know the true God, for although no specific day or manner of worshipping Him would apply, due to their ignorance of His detailed precepts in that regard, they would still be obligated to worship Him as best they could, according to their knowledge. The last seven of the Ten Commandments, so far as their objects and the actions they dictate are concerned, would have to be held even by atheists, if they had any hope of having even a merely secular happiness.

As St. Paul says:

> For when the Gentiles, who have not the law [given in detail to Israel in addition to the Ten Commandments], do by nature those things that are of the [Natural] law [of the Ten Commandments]; these, having not a law of that [detailed] kind, are a law to themselves, who show the work of the [Natural] law written in their hearts, their conscience rendering them witness... (Rom. 2:14)[11]

Thus someone who is ignorant of the True God is still obligated to be a "law unto himself", which means indeed *not* that he create his *own* law by the exercise of a false freedom, as driven by his fallen nature, but that he simply recognize and live by that which is already found in himself; in his true nature as given by the Creator. It matters not if one even recognizes the true Creator, or any creator; recognition of Nature itself is sufficient to recognize that Natural Law exists.

> **PRINCIPLE 11: No contradiction exists between Natural Law and Divine Law, as both are expressions of the Eternal Law, and have God as their Author. The Ten Commandments are both Natural and Divine Law.**

---

[11] The "law written in their hearts" is those natural inclinations to good which St. Thomas calls *inclinations toward their proper acts and ends.*

Ecclesiastical Law

2.9 – Since Natural and Divine Law make general mandates, and do not descend to prescribing details of their application to circumstances of time and place, and since the manner of such application is often disputable among men, but just as often attended by serious consequences, it was necessary that the Eternal Lawgiver provide an earthly temporal authority that could reliably decide these details. This He did by establishing the Catholic Church, the hierarchy of which is charged with this task.[12] Thus He added Ecclesiastical Law to Natural Law and Divine Law. Since Ecclesiastical Law comes to us through the mediation of men and not directly from God, it has not the same authoritative force as Natural or Divine Law. Nevertheless, it is a moral necessity to mankind, in order that he reliably tend toward his supernatural end.

2.10 – The traditional division and distinction of law is from the standpoint of the source (or efficient cause) of the laws; Natural Law comes from nature (created reality),[13] Divine Law comes directly from God, Ecclesiastical Law comes from the Church. But our purpose is the study of social order. Order only exists so as to achieve a goal. Thus our study is "goal oriented". Chapter 1 (1.8) made the crucial observation that man has both natural and supernatural goals, highlighting the infinitely greater value of the latter. This distinction of goals must be carried over into all the rest of our work, and so it is suitable to introduce a classification of laws according to their purpose (final cause) rather than their source. We therefore consider Natural Law not only as being *from* nature, but also and even primarily as directing us *toward* our natural happiness. Consonant with this, we introduce the term Supernatural Law.[14] Supernatural Law is so named not from its source, but from its purpose; *Supernatural Law is any and all laws whose purpose is to direct us to supernatural happiness.*

We must add that a law can be supernatural also in respect of what we call the formal motive; that is, the *reason* why we obey the law. Hence Natural Law is supernatural neither in its origin (which is Nature) nor in its purpose, which is natural happiness. Nevertheless, it can be supernatural*ized* in respect of a supernatural *motive* on the part of those keeping it. When our *reason* for keeping Natural Law is primarily love of the Supernatural God (rather than love of self and/or neighbor), the Natural Law (in that aspect only) becomes supernatural.

> **Supernatural Law is any and all laws of God or His Church that help us to attain supernatural happiness. It includes Divine Law, Ecclesiastical Law, and even the Natural Law (only so far as motivation for keeping the latter is primarily love of the True God).**

---

12 For example, the Fifth Commandment as it stands, "Thou shalt not kill", would seem to forbid capital punishment and even killing in self defense. The Tradition of the Church shows, however, that it has never been understood that way. See Rom. 13:4, and any catechism in use before Vatican Council II; e.g. the *Catechism Of The Council Of Trent* (the chapter on the Fifth Commandment).

13 God is, of course, the cause of nature itself, and is thus the ultimate efficient cause even of the Natural Law, so that nature is really only the immediate efficient cause of Natural Law, but for several reasons it has historically been found convenient to treat nature *as if* it were a cause independent of God. One of these reasons is that atheists and pagans do not accept the True God, but generally do accept nature.

14 This of course in no way invalidates the traditional distinctions according to efficient cause. We have used them, and will continue to do so.

Ecclesiastical Law includes the six commandments of the Catholic Church, the Church's Canon Law, and other legitimately promulgated mandates of the Church.[15]

Man's Social Nature[16]

It should be clear that all the kinds of law mentioned above, which help man to achieve both natural and supernatural happiness, find their full effectiveness only within a social setting. Human society both explicitly mandates and authoritatively enforces these laws. Additionally, traditions within a society provide a moral encouragement to keep them, even without physical force.

WHAT IS *SOCIETY*?

2.11 – But what *is* society? Men very frequently use the term 'society'. Common speech, however, when it comes to all but the simplest and most concrete notions, is also frequently inaccurate or vague. Here we must be perfectly clear.

> *A society is a stable union of a number of persons in fellowship and cooperation for a common purpose of benefit to all.*[17]

In a family, city, nation or State, the common purpose, of course, ought to be the striving for common goods, especially natural and supernatural happiness.

We must note that cooperation among persons for a common purpose requires an ordering of the actions of those persons toward the common goal. This order cannot be achieved or maintained unless there is someone definitively directing it. Therefore every society must have an authority.

Men have formed societies since time immemorial, and with any number of purposes. It is clear from this definition that even the little group that composed this document is a society. Through history, none but a few raving fools (e.g. J.-J. Rousseau) have ever denied that man is by nature a social being.

Man : A Social Being By Design

2.12 – Nevertheless, here we must assume as little as possible. How can man's social nature be proven?

1. Ontologically; i.e., by certain realities of man's very being.

    a) Man has intellect. This gives him the power of speech. Man is thus able to share ideas. This ability is evidently extremely useful as well as pleasant, but only when man lives in society.

---

15 The commandments and laws of the Church are infallible only so far as they derive directly from infallible doctrine, and/or have been approved by Tradition (i.e., at least 200 years of universally accepted use). A full treatment of the conditions of infallibility of Catholic Church doctrine would be off topic in this book, but the reader is highly encouraged to familiarize himself with this matter. An approachable and reliable exposition can be found in the *Catholic Encyclopedia*, art. Infallibility (Robert Appleton Co., New York, 1910-1914).

16 See the *Catholic Encyclopedia*, art. Society, for a good overview of this subject.

17 Celestine Bittle, O.F.M. Cap., *The Whole Man* , p. 600 (Bruce Publishing Co., Milwaukee, 1945).

To live in solitude frustrates the advantages of this natural power.[18]

    b) Man's development to maturity is very slow. At birth he is entirely helpless. He does not become a truly viable and independent rational creature until probably ten years of age, at a minimum. And if he is to be raised to a high level of rational development, he requires correspondingly more time, among teachers, within an educational (and that means social) environment.

2. Historically, man's social nature can be proved from the fact that nearly all men have lived, and still do live, in a society. The very rare exceptions prove the rule. (Catholic hermits are not an exception, as nearly all of them did have occasional contact with others, often even formed groups living under a common rule, had daily converse, through prayer, with God and the saints, and in any case, were members of the Mystical Body of Christ, which is certainly a society.)

PRINCIPLE 12: That man live in society is a precept of the Natural Law, and admits of no exceptions. Those few who do not do so are spiritually perverted or psychologically ill. Though the eremitic life is permitted by Supernatural Law, and even encouraged in some cases by counsel, the Catholic eremitic life is *not* asocial.

THE COMMON GOOD : THE GOAL OF SOCIETY[19]

2.13 – As said (2.3 – 2.6), persons naturally seek their individual good, but it is evident also that they naturally prefer the good of the society they belong to, or some other good higher than themselves. These higher goods are common goods, and since this is built into the nature of individuals as a preference, it follows that a person cannot achieve his own true individual good, and the consequent complete happiness, without preferring and promoting the common good.

Many who talk about the common good, and think they are acting to advance it, have vague or erroneous notions of it. What they advance can be highly questionable.

---

18 St. Thomas speaks to the conveniences that the sophisticated communication we call language affords: "...[T]he use of speech is a prerogative proper to man. By this means, one man is able fully to express his conceptions to others. Man [as compared to animals] has a natural knowledge of the things which are essential for his life only in a general fashion, inasmuch as he is able to attain knowledge of the particular things necessary for human life by reasoning from natural principles. But it is not possible for one man to arrive at a knowledge of all these things by his own individual reason. It is therefore necessary for man to live in a multitude so that each one may assist his fellows, and different men may be occupied in seeking, by their reason, to make different discoveries – one, for example, in medicine, one in this and another in that." (*De Regno*, Bk. 1, ch. 1, 7 & 6. Trans. Gerald Phelan & I. Th. Echmann, Pontifical Institute of Mediaeval Studies, Toronto, 1949. This work is also called *De Regímine Príncipum*.)

19 For our treatment of the common good we are indebted to Edmund Waldstein, O. Cist., for his essay *The Primacy Of The Common Good* (https://thejosias.com – accessed 11 Nov. 2025), and even more for the book upon which that essay is based: *On the Primacy of the Common Good: Against the Personalists*, by Charles de Koninck, 1943.

The common good is not simply the sum total of the private goods of the individuals in a community. It is not the provision of equal opportunities to individuals within a society to acquire such private goods, as desired by Libertarians. It is not an equal distribution of goods to individuals in a community, as purportedly desired by Socialists and Communists. Nor is it the collective of individuals taken as some sort of moral super-person called the State, as in totalitarianism. Rather,

> *A common good is a single good that is enjoyed simultaneously by two or more beings.*[20]

2.14 – This definition applies not only to man, but to all creatures. It would perhaps be of interest to consider this concept in some detail as it applies to all kinds of creatures, but the scope of our work is restricted to the social order of mankind. We will therefore turn our attention and emphasis in that direction.

As far as common goods of mankind are concerned then, we can say that we have not far to look for them, but our eyes are not trained to do so. They can be divided into two broad categories: material common goods and spiritual common goods. Here are some examples:

- Of Material Common Goods: The air we breathe; the benefit of division of labor (see 9.8); public roads; police and military forces that provide physical security; judicial systems that provide the human rules for peace and order; peace and order themselves (so far as these words refer only to material conditions).

- Of Spiritual Common Goods (i.e. intellectual and moral common goods): The physical peace and order mentioned above also lead to peace of mind, which is a moral good. The historical fund of common knowledge – any kind of knowledge – is an intellectual good. Some categories are: knowledge of history itself, culture, the empirical sciences, philosophy or theology. There is also the moral support that this knowledge as such can give, and (as we may

---

20 See St. Thomas, *Super Sent.*, lib. 4, d. 49, q. 1, a. 1, qc. 1, ad 3 (online edition found here: https://www.corpusthomisticum.org/snp40491.html – accessed 5 Nov. 2025), where he says: "In another way, [something can be said to be common] according to participation in one and the same thing [and] according to a number [of participants]." Also see *De Veritáte* Q.7 a. 6, ad 7: "[something can be said to be common] in the mode of a cause, as a cause which, remaining one in number, extends itself to many effects; and thus that which is more common is more noble, as the conservation of a city is [more common and noble] than the conservation of a family." Some restrict the meaning of 'common good' to goods that are not diminished no matter how many share in them, but these quotes clearly prove that St. Thomas admitted of *degrees* of excellence, and even that material things can be common goods, albeit of a lower sort. This latter is definitively proved by II-II, Q.61, a1, the whole tenor of which concerns material common goods, distributed by rulers to their subjects. Moreover, the line of thinking here often cites Aristotle in support. Then too, St. Thomas makes clear elsewhere that animals have and seek a common good for their species, but animals are material beings, thus the common good that their species is for them is neither rational nor undiminishable, since matter is limited.

The *Compendium Of The Social Doctrine Of The Church,* 2004, commissioned by John Paul II, has a good definition of 'common good': "the sum total of social conditions which allow people, either as groups or as individuals, to reach their fulfillment more fully and more easily". However, this definition applies only to the *combined* common goods found in a larger society. It does not define what **a** common good is, *as such*. It also fails to mention that a good part of that very fulfillment is the satisfaction of nature that the individual part receives from *serving* the good of the whole.

Some make a distinction between 'public good' and 'common good', but a public good is simply a common good that is publicly (governmentally) owned. See 8.1.

say) the fund of moral fiber that a community may have due to the example of its predecessors.

These are only a few instances out of many common goods that naturally grow out of a human society, and even these examples only give food for thought concerning the full reality of the value they provide. A mere list of the different kinds of intellectual and moral common goods, beyond the few major categories mentioned above, would alone be extensive, even without any explanation of their particular values. A full treatment of the common good would be a book-length work in itself.

COMMON GOODS IN SOCIETY AND FALLEN HUMAN NATURE

2.15 – As said in Chapter 1 (1.9), man's nature is fallen, and tends to evil. This tendency to evil is *not* part of man's nature as originally constituted by God (*Summa Theol.* I-II, Q.109, a3). The authorities in every human society must take this fact into very serious account if they want to accomplish their chief task: the promotion of the common good. It is a grave mistake to assume these evil tendencies as being part of Natural Law.

> [M]an in the state of integral nature used to refer the love of himself to the love of God as to the purpose, and likewise the love of all other things, and in that way loved God more than himself, and above all things. But in the state of corrupted nature man falls short of this according to the appetite of the rational will, which on account of the corruption of nature [=original sin] follows the private good, unless it be healed by the grace of God.[21]

Here, following the "private good" simply means being shortsightedly selfish. As said before, one's *true* good as an individual includes *preferring* the common good to the individual good. History is rife with examples of societies that did not do this, and became disordered and/or eventually destroyed by allowing God's Natural Law to be supplanted in some points by toleration of certain selfish evils.

2.16 – The evil tendencies in man reside either in his intellect or in his will and bodily appetites; in the intellect as an attenuation of its capabilities, in the will as an inclination to serve Self rather than the common good (and ultimately God). The ways in which the will's self-serving habit manifest itself are conveniently categorized into what are called the Capital Sins. These tendencies are called capital because they are the heads (Lat. *caput* = head) or main categories into which such inclinations can be divided. They are sloth, lust, anger, pride, avarice, gluttony, envy.

While not within the scope of our work to give a complete enumeration, it may be useful to mention a few examples of socially impactful evil acts that arise from these tendencies: living off the public dole because of laziness rather than need; divorce, homosexuality and transgenderism; cruel and unusual punishment; excessive nationalism, racism; usury; marketing of harmful foods; class strife.

2.17 – It may be useful to point out that original sin, or flawed human nature, is not only a dogma of Catholic Faith, it is a self-evident fact. Therefore, for those (especially atheists) who would refuse to accept any supernatural goal for man, and

---

21 *Summa Theol.* I-II Q.109, a3, resp.

yet would pretend to solve man's social problems, it is expedient that they consider a purely Natural-Law purpose for man's existence. For there is clearly no hope for a unified social order without an agreed upon goal, and that is the only rational and scientific alternative. The best of the natural philosophers, Aristotle, posed an answer to this question:

> The purpose of human existence is human happiness, which is the perfection of human nature, consisting in the lifelong exercise of virtue. Since man's reason is his distinctive feature, the exercise of proper reasoning, and the contemplation of truth, are essential to happiness.[22]

2.18 – Since under this conception the general common good of man would be that all persons, so far as possible, would have what is necessary to exercise these virtues, for Aristotle, political law would be in conformity to Natural Law, and would be all the reasonable ordinances of those in charge of society that would permit and induce the widest exercise of natural virtues.

Note that there is no assertion here of any kind of afterlife, whether with God as goal (supernatural end), or merely natural goods as an afterlife goal. There is only proposed the limited happiness of the *saeculum* (this earthly time). Nevertheless, we see that the evil tendencies of sloth, lust, anger, pride, avarice, gluttony and envy are excluded. This is simply because they are vices, and hence by definition also opposed to the virtue which Aristotle requires. Consequently also, the actions flowing from these vices are excluded. Vices lead away from natural happiness; thus actions flowing from them are forbidden by Natural Law.

> **PRINCIPLE 13: No society can hope to maintain order or achieve any sort of happiness without substantially conforming to Natural Law.**[23]
>
> **PRINCIPLE 14: No actions coming from the evil tendencies of original sin (tendencies in man's *fallen* nature) are of the Natural Law.**

THE ORIGIN OF SOCIETY

2.19 – If the formation of society among humans is a precept of the Natural Law, how does this actually happen? How do men really come together to form a society?

One thing is certain. A human society never arises except through a *preexisting* human society. For example, our experience with feral children shows that human beings, when from a very young age they are left among beasts, rarely learn to actualize the potential of their intellect; they have a very strong tendency to remain at the level of the beasts in whose "society" they were raised, and this even when they are brought into human society and given special training. And if not brought into human society and given special training, they *never* actualize their rational potential.

---

22 Condensed from various places in the *Nichomachean Ethics*.
23 Cf. Encyclical of Leo XIII, *Libértas Praestantíssimum*, §§8-10. Unless otherwise noted, all citations from papal encyclicals are from the English versions at www.papalencyclicals.net.

This fact of scientific experience is reinforced by another observation, and a bit of logic.

We note that all children learn a language by imitating their parents, or other people in whose society they are raised. If they grow up alone, or among beasts, how will they learn any language? It is inconceivable that they will invent one on their own. Firstly, why would they do so, when they have no one to talk to? Secondly, in order to invent a language, one must already know, at the very least, what a language is. Further, this involves other prerequisite concepts: one must know what a 'word' is, what 'grammar' is, what a 'noun' is, what a 'verb' is, etc. All these fundamental concepts by which one might construct a language are themselves expressed and understood through language itself. In fact, thirdly, language is the very vehicle of rational thought. To produce a language requires rational thought, which only happens through language itself. In short, the very thing needed to invent a language is language itself; one has to already have one in order to invent one.

Thus there is a reasonable scientific basis for the Catholic doctrine that Adam was given infused (unlearned and inborn) knowledge. Language would have been included in this. It follows that all human societies developed from our first parents; from the family of Adam and Eve.

First Level Of Society : The Family

2.20 – The family fits the definition of a society given above (2.11). Out of that general definition we can derive a definition of that species of society called the family:

> **PRINCIPLE 15: A family is a permanent union of one man and one woman, with their children.**[24]

2.21 – As was said concerning the definition of society in general, every society must have an authority, as an organizing principle (cf. *Summa Theol.* I-II Q.96, a4, resp.). Therefore the family must have one also. The man is this authority, and for several reasons:

1. By Natural Law (i.e. by the nature of creation)

St. Thomas Aquinas says in the *Summa Theologiae*:

> Subjection is twofold. One is servile, by virtue of which a superior makes use of a subject for his own benefit; and this kind of subjection began after sin. There is another kind of subjection, which is called economic or civil, whereby the superior makes use of his subjects for their own benefit and good; and this kind of subjection existed even before sin. For good order would have been lacking in the human multitude if some were not governed by others wiser than themselves. And so, by such a kind of subjection woman is

---

24 For the proper final cause (purpose) of this union, see Ppl. 47. The final cause was not stated because not all families pursue it. 'Permanent' here does not mean everlasting, but means (at least normally) as long as either the man or woman is alive. It will sometimes happen in this work that a definition is also a Principle. That is the case here, for what the family *is* will also determine what policies one should establish in its regard.

naturally subject to man, because in man the discretion of reason is naturally more abundant. (I Q.92, a1, ad2)

And in the *Summa Contra Gentíles:*

...[O]n account of the force of passions, by which the reckoning of prudence is corrupted, [children] need not only instruction, but also repression. But a woman alone does not suffice for these things, but rather the work of a male is required, in whom is a more perfect reason for instructing, and a more potent virtue for punishing.[25]

Throughout all history, the judgment of Aquinas is validated by experience. If anything, modern times prove this even more, for in spite of the fact that women largely receive the same education as men, and there are hardly any social taboos against them taking on any task they might like, and in spite of a moral training in many countries that attempts to effeminize men and masculinize women, we find that the occupations that require deep philosophical inquiry and understanding and/or precise analysis on the theoretical level are still – as they always have been – heavily dominated by men. The vast majority of women are not even *interested* in such kind of thought, and very few of those that are can produce any original studies of their own. On the practical level, we have a similar finding: wherever hard and imaginative thinking concerning cause and effect, and the means to solve a problem or achieve a difficult end are concerned (e.g. engineering, repairing or improving machines), women are rarely either apt or *even interested*.[26]

2. By Supernatural Law (i.e. by declarations of Revelation and of the Church)

Sacred Scripture and Tradition are perfectly clear on this point.
   a) Scripture: 1Pet 3:1-7; 1Cor 11:3-9; 1Tim 2:11-14; Eph 5:22-33; Col 3:18-20.

   b) Tradition: All the Fathers and Doctors agree. This Tradition is authoritatively stated in the encyclicals *Arcánum*, §11; *Rerum Novárum*, §13; *Casti Connúbii*, §§ 26-29.[27]

---

25   *SCG*, Bk. III, c.122,8. Online edition: https://aquinas.cc/la/en/~SCG3.C122.8 (accessed 11 Nov. 2025). Translation from the Latin is our own. It must not be thought that St. Thomas thinks demeaningly of women. In the following two chapters of *SCG*, he speaks of the "intense friendship" there ought to be between man and wife, that friendship itself requires a "kind of equality", and that man and wife should be joined "not only by the act of carnal copulation...but also for the sharing of all domestic conversation".
26   See also Pius XI, *Divíni Illíus Magístri*, §31 (Dz 2207)
27   We say "*all* the Fathers and Doctors agree" in the sense of moral unanimity, not necessarily numerical. In any case, our own research reveals no exceptions, but also and more tellingly, the writings of "feminist" researchers apparently don't either. One would think that these writers would specifically try to find and exploit dissenting opinions among the Fathers that would support their desire to overthrow the patriarchy. It seems they have not been successful in doing so, although there has been much research done by them. See for instance https://www.scielo.org.za/scielo.php?script=sci_arttext&pid=S2074-77052017000100005 (accessed 11 Nov. 2025)
John Paul II illegitimately exposed Tradition to question on this point, in his Apostolic Letter *Mulíeris Dignitátem*, §24. He directly contradicts the teaching of Pius XI (*Casti Connúbii*, §§26-29). He also blatantly misuses Scripture, saying that Eph 5:21 "Being subject one to another, in the fear of Christ" applies to man and wife (both). It clearly does not, for it is connected to the *preceding* context, which speaks of Christians in general, in respect of each other. It is in the very **next** verses that St. Paul

PRINCIPLE 16: According to Natural and Supernatural Law, the husband is the final authority in the family. The wife has authority over the children, but she herself is subject to her husband. The husband has the right to act as the head of the entire family. The wife has the right to authority over the children.[28]

2.22 – Throughout history, most have acknowledged that the family is the fundamental societal unit. However, in recent years the traditional notion of family has been under severe attack, because the sexual Natural Law itself is under attack.

PRINCIPLE 17: All sane persons recognize that homosexual or transgender tendencies are radically unnatural, and that there can be no marriages and no families based on homosexual or transgender unions. The State should not allow children to be raised in such unions. It is the severest form of psychological child abuse, and will deform the sense of the Natural Law in these children, which will with great difficulty, or never, be corrected.[29]

In 2.25 below we will speak of Human Law, which, briefly stated, is the detailed rules for practical living that a human authority must add to Natural or Supernatural Law, in order to resolve questions or disputes and keep life organized. From what has been said in the preceding sections, it is clear that even the lowest level of society, the family, requires Human Law.

Second Level Of Society : The City, Nation, Or State

2.23 – The fundamental social unit of the family provides some critical necessities. Among these are basic material survival in the form of food, shelter, mutual aid in illness or danger, etc., also the continuation of the species through procreation, the imparting of the most basic tool of rational development to the children (that is, a language), and the rudiments of other aspects of human culture (e.g. cooking, basic crafts, and a moral sense, especially of mutual love and duty among the family members themselves). It cannot of itself, however, produce a real civilization; a "big picture" sort of culture, with its sense of a larger purpose, detailed moral code, educational, fine art, and governmental traditions; all deeply rooted in a history which is preserved and passed on to future generations.

---

specifies the man/wife relationship, and there he says: "Let women be subject to their husbands, as to the Lord: Because the husband is the head of the wife, as Christ is the head of the Church. He is the Savior of his Body. Therefore as the Church is subject to Christ: so also let wives be to their husbands in all things." The attempt to apply v. 21 to the man-wife relationship is also senseless for another reason, for how is a wife to be subject to her husband "in *all* things" if the husband is also subject to the wife in *any* authoritative way at all? Further, if the man and wife are "subject to each other", but a woman is to be subject to her husband "as to the Lord", this means Christ and the woman are mutually subject to each other just as the woman and her husband are. Since Christ is God, and can be subject to no creature, this is a blasphemy. Finally, 1 Pet. 3:1 supports Tradition against John Paul II's Modernist interpretation, saying: "...let wives be subject to their husbands..."

28 These are not absolute rights, but contingent on the spouses fulfilling at a minimum level their duties as parents. If there is sufficient cause, they can be taken away by a higher authority. See 2.29 below on Human Rights; also H. Denzinger, *Enchiridion Symbolorum (The Sources of Catholic Dogma)*, §2209, 30th ed., trans. Roy J. Deferrari, Marian House, Powers Lake, ND. In our work, Denzinger will be cited as *Dz*.
29 Cf. *Summa Theol.* I-II Q.94, a6.

The most natural way of developing a civilization as such would be that a family would produce progeny, all morally bound to each other by blood relations. This moral bond would lead to mutual cooperation, first at a village level, and eventually a national level, under the leadership of some experienced, knowledgeable, talented men, who would rise to their position simply from the natural respect their qualities would elicit from others. Such was the way the Hebrew nation was born, under the patriarch Abraham.[30]

2.24 – There are secondary types of natiogenesis. For instance, a nation may arise from several mutually friendly families banding together, or from an already established nation conquering another (or others), with the latter gradually being accepted and integrated into the former. It may be mentioned in passing that aberrant theories of natiogenesis (e.g. Rousseau's Social Contract, or Hobbes' Leviathan) have been driven by original sin; the desire to put a supposed private good before the common good.

It is self-evident that a nation born from a single religious tradition will be more unified than one formed from different elements. This will be fully explained in 4.5 – 4.12 below. However, it is also true that not only religious but other cultural traditions help to unify a country.

> **PRINCIPLE 18: It is in man's nature to form nations held together by bonds of religion, culture, kinship and history. The Catholic State has the right to preserve and defend the nation's identity against antagonistic forces.**
>
> **PRINCIPLE 19: By necessary corollary to the reasons leading to Principle 16, primarily men should hold positions of authority in a larger society. Excepted would be communities composed only of women, or of women and children, or special cases where God has clearly called a woman to an extraordinary role.**

HUMAN LAW

2.25 – Although we have seen that Natural Law is essential to any human society, and that in a Catholic society Supernatural Law (which includes Divine and Ecclesiastical Law) is also essential, these are not enough by themselves to produce sufficient order and peace. Divine Law is either not detailed enough (e.g. the Ten Commandments) or it concerns purely religious matters that are not the province of the State. Ecclesiastical Law, while quite detailed, also mainly concerns purely religious matters, and although its moral principles (coming largely from the Ten Commandments), and even many details derived from those principles, apply also to secular society, that application must be done in a clear and distinct way, in a separate legal code capable of addressing the complicated and changing circumstances of workaday life in particular. The body of law that does this is called (secular) Human Law (*Summa Theol.* I-II Q.95, a1).

Such law cannot be effected without a political authority to enforce it, and so it is also called Political Law, and St. Thomas defines it thus:

---

30 The authors later discovered that this idea was proposed by Aloysius Taparelli, S.J., in the work *Saggio Teoretico di Diritto Naturale Appoggiato sul Fatto,* published ante 1845. See also 3.3.

Political law is an ordinance of reason for the common good, promulgated by him who has charge of a community.[31]

This is the sense we will be using henceforth, when considering law in terms of the secular social order. The understanding of 'common good', as we have explained it above (2.13 and following), is essential to the understanding of this definition of political law.

2.26 – Human Law is also called Human Positive Law, because it has to be posited, that is, published or declared in some clear manner. Human Law is of course subject to error on account of its fallible efficient cause, which is man, and it must be remembered that even that portion of Ecclesiastical Law not yet confirmed by Tradition as to its divine source, while still supernatural in its purpose, is not Divine Law, and must be considered Human in its source. No human-proposed law can ever legitimately contradict the Natural Law or Divine Law (which includes that part of Ecclesiastical Law which is confirmed by Tradition), for these have God for efficient cause, and are therefore infallible. And since our definition of (human) political law stated above stipulates that a law must be an ordinance of reason, a clearly irrational and harmful law cannot be a true and real law. (*Summa Theol.* I-II Q.95, a2, resp.)

> **PRINCIPLE 20: Human laws are not laws if they are contrary to the Natural Law or Divine Law, or the Ecclesiastical Law of Catholic Tradition. Pretended laws contrary to these must not be obeyed. Pretended laws that are evidently irrational are not binding in themselves, but they can be obeyed if they do not directly command what is evil, and should be obeyed if by doing so a greater evil will be avoided.**[32]

(Social) Justice

2.27 – There are four cardinal moral virtues: Prudence, Justice, Fortitude and Temperance.[33]

> *Justice is the virtue that inclines one to render to others what is their due.*

Clearly, Justice is the virtue most applicable and most necessary within a society (even if it is not possible to apply it correctly without Prudence, or sometimes also one or more of the other virtues).

A society will thrive or disintegrate in proportion to how well the members as a whole are fulfilling their duties toward each other.

---

31 St. Thomas Aquinas, *Summa Theol.*, I-II Q.90, a4. All citations from the *Summa* are taken from the Marietti edition, Turin, Italy, 1948. All translations are our own.
32 *Summa Theol.* I-II Q.96, a4; see also 4.14, 4.15 & 4.23, and Appendix 2.
33 'Moral' means having to do with the goodness or badness of human acts. Any dictionary will confirm this meaning. But goodness or badness themselves mean nothing other than whether an act helps man fulfill his ultimate purpose in life (see for example J. Maritain, *Introduction to Philosophy*, p. 184f, Christian Classics, 1989). This is because 'good' and 'bad' actions, like absolutely all others, have meaning only so long as they impact someone's everlasting fate. For if the person impacted ceases at any time to exist, his entire previous existence, with all that happened in it, is meaningless to him, since he himself no longer exists to know or care about it.

A society cannot survive unless it follows at least the Natural Law, at least in greater part. Since the Natural Law comes from the Creator, the first justice that must be done is that the creature (man) render to the Creator the obedience due to His Natural Law (cf. Principles 1 & 2).

2.28 – It is not without reason that the first three of the Ten Commandments stipulate man's basic duties to God. There will be no justice between men if there is not first justice from man to God.

Nor without reason does the Fourth Commandment declare that honor and obedience are due to one's earthly father and mother. If children do not do justice to parents, to whom else will they do so?

Fittingly too, since life is the capital individual good, the Fifth Commandment requires that human life, once given by God through the mediation of the parents, cannot be taken away by men unless the person from whom it is taken has forfeited his right to life by a serious offense. Since the parents do not create life, but only mediate its creation by God, that they kill their innocent children is a grave crime, since they sin not only against the Fifth Commandment, but directly against the dignity of procreator with which God honored them.

The Sixth Commandment expresses the primary justice which the spouses in a marriage owe to each other, which is singular mutual love and dedication, and what they owe to their children, which is a stable home, and good example in fulfilling duties, especially the most important. This Commandment begins also to introduce those duties that apply in the society outside the family as well, for the person with whom an adulterer sins has his/her chastity taken away (which no one has a right to give away even willingly), and if that person is also married, the adulterer further sins by stealing from someone else the faithfulness of his/her spouse.

The Seventh Commandment begins to extend justice farther outside the family, for stealing is more commonly perpetrated against those outside the family.

Likewise with the Eighth Commandment; bearing false witness.

The Ninth and Tenth Commandments safeguard the Sixth and Seventh, by forbidding that we even entertain thoughts of sinning against the Sixth and Seventh.

In the above exposition, we have begun to speak of human "rights". This term figures prominently in questions of social order, so it is absolutely required to have a clear idea of what it means.

HUMAN RIGHTS[34]

> **2.29** – *A 'right' is a law commanding that what is owed to a person be allowed or given to him, provided that he has fulfilled on his part any associated duties.*

From this definition one can infer that a human right is simply justice considered passively rather than actively; i.e. it is justice experienced by a person who is the recipient of that justice rather than being the renderer of justice to another. A right is

---

[34] For an interesting introduction to this question, presented in the Thomistic context, see the essay by Anthony Lisska, *Human Rights Theory Rooted In The Writings of Thomas Aquinas*: https://diametros.uj.edu.pl/diametros/article/view/542 (accessed 4 Nov. 2025)
The foundational text for St. Thomas' ideas on rights is in the *Summa Theol.*, II-II Q.57. For a practical though rather complicated discussion of rights, see J. McHugh & C. Callan, *Moral Theology*, §§1690ff (Joseph Wagner Inc., New York, 1958).

therefore based on a preexisting precept of the Eternal Law (whether Natural or Divine), or of Human Law in conformity to the same.

Example: The right to life.
Its foundation in the Eternal Natural Law is the Fifth Commandment (thou shalt not kill), which itself is given because

1. One cannot work to fulfill one's God-given purpose unless one is alive.

2. God alone, as Author of life itself, has the right to take life away (even without apparently adequate reason, such as a grave crime on the part of the person).[35]

Therefore, one has the right to be allowed to live. However, this right is contingent upon fulfilling duties. Persons who are themselves guilty of the crime of breaking the Fifth Commandment (or an equally or even more serious commandment) have so far failed in their social duties as to merit the loss of their right to life. To say it in the most merciful way possible: All persons, including such criminals, have an absolute right to justice, to what is their due. In the case of these criminals, what is due to them is death. The death of the criminal is also due to the victims of their crimes, and to society as a whole, the security of which has been compromised, and which will be further damaged when the injustice and scandal of a false mercy emboldens the criminals.[36]

2.30 – There are some rights that are absolute; that is, they do not carry with them any associated duties. For instance, the right to serve the true God – which is the same as a right to pursue true happiness – is an absolute right. As we noted in the previous paragraph, the right to justice is also an absolute right.

Catholic spiritual theology makes a distinction between merit *de rigóre justítiae* (reward or punishment in strict justice) and merit *de condígno* (reward or punishment based on a promise or privilege granted by one party). This distinction can be applied to human rights.

Human rights strictly speaking would be those that are given in strict justice (*de rigóre*), in virtue of the Eternal Law. The right to life and the right to serve the true God are examples of such rights.

2.31 – There is a quasi "right" however, that comes not from justice *per se*, but from a certain fittingness (or worthiness, in a non-strict sense of the word). For example, in virtue of the Divine Law, we have a "right" to the possession of God if we obey His laws in all serious matters. But this is in reality only by a concessive kindness of God. Only Christ, by His death on the Cross, has strictly merited (*de*

---

35 We say "apparently adequate reason", because God always in fact *has* quite adequate reasons, but they are often known only to the infinite and eternal Intellect, which sees the whole context of the Divine Plan. God never arbitrarily slays anyone. This would be contrary to His Wisdom and Goodness.

36 This is not to say that mercy is therefore by nature injustice, and thus should never be granted. It is to say that *true* mercy must be reconcilable with justice. Mercy must be done only when circumstances indicate that the mitigation of the strict rigors of justice will bring about a greater good, which greater good will actually help to repair the damage done by a crime, and thus help to restore the very justice which mercy *seems* to be mitigating. For more on this very complicated point, see Romano Amerio, *Iota Unum*, ch. 26 (Sarto House, Kansas City, MO), and John Senior, *The Death of Christian Culture*, ch. 7 (IHS Press, Virginia).

rigóre) forgiveness of sins, because sin in itself is an infinite offense, since the God offended is infinite, and thus an infinite reparation is due to the Father, which only a being of equally infinite dignity (the Son) can render. But if we obey God's laws in a spirit of union with Christ, or if Christ requests it of the Father, it is fitting (*de condígno*) that God consider us as partakers in Christ's infinite merits. Our "right" to salvation then ought to be called, in strict terms, a privilege.

Similarly, Human Law sometimes concedes us a "right" (really a privilege) of this sort. For example, a city ordinance may stipulate that if your neighbor is neglecting his property, and you maintain it for him for a certain number of years without the neighbor objecting, you have a "right" to take possession of that property.

> **PRINCIPLE 21:** "Rights" given by Human Law are, strictly speaking, privileges, not rights; they are true rights only to the extent that they facilitate or confirm a right that is already contained in the Eternal Law.

2.32 – Liberals act as if the will takes precedence over the intellect; that there is no certainly knowable objective truth (at least not concerning the purpose of human life), but rather each individual must choose by an arbitrary act of will what he will believe. Since they agree only that all must be free to disagree regarding theories of human nature and the purpose of human life, it is impossible for them to form any theory of law or rights, much less impose it upon anyone. By their own principles, there is no objectively true and knowable Law, therefore there is no foundation for imposing any law, unless it be the highly changeable and manipulable "will of the people", which is more often the mere will of some demagogue in bad disguise. These are no foundations at all. Consequently there is no foundation for any rights.

> **PRINCIPLE 22:** There is NO right to do or have anything unless it is founded in the objective Eternal Law, nor can even a privilege be conceded by Human Law to things contrary to Eternal Law.

Hence most of the slew of newfound human "rights" are either mere privileges (e.g. the right to vote), or even criminal usurpations (e.g. LGBTetc "rights" to free expression and respect of unnatural "lifestyles").

CHAPTER 3

MAN AND THE STATE

Introduction

3.1 – This Chapter follows the one on the relationship of man to his fellow man. The extension of that topic is how men relate to others in a communal, political, and governmental environment. We will unfold the Catholic position on government and the State. There is some overlap between this Chapter and the previous one, and no attempt is made here to catalog and differentiate the different forms of government, as this will be covered in Chapter 5.

The term 'government' covers such a wide range of topics that it is difficult to discuss it without narrowing the scope of the meaning of the word. Referring to an early 19th century English dictionary, we find the following:

> *Government is the exercise of authority over the actions of men in communities, societies or States; it is the direction and restraint exercised in the administration of public affairs, according to established constitutions, laws and usages, or by special edicts.* (*Webster's Dictionary*, 1828)

The State itself is simply a society on a large scale, as in a nation or country. By long-standing custom, the term can refer to the nation itself (e.g. "Mexico is a socialist State"), or only to those who govern the State (e.g. "The Mexican State decreed the nationalization of the oil industry"). It can also be used in a combined sense, to mean both at the same time. In modern times the word 'State' is too often understood to mean only the government. As said in the Glossary, we will in this work normally use the word 'State' solely in the *combined* sense, as meaning both the government and the people. When speaking of the government alone, we will usually say 'government', 'authorities', 'rulers', etc., and when speaking of the people alone we will say 'people', 'nation', 'citizens', etc. There will be a few times when 'State' will be used alone to mean one of these single senses, but if so, context should make our intent clear.

The Framework Of The State

3.2 – A State is ultimately composed of a great number of individuals, and there are relationships that exist between these individuals that are important to the societal structure of the State. As with all other organisms, there must be replenishment of the individuals in order for the State to continue to exist. The union of a man and a woman in creating and nurturing new life is so fundamental to man's nature that this bond of marriage is universally recognized by all civilizations, even the most primitive of pagans. Confucius taught that marriage is one of the pillars of government.[37] Marcus Tullius Cicero stated:

---

37   *Li Ki*, Bk. XXIV, 11: "This ceremony [*i.e.*, marriage] lies at the foundation of government."
    (http://www.sacred-texts.com/cfu/eoc/eoc09.htm – accessed 9 Nov. 2025)

> The first society is marriage itself, the next our children, then one household with all things in common; but that is the beginning of a city, and a sort of nursery of the State.[38]

It is painful to observe the chaos that results in society when the stability that marriage brings does not exist.

PRINCIPLE 23: The family is the fundamental unit of society, and forms the basis of the State.

3.3 – Although the family has the immediate means of sustaining and perpetuating itself, it lacks the ability and the wherewithal to do many of the things that will lead to fulfilling its temporal and spiritual ends. Man's highest end, of course, is to be united with God. For this purpose, Christ instituted His Church and ordained her priests, for functions that individual families cannot provide. However, even in the family's temporal existence, it falls short of providing for all its needs. Pope Pius XI summarized this when he said:

> In the first place comes the family, instituted directly by God for its peculiar purpose, the generation and formation of offspring; for this reason it has priority of nature and therefore of rights over civil society. Nevertheless, the family is an imperfect society, since it has not in itself all the means for its own complete development; whereas civil society is a perfect society, having in itself all the means for its peculiar end, which is the temporal well-being of the community; and so, in this respect, that is, in view of the common good, it has pre-eminence over the family, which finds its own suitable temporal perfection precisely in civil society.[39]

PRINCIPLE 24: The family is an imperfect society, since it does not have at its disposal all the means necessary to carry out its end.

PRINCIPLE 25: Civil society is a perfect society, that is, it has in its power all things necessary to achieve its destined end, namely the common good of its citizens in this earthly life.

Functions Of State Government

3.4 – The primary duty of the State is to facilitate the common temporal good. St. Thomas Aquinas tells us:

> The aim of any ruler should be directed toward securing the welfare of that which he undertakes to rule.[40]

Just as the father of a family puts aside his own selfish interests for the betterment of his family, so it should be for a good ruler.

---

38 *De Officiis*, Bk. I, ch. 1, §54. (https://www.thelatinlibrary.com/cicero/off1.shtml – accessed 9 Nov. 2025). Our translation.
39 Pope Pius XI, Encyclical *Divíni Illíus Magístri*, §12
40 *De Regno*, Bk. 1, ch. 3, §17

3.5 – The principal means through which the common good is achieved is through the promotion of justice, which is to give each person that which is due him.

As we have seen before with other moral principles, this concept predates Christianity, and is universally recognized in all civilizations. Our first parents were imbued with a sense of justice at their creation. It is easy to see how justice exists in the temporal realm, and it is quite interesting to see that even pagan societies understood that justice had a place in relation to religion. To quote Cicero:

> Justice is a habit of mind giving to each person what he is worthy of while preserving the common utility. Its beginning came forth from nature; afterword, certain things came into custom by reason of their usefulness; after that, the fear of the laws, and religion, sanctioned the things approved by both nature and custom. The law of Nature is that which opinion did not beget, but a power in nature implanted certain things [in men], such as religion, piety, gratitude, revenge, respect [and] truth. It is religion that brings on the care and ceremony of a certain higher nature which [men] call divine.[41]

3.6 – As the highest end of mankind is to be with God, St. Augustine describes the highest form of justice being directed toward God; if this is achieved, temporal justice will also be served.

> Justice is love serving God alone, and on that account rightly ruling... But we have said this love is not of anything, but of God, the supreme good, the highest wisdom and the perfect harmony. For which reason [justice] can be defined thus:...justice is love serving God only, and on this account ordering well other things that are subject to man...[42]

3.7 – Placing them in order of dignity and highest ultimate value, the responsibilities of the State government toward its citizens can be summarized as follows:

1. Support and defense of the mission of the Catholic Church.

2. Recognition, protection and advancement of truth and virtue.

3. Promotion of institutions for education, health, and the arts.

4. Promotion of economic stability and prosperity.

5. Providing for protection, both internal and external.

6. Creating peace and order through Human Law.

---

41 *De Invéntione*, II, §§160f. (https://www.intratext.com/IXT/LAT0922/_PX.HTM – accessed 31 Oct. 2025). Our translation.

42 St. Augustine, *On the Morals of the Catholic Church*, Bk. 1, ch. 15 (Migne edition). Our translation from the Latin. Augustine is here defining the *supernatural* virtue of justice, not the natural. In this case, justice is, in other words, the rendering to (the supernatural) God what is His due service, and that is primarily to love Him. Augustine then adds that, if this is done, it will include natural justice, which renders what is due to creatures.

As will be said later (4.2), from the standpoint of practical and immediate necessity, this order of duties would be reversed.

Subsidiarity And Solidarity

SUBSIDIARITY

3.8 – One of the most fundamental social teachings of the Church is that of the principle of subsidiarity. This principle was formally developed by Pope Leo XIII in the encyclical *Rerum Novárum*, of 1891. We can recall that two polar opposite economic systems, Laissez-faire Capitalism, and various forms of Communism, were rampant at the time. The abuse of the first system favors greed of the individual, whereas the basic premise of the second system makes the government supreme over the just rights of the individual. Pope Leo XIII sought to define a just system as a middle ground between these two systems. Forty years later, Pope Pius XI mentioned this principle:

> Just as it is gravely wrong to take from individuals what they can accomplish by their own initiative and industry and give it to the community, so also it is an injustice and at the same time a grave evil and disturbance of right order to assign to a greater and higher association what lesser and subordinate organizations can do. For every social activity ought of its very nature to furnish help to the members of the body social, and never destroy and absorb them.[43]

This is akin to the development of a child in a family; in order to mature, he must be given enough independence to develop habits of initiative and responsibility, without being stifled. At the same time, he must be given the support of other family members when he needs it. One hundred years after *Rerum Novárum*, subsidiarity was again clearly enunciated by John Paul II:

> A community of a higher order should not interfere in the internal life of a community of a lower order, depriving the latter of its functions, but rather should support it in case of need and help to coordinate its activity with the activities of the rest of society, always with a view to the common good.[44]

Subsidiarity also fosters the development of trade groups and other voluntary organizations that help connect individuals with the life and welfare of civil society. The abuse of this principle can best be shown by example. The centuries old Catholic hospital system, which was the most advanced, efficient, economical, and charitable medical system ever devised, has been all but totally destroyed by modern governments.

PRINCIPLE 26: A social body of a higher order should not exercise its authority in the affairs of a lower order of society, whether public

---

43 Encyclical *Quadragésimo Anno*, §79; see also §80
44 Encyclical *Centésimus Annus*, §48, ph. 4

or private, if that lower level is competent to deal with those affairs so as to achieve the common good.

SOLIDARITY

3.9 – A balancing principle to subsidiarity is that of solidarity, which is respect and affection for the entire human family. Pope Leo XIII used the term "friendship", and Pope Pius XI refers to it as "social charity" in the following excerpt:

> Just as the unity of society cannot rest on mutual opposition of classes, so the right ordering of economic affairs cannot be given over to the free competition of forces... Therefore, higher and more noble principles are to be sought, with which to control this power firmly and soundly; namely, social justice and social charity. Therefore, the institutions of the people, and of all social life, must be imbued with this justice, so that it be truly efficient, or establish a juridical and social order, by which, as it were, the entire economy may be fashioned. Social charity, moreover, should be as a soul of this order, and an alert public authority should aim to protect and guard this effectively...[45]

> **PRINCIPLE 27: In any society, subjects should practice solidarity for the common good; they should obey superiors, unless such obedience will clearly be false obedience because it conflicts with a higher authority, especially God Himself. A lower order of society, whether public or private, should always act with the intention of placing first the common good of the larger society of which it is a part.**

3.10 – Since the Church was instituted for man by Christ, who was both man and God, it has both human and divine elements. Being from God, the Church was given the fullness of grace and truth. As we have seen in several instances before, even pagan societies sometimes do an admirable job of discerning moral truths. The Church has never held that outside of her teaching man cannot arrive at any moral truths, but that she has the whole of moral truth needed for salvation: *omnem veritátem*. Pope Pius XI tells us the completeness of the Church:

> The third society, into which man is born when through Baptism he reaches the divine life of grace, is the Church; a society of the supernatural order and of universal extent; a perfect society, because it has in itself all the means required for its own end, which is the eternal salvation of mankind; hence it is supreme in its own domain.[46]

---

[45] Encyclical *Quadragésimo Anno*, §88. It should be plain that this unity and charity in a society can neither exist nor be maintained without a substantial agreement by its members on man's purpose in life. In fact, there cannot even *be* a State society without this common purpose (cf. the definition of 'society' given in 2.11).

[46] Encyclical *Divíni Illíus Magístri*, §13

Since the spiritual end of man is more exalted than the temporal end, the Church is superior to the institution of the State.

This principle is self-evident and hardly needs any justification. Pope Boniface VIII made this comment:

> We confess the more clearly that spiritual power precedes any earthly power both in dignity and nobility, as spiritual matters themselves excel the temporal. (Bull *Unam Sanctam*, Dz 469)

PRINCIPLE 28: The Church, like the State, is a perfect society, since she has been given everything she needs to attain her end, namely the salvation of man.

3.11 – But since political power comes from God, government is in accord with human nature, and is therefore intrinsically good.

> Let every soul be subject to higher powers: for there is no power but from God: and those that are, are ordained of God. (Romans 13:1)

> God imposed upon mankind the fear of man, for mankind did not acknowledge the fear of God... Earthly rule, therefore, has been appointed by God for the benefit of nations...[47]

> ...[B]y this choice [of the people], in truth, the ruler is designated, but the rights of ruling are not thereby conferred.[48]

> Modern writers in great numbers, following in the footsteps of those who called themselves philosophers in the last century, declare that all power comes from the people; consequently those who exercise power in society do not exercise it from their own authority, but from an authority delegated to them by the people and on the condition that it can be revoked by the will of the people from whom they hold it. Quite contrary is the sentiment of Catholics who hold that the right of government derives from God as its natural and necessary principle.[49]

The best known and also most authoritative statement of the source of political authority is from Jesus, when he replied to Pilate's question:

> Pilate therefore says to him, "Speakest thou not to me? Dost thou not know that I have authority to release thee and have authority to crucify thee?" Jesus answered: "Thou shouldst not have any power against me, unless it were given thee from above." (John 19:10-11)

In their turn, authorities of Christ's Church have explained His words:

---

47 St. Irenaeus, *Adversus Haereses*, Bk. 5, ch. 24, §2 (from *Ante-Nicene Fathers*, Vol. 1, trans. A. Roberts & W. Rambaut, www.newadvent.org/fathers/0103524.htm – accessed 9 Nov. 2025)
48 Pope Leo XIII; *Diuturnum Illud*, §6.
49 Pope St. Pius X, Encyclical *Notre Charge Apostolique*, ph. 22, citing Leo XIII.

> For it is certain that political power is of God, from Whom proceeds nothing that is not good and lawful. St. Augustine proves this. For the [Book of] Wisdom of God proclaims, "By Me kings reign." And below, "By Me princes rule."[50]
>
> First, political power considered in general...comes directly from God alone; for this follows of necessity from the nature of man, since that nature comes from Him Who made it.[51]
>
> For even if servile subjection began after the sin of Adam, nevertheless there would have been political government even while man was in the state of innocence. And this is proved, firstly, because even then man would have been by nature a political and social animal, and hence would have had need of a ruler.[52]
>
> From these pronouncements of the Popes it is evident that the origin of public power is to be sought for in God Himself, and not in the multitude...[53]

PRINCIPLE 29: Political leaders of a State derive their authority from God, not from the people over which they rule.

3.12 – Nevertheless, this does not mean that the people have no role to play in political or governmental affairs.

> But, in general, as we have said, to be willing to take no part in public affairs would be as much at fault as to have no interest and to do nothing for the common good, and even more, because Catholics by the admonition of the very doctrine which they profess are impelled to carry on their affairs with integrity and trust. On the other hand, if they remain indifferent, those whose opinions carry very little hope for the safety of the State will easily seize the reins of government. And this also would be fraught with injury to the Christian religion, because those who were evilly disposed toward the Church would have the greatest power, and those well disposed the least.
>
> Therefore, it is very clear that the reason for Catholics entering public affairs is just, for they do not enter them nor ought they to do so for this reason: so as to approve that which at the moment is not honorable in the methods of public affairs, but to transfer these methods, insofar as it can be done, to the genuine and true public good, having in mind the purpose of introducing into all the veins of the State, as a most healthful sap and blood, the wisdom and virtue of the Christian religion...

---

50 St. Robert Bellarmine, *De Láicis*, ch. 6, §1 (https://catholicism.org/de-laicis.html/6 – accessed 9 Nov. 2025)
51 Ibid., ch. 6, §2
52 Ibid., ch. 7, §1
53 Leo XIII, Encyclical *Immortále Dei*, §35 (Dz 1868), after quoting Gregory XVI and Pius IX.

> In this way Catholics will obtain two very excellent results: one, that of establishing themselves as helpers of the Church in preserving and propagating Christian wisdom; the other, that of bestowing upon civil society the greatest blessing, the preservation of which is imperiled by evil doctrines, and passions.[54]
>
> Unless it be otherwise determined by reason of some exceptional condition of things, it is expedient to take part in the administration of public affairs. And the Church approves of every one devoting his services to the common good, and doing all that he can for the defense, preservation, and prosperity of his country.[55]

3.13 – In forms of government in which the privilege of voting is established, the *Baltimore Catechism* gives a good summary of the Church's teaching regarding the duty to vote.

> Question 246: How does a citizen show a sincere interest in his country's welfare?
>
> Answer: Citizens should exercise the right [sic] to vote. This is a moral obligation when the common good of the State or the good of religion, especially in serious matters, can be promoted...[56]

3.14 – Finally, the most important reason to be involved with the affairs of government is to ensure that it does not violate one of its most important functions: that of promoting and protecting the Church. Pope St. Pius X chastised the French Catholic action group, the Sillon, for its indifference in defending the Church against political assault:

> Certainly, it is not the Church that has gone into the political arena: they have dragged her there to mutilate and to despoil her. Is it not the duty of every Catholic, then, to use the political weapons which he holds, to defend her? Is it not a duty to confine politics to its own domain and to leave the Church alone except in order to give her that which is her due?[57]

PRINCIPLE 30: Citizens must take an active interest in the commonweal and participate according to their station in life.

Summary

3.15 – The State is the interrelationship of men with each other in the public, national realm. Government is an artifact of man's very nature, and as such is inherently good. It is only misdirection of political force by those in power that turns State authority into a vehicle for evil rather than for the betterment of its citizens.

---

54 Pope Leo XIII, Encyclical *Immortále Dei*, §44f (quoted from Dz 1883-1888)
55 Leo XIII, Encyclical *Libértas Praestantíssimum*, §45
56 Rev. Francis J. Connell, C.Ss.R., ed., *The New Confraternity Edition: Revised Baltimore Catechism and Mass*, No. 3, p. 145 (Benziger Brothers, New York, 1949)
57 Letter of Pope St. Pius X to the French Archbishops and Bishops on The Sillon, *Notre Charge Apostolique*, ph. 38.

CHAPTER 4

THE CHURCH AND THE STATE

Review And Preview

4.1 – Chapter 2 had defined that a society is a stable union of a number of persons in fellowship and cooperation for a common purpose of benefit to all.

'Church' and 'State' fit this definition, and both are therefore societies.

Chapter 3 touched upon the fact that Church and State are both perfect societies; that is, each has everything it needs for the attainment of its purpose. Their respective purposes were declared.

We will restate these purposes here, but since Church-State relations are an eminently practical affair so far as the State government is concerned, we will list the civil leaders' general duties in order of the urgency of needs that the State must address.

4.2 – Purposes Of The State

1. Creating peace and order through Human Law. (The formulation and enforcement of Human Law is the government's main instrument for achieving a basic level of justice, without which a society cannot even exist.)

2. Providing for protection, both internal and external.

3. Promotion of economic stability and prosperity.

4. Promotion of institutions for education, health, and the arts.

5. Recognition, protection and advancement of truth and virtue.

6. Support and defense of the mission of the Catholic Church.

Immediate Purposes Of The State

4.3 – The first four above are the immediate purposes of the State, but there are others, less pressing but more elevated.

Remote Purpose Of The State

As was said in Chapter 2, Aristotle declared a deeper goal of the State to be the perfection of human nature, consisting in the lifelong exercise of virtue. He adds that proper reasoning, and the contemplation of truth, are virtues essential to man's natural happiness. The immediate goals of the State simply provide the conditions whereby this remote purpose, natural happiness, can be realized, and this natural happiness is therefore listed as number 5 in the State's priorities.

However, even this remote purpose is not the deepest, or ultimate, purpose of man.

Ultimate Purpose Of The State

4.4 – Chapter 1 said that, while man through his natural power can attain a limited satisfaction in the limited truth and good found in nature, his true and full happiness can be found only in the possession of the supernatural vision of God. (Principle 7)

Providing for this ultimate happiness is the *entire* purpose of the Catholic Church. (Principle 28)

But the State actually shares with the Church that same ultimate purpose, for all men are called to the same ultimate end. The Church, however, has the salvation of souls as its sole, direct, and proper end, whereas the State properly and directly has the immediate and remote ends named above, and has the salvation of souls as ultimate end only in an indirect and auxiliary manner. This is the way to understand goal number 6 in our above order.

The very reasons for the existence of the two societies of Church and State being clarified at the foundation, we can proceed to study their relations.

Defining Terms : Religion, Pseudo-Religion, Church

4.5 – In this discussion we must define three terms: religion, pseudo-religion and Church. The terms 'government' and 'State' have already been addressed in the Introduction to Chapter 3.

> *A religion is any comprehensive and organized system of beliefs, and/or a corresponding society that practices that system, centered on man's ultimate purpose, including his relationship to God or gods, and including the practice of some kind of worship of God or gods.*

Thus, an essential element of any religion is an acknowledgment of a Deity or deities, one or more beings transcendent to and superior to human society and nature.

> **4.6** – *A Pseudo-Religion is any comprehensive system of beliefs that purports to give explanations of man's ultimate purpose and highest ideals, including moral values, but which does not acknowledge the existence of any God or gods, and/or pretends to make man himself a god.*

Communism and Secular Humanism are examples of pseudo-religions.

> **4.7** – *A Church is an organized Christian society existing to offer worship to the God of the Old and New Testaments, to instruct its adherents in all spiritual matters, and to define doctrines of a Christian faith.*

When it is not sufficiently clear from context, and when the word 'Church' refers to the one, true, holy, Catholic and apostolic Church (the Roman Catholic Church), we will use the term 'Catholic Church'.

When we speak of Church-State relations, then, it is important to remember that we are really speaking of Religion-State relations. 'Churches', as we see, are simply a subset of the larger set called 'religions'. It is obvious that Christian religions are not the only ones that have relations with the State in which they are found.[58]

Cooperation Of The State With A Religion Or Pseudo-Religion

GOVERNMENT AND SUBJECTS MUST AGREE ON MAN'S ULTIMATE PURPOSE

4.8 – It is possible that a Religion or Church's relation to the State authorities be simply that of conflict; the two do not cooperate at all, but have goals entirely at odds with each other. For instance, the theocracy that is Islam has militarily conquered other States and imposed its own religion upon the subjects. Since the vast majority of the inhabitants of the conquered territory were of other religions, the inevitable result was that the Islamic government and the religion(s) of the inhabitants were profoundly inimical to each other. Islamic rule could be maintained only through sheer force.

Again, in modern times, Communist revolutions staged military takeovers of nations where the majority of citizens did not share the atheist pseudo-religion of their new "leaders".

In these cases, there must follow a persecution by the rulers (usually one both physical and moral) of non-conforming religions. The result is a schizophrenic society which cannot long endure. The situation usually resolves itself by the population little by little being converted to the conqueror's religion or pseudo-religion, or at least becoming entirely acquiescent.

Historically, every stable nation has had of necessity a rather good cooperation between Religion and State.

SEPARATION OF CHURCH AND STATE?

4.9 – Apologists for modern democratic republics, however, claim to practice the "separation of Church and State"; that is, the separation of religion from the State. In most of the world it is now accepted that this separation is a good thing because it allows all citizens the freedom to practice the religion of their choice without having the government impose any particular set of beliefs on them.

However, consider the following reasoning:

1. Every deliberate act of man is either good or evil; either ordered to his true final end or to a false final end. (*Summa Theol.* I-II Q.18, a9, resp.)[59]

---

[58] The framers of the First Amendment of the United States Constitution clearly recognized this fact, for they used the word 'religion', not 'Church': "Congress shall make no law respecting an establishment of **religion**, or prohibiting the free exercise thereof..."

2. All man's deliberate acts are therefore moral, and impact man's ultimate purpose.

3. And man's ultimate purpose is the province of a religion (or Church) to decide.

4. And for that reason, religions also establish laws to encourage or discourage certain deliberate acts.

5. But a government, by its own laws, also encourages or discourages certain deliberate acts.[60]

6. The laws of the Religion/Church and of the government affect the same citizenry.

7. Therefore, most civil laws either support or oppose a given religion (or Church).

An example is needed to make this more clear.

In 1973, the United States legalized abortion. By this action it unmistakably declared that abortion was not a crime. By so doing, it put itself at total variance with many Churches or Religions in the U.S., which hold the opposite view. To put it another way, the government declared that abortion is either a good thing to do, or, at worst, that it is morally indifferent. This in turn meant that the civil rulers declared that abortion does no harm to man's well being (and perhaps even helps it).

Many Churches or Religions, however, hold the opposite view; they claim that the law of God (or of nature) forbids abortion; that the aborted child is in fact a child and not merely a soulless blob of tissue, and thus the child itself is obviously harmed, and more, that perpetrators of abortion have gravely damaged their own souls, and risk going to everlasting misery in hell. Thus these Churches or Religions hold that abortion negatively impacts man's purpose.

The United States established a totally contrary law, that enabled and encouraged abortion. Thus it set its own law as true, and that of the opposed Churches or Religions as false. This means it set itself up as the ultimate moral and therefore *religious* authority in the land, which in turn means it acted as both State and State Religion.[61]

4.10 – For these reasons (and others), the authority of the Church declares:

> [It is a *condemned* proposition that] the Church is to be separated from the State, and the State from the Church.[62]

---

59 "For since it belongs to the reason to direct [things], if an action that proceeds from deliberate reason be not directed to the due end, it is, by that fact alone, repugnant to reason, and has the character of evil. But if it be directed to a due end, it is in accord with reason; wherefore it has the character of good. Now it must needs be either directed or not directed to a due end. Consequently every human action that proceeds from deliberate reason, if it be considered in the individual, must be good or bad."

60 Cf. Chapter 2, 2.2 – 2.4.

61 This passage was written before the U.S. Supreme Court, in 2022, overturned Roe vs. Wade. This reversal, of course, has no impact on the force of our example, unless to enhance it.

62 Pius IX, *Syllabus of Errors*, (condemned proposition from the Allocution *Acerbíssimum*. Dz 1755)

[A]t this time men are found not a few who, applying to civil society the impious and absurd principle of "naturalism", as they call it, dare to teach that the best constitution of public society, and civil progress, altogether require that human society be conducted and governed without regard being had to religion any more than if it did not exist; or, at least, without any distinction being made between the true religion and false ones.[63]

...[S]o far from one of the powers [of Church or State] separating itself from the other, or still less coming into conflict with it, complete harmony, such as is suited to the end for which each power exists, should be preserved between them.[64]

PRINCIPLE 31: In the fulfillment of its duties, State government passes laws with moral implications. Those laws are either in accord with God's Law or reject God's Law. Therefore, it is not possible for the State to be neutral regarding matters of religion.

We can add that, every time a State passes an important law, then, simply because that law has moral implications, it necessarily discriminates against any other religions that do not agree with those moral implications.

4.11 – Since it clashes so harshly with the mindset of so many people today, we would like to show the origins and development of the delusion that it is possible to separate Religion/Church from the State, and the inevitable result of trying to do so. We can, however, give only an extremely brief outline, as follows:

1. Martin Luther introduces the idea of private interpretation of Scripture. Since private persons don't agree in their interpretations, the logical consequence is that each person must invent his own religion; we have unconditional liberty of conscience.

2. The Anabaptists take this principle and apply it rigorously; all men are of equal authority; existing religious and secular laws are thus invalid; democracy is the only legitimate form of government in both Churches and States.

3. Anabaptist anarchic logic is first met with horror and persecution, but since Protestant society at large wishes to retain its "right" to private interpretation in religious matters, it remains blind to the fact that the associated social anarchy follows necessarily from that very "right". Thus the anarchy remains unchecked.

4. Necessarily then, nations are disintegrated by religious factions and wars. European nations north of Spain are forced to grant more and more

---

63 Pius IX, *Quanta Cura*, 1864, §3 (Dz 1689)
64 Leo XIII, Encyclical *Immortále Dei*, §35. See also Gregory XVI, Encyclical *Mirári Vos*, §20 (Dz 1615); Pope St. Pius X, Encyclical *Veheménter Nos*, 1906, §3; St. Augustine, quoted by Pius XI in the encyclical *Quas Primas*, §18 (Dz 2196); Pius IX, *Syllabus of Errors*, §77 (condemned proposition from the Allocution *Nemo Vestrum*. Dz 1777); Pope Leo XIII, *Immortále Dei*, §47 (Dz 1885).

religious liberty; to agree to disagree, in order to keep internal material peace.

5. "Enlightenment" philosophers, especially Locke, Bayle and Voltaire, rationalize and recommend this religious "tolerance" – while of course, unavoidably, showing intolerance of any disagreement with their own view.

6. Meanwhile, a mishmash of European emigrants, many of whom have fled religious persecution, come to North America. The United States is formed, being the first major nation to adopt religious liberty as a principle: the first non-confessional State. A supposed separation of Religion and State is declared and practiced – which in reality is the establishment of the pseudo-religion of Agnostic Secular Humanism, but which fact few are aware of.

7. The material and temporary success of Agnostic Secular Humanism causes it to be adopted through most of Western civilization. During all this time, this success, as also love of self and one's "liberty", keep the world blind to the fundamental impossibility of the separation of the State from religious matters. Ironically, the Anabaptist anarchic liberty of conscience is going from being persecuted to being the persecutor; those who are "intolerant" are no longer tolerated.

8. Presently, this blindness continues, but Secularism is the all-but-official pseudo-religion of Western nations. Sensing its power, it is now repudiating the same liberty of conscience it made use of to gain its position; liberty of conscience is being denied to many religions, and to the Catholic Faith in particular. Examples of this denial of liberty of conscience are everywhere: coercion of Christian bakers to force them to bake wedding cakes for homosexuals; forced sex and transgender "education" in public schools; strictly enforced codes of "politically-correct" speech on college campuses; requirements to participate in health plans which provide abortions; not to mention institutionalized, publicly-funded usury and never-ending rounds of unjust wars.

4.12 – We can also argue that there is no such thing as separation of Religion and State because no laws can even be made unless they come from religious or at least pseudo-religious principles. A religion by definition tells us what our ultimate purpose is, and how to achieve it. Even a pseudo-religion does this, though the purpose it proposes is false. If a State were truly to operate without such ultimate life principles at all, it would act without any goal in mind at all. Thus its laws could only be formulated at random, by the alternate personal campaigns of demagogues, and the nation would be in chaos, with no order, peace or happiness possible.[65]

As a corollary then, the more strongly the ultimate principles of life are held by the rulers together with the citizens, the more efficient will be the State's lawmaking.

---

65 In practice, of course, this can never happen. Since nature abhors a vacuum, the reality is that, even in a mass of individuals thrown together by circumstance, some leader, along with a leading idea, always rises up to unite the individuals into a society, with one common purpose. We see this even in the simplest everyday situations, such as on the elementary school playground, where all generally participate in one recreational activity, at the instigation of one person.

Unfortunately, these laws will be efficiently destructive if the life principles in question are false.

On the other hand, they will be efficiently helpful if they are true.

Thus we have:

> **PRINCIPLE 32: To the extent that the religion professed by the State is true, and assuming that Church and State are pursuing their purposes correctly, then the more closely they cooperate, the more functional is the nation, and the more peace and happiness for the citizens will result.**

Of course, the greatest possible peace and happiness will follow from the most effective application of the truest religious principles, and so only a Catholic State can hope to achieve this maximal happiness.

THE CATHOLIC MODEL OF CHURCH-STATE COOPERATION

Church And State Authority : Distinct But Overlapping

4.13 – Authoritative declarations of the Catholic Church maintain both the distinction between ecclesiastical and civil power, and the need for close cooperation between the two.[66]

The following will serve as an excellent preamble to this subject:

> The Almighty, therefore, has given the charge of the human race to two powers, the ecclesiastical and the civil, the one being set over divine, and the other over human things. Each in its kind is supreme, each has fixed limits within which it is contained, limits which are defined by the nature and special object [i.e. purpose] of the province of each, so that there is, we may say, an orbit traced out within which the action of each is brought into play by its own native right. But...each of these two powers has authority over the same subjects, and...it might come to pass that one and the same thing – related differently, but still remaining one and the same thing – might belong to the jurisdiction and determination of both...
>
> In matters, however, of mixed jurisdiction, it is in the highest degree consonant to nature, as also to the designs of God, that so far from one of the powers separating itself from the other, or still less coming into conflict with it, complete harmony, such as is suited to the end for which each power exists, should be preserved between them.[67]

Because these two powers, Church and civil government, rule over the same subjects, the possibility at least of conflict between them is ever-present. It is therefore obviously desirable to be clear about the said "fixed limits", wherever

---

[66] E.g. Pius IX, Encyclical *Quanta Cura*, §5 (Dz 1698), where the opinion that Church power is not distinct and independent of civil power is condemned as heretical, and Leo XIII, Encyclical *Immortále Dei*, §14: "There must...exist between these two powers a certain orderly connection, which may be compared to the union of the soul and body in man."

[67] Leo XIII, *Immortále Dei*, §§13, 35

possible, which will also make clear which issues overlap, and "belong to the jurisdiction and determination of both".

As will be said (Principle 33), of the two powers, the Church is higher than secular rulers. Therefore, the Catholic Church can authoritatively define her own manner of cooperation with them. She has already made definite statements regarding this, and thus we shall present these as the "fixed limits" mentioned by Leo XIII. Knowledge of these limits, though necessary, will never suffice, however. As said in our General Introduction, the virtue of prudence will be needed, and in both Church and State rulers. It will also be found that the balancing principles of subsidiarity (Principle 26) and solidarity (Principle 27) become essential to the practical maintenance of relations between the Catholic Church and civil governments.

DOMAINS OF AUTHORITY RESERVED TO THE CATHOLIC CHURCH : IN GENERAL

> **4.14** – Since *everything which is not from faith is a sin* (Rom. 14:23)...we define that no precept either canonical or civil, without good faith, has any value, since that which cannot be observed without mortal sin must in general be rejected by every constitution and custom. (Lateran Council IV, Dz 439)

The meaning here is that no law, whether canonical (i.e. ecclesiastical) or civil, is valid unless it conforms to the moral teaching of the Catholic Faith.

Consider these propositions *condemned* by Pope Pius IX:

> Kings and leaders are not only exempt from the jurisdiction of the Church, but they are also superior to the Church in deciding questions of jurisdiction.[68]

> In a conflict between the laws of both [Church and State] powers, the civil law prevails.[69]

> The civil authority can interfere in matters pertaining to religion, morals, and spiritual government.[70]

Since these three quotes assert what is condemned, Pius IX means that in a conflict between civil laws and Church laws, the Church has jurisdiction, and her law prevails. Civil authority cannot interfere in matters pertaining to religion, morals, and spiritual government.

> Whatever therefore in things human is of a sacred character, whatever belongs either of its own nature or by reason of the end to which it is referred, to the salvation of souls, or to the worship of God, is subject to the power and judgment of the Church.[71]

68　*Syllabus of Errors*, §54 (condemned proposition from *Multíplices Inter*. Dz 1754)
69　*Syllabus of Errors*, §42 (condemned proposition from the Apostolic Letter *Ad Apostólicae*. Dz 1742)
70　*Syllabus of Errors*, §44 (condemned proposition from the Allocution *Máximae Quidem*. Dz 1744)
71　Leo XIII, Encyclical *Immortále Dei*, §14 (Dz 1866)

> [I]t is the Church, and not the State, that is to be man's guide to heaven. It is to the Church that God has assigned the charge of seeing to, and legislating for, all that concerns religion.[72]

4.15 – Given the definition of 'religion' stated above (4.5), the phrase in the latter quote, "all that concerns religion" means all that concerns man's ultimate purpose and how to serve it.

This includes all moral laws. Questions of abortion and homosexuality, for example, "refer to the salvation of souls", and it follows that any laws concerning them must be in conformity to the laws and teachings of the Catholic Church.

> [I]nstances occur where the State [government] seems to require from men as subjects one thing, and religion, from men as Christians, quite another; and this in reality without any other ground than that the rulers of the State either hold the sacred power of the Church of no account, or endeavor to subject it to their own will. Hence arises a conflict... The two powers confront each other and urge their behests in a contrary sense; to obey both is wholly impossible. "No man can serve two masters", for to please the one amounts to contemning the other. As to which should be preferred no one ought to balance for an instant. It is a high crime indeed to withdraw allegiance from God in order to please men, an act of consummate wickedness to break the laws of Jesus Christ, in order to yield obedience to earthly rulers, or, under pretext of keeping the civil law, to ignore the rights of the Church: "we ought to obey God rather than men".[73]

Thus it is clear that the traditional teaching of the Catholic Church gives us this principle to guide Church-State relations:

> **PRINCIPLE 33: In case of a conflict between laws of Church and State regarding religion, morals, and spiritual government (i.e. Church discipline), the Catholic Church is the final judge.**[74]

DOMAINS OF AUTHORITY RESERVED TO THE CATHOLIC CHURCH : IN PARTICULAR

4.16 – From certain more specific judgments of the Church, we can add some details as to what falls under Church jurisdiction. In what follows, in order to avoid cumbersomeness, we shall give only a condensed summary of Church teaching, using few or no direct quotes. If found in Denzinger, references will be cited only by their Denzinger number; that is, the exact papal or conciliar source will not be given. These exact sources can be found in Denzinger itself, if needed.

---

72 Ibid., §11
73 Leo XIII, Encyclical *Sapiéntiae Christiánae*, §§6 & 7 (Dz 1936b). See also Pius XI, Encyclical *Quas Primas*, §32.
74 See also Dz 1719, 1842 & 1869.

On Various Temporal Affairs

Dz 361: Laymen have no faculty for determining anything concerning ecclesiastical possessions.

Dz 401: The Church does not employ bloody punishments, but Catholic rulers sometimes should do so if the Church hands criminals over to them.

Dz 469: The State [government] should safeguard the liberty of the Church to teach and act for the salvation of souls. (Also Leo XIII, Encyclical *Immortále Dei*, §11f).

Dz 495: Temporal affairs of the Church are not subject to the secular ruler.

Dz 1692, 1693: The right of citizens and the Church of asking for alms openly in the cause of Christian charity cannot be taken from them by the State [rulers].

Dz 1693: The Church can establish Holy Days, on which servile work is prohibited.

Dz 1696, 1726, 1727, 1734: The Church has the right to acquire property, and cannot be excluded from administration and dominion over it.

Dz 1697: The Church can make laws binding in conscience concerning the use of temporal goods.

Dz 1728, 1749: Bishops can issue letters without the permission of the State [government], and bishops and faithful cannot be hindered from communicating with the Roman Pontiff.

Dz 1850, 1936, 2278: Citizens can fight against the State [authorities], morally and even physically, if the State is gravely and continuously violating their rights, and provided that Catholic moral principles are followed.

Dz 439, 1842, 1857: However, members of the Church, and even its hierarchy, are subject to civil law so far as it conforms to Natural and Divine Law. (Cf. Ppl. 35)

4.17 – On Marriage

Dz 971-981, 982, 1500a, 1558-1560, 1640, 1765-1774: Since marriage is a sacrament, matrimonial and betrothal cases belong to the Church, even in infidel countries.

4.18 – On Education

Dz 2202: Like all human endeavors, education has a purpose. The ultimate purpose is salvation.

Dz 2203: This is greater than the immediate purpose, which is useful skills; e.g. family living, or the remote purpose, which is societal living; i.e. the common good of this earthly life.

Dz 2204: Therefore the Church is the supreme authority in matters of education.

Dz 2209–2211: (The roles of Church and State in education are described.)

Further particulars:

Dz 1694: Rights of parents over the education of their children do not come from the State.

Dz 1695: The Church cannot be obstructed from educating youth.

Dz 1733, 1746: The Church has the power to direct the teaching of theology.

Dz 1745, 1747: The State cannot take over Catholic schools, or interfere in discipline, the system of studies, conferring of degrees, or choice or approval of teachers.

Dz 1746: Nor can the State [rulers] interfere in the plan of studies for seminaries.

Dz 1748: The Catholic Faith should be taught in all schools.

4.19 – On Public Speech

Dz 1690, 1867, 1868: No law can be made granting liberty of conscience to the expressing of error.

Dz 1932f: But expression of error may be tolerated wherever there is just cause, and only with such moderation as will prevent its degenerating into license and excess.

4.20 – On Public Worship

Dz 411, 1875: The Church does not, and the State [government] may not, make a law forcing conversion, or baptism or any other Catholic sacrament, on anyone.

Dz 1690, 1778, 1779, 1867, 1868: No law can be made *approving* liberty of worship to false religions.

Dz 1874: But, for some great good, or the prevention of some evil, false worship may be tolerated.

4.21 – On Church Discipline

Dz 333: "...[W]ithout doubt, every administrator of mundane [worldly and temporal] affairs ought to be removed from sacred affairs, just as it is proper that no one from the group of clergy...be implicated in any secular affairs."

Dz 339, 341, 497, 1750, 1751: Secular power cannot correct, appoint or depose the pope or bishops.

Dz 340: The presence of a civil ruler is not necessary in order to hold a synod.

Dz 1731: The Church can run its own courts to try clerics for civil or criminal cases.

Dz 499, 1504, 1505, 1697, 1724: The Church can use force to punish her subjects, even without State [authorities'] permission.

Dz 1736: The State [power] cannot enforce definitions of a national ecclesiastical council against a counter-ruling of the Holy See.

Dz 1737: National Churches which are exempt from the authority of the Holy See cannot be established.

Dz 1744: The State cannot interfere in matters pertaining to instructions of pastors to souls, administration of the sacraments, or dispositions needed to receive them.

Dz 1752, 1753: The civil power cannot set legal ages for, nor require that persons wishing to enter religious life in the Church ask State permission, nor does it have power over laws concerning the rights and duties of religious persons.

Dz 1842: The State [authority] has no power over bishops in matters which pertain to the holy ministry.

4.22 – On Military Matters

Dz 469: The Church has both a spiritual and material sword. The latter should be exercised by the State [power], but with the will and sufferance of the Church, for spiritual power must judge of earthly power, whether it acts well or not.

Dz 1732: Clerics cannot be conscripted.

Dz 1936b: If a war is clearly unjust, citizens must object in conscience, and even refuse service. (See also the context of Dz 1936b: *Sapiéntiae Christiánae*, §§7ff)

4.23 – It may sometimes happen that it is not clear to civil authorities what the Catholic Church teaches on a particular and current public matter about which those civil authorities must legislate or otherwise establish policy. Extended periods of persecution of the Church, or of breakdown in communications caused by war, civil upheaval or natural disaster, or even temporary turmoil or confusion among authorities in the Church Herself, are examples of such situations. Those people in authority who wish to do the will of God in this case will not go far wrong if they hold to, and strive to reason from, the Tradition of social and moral doctrines of the Church, for these cannot possibly be overturned or altered by any authority whatsoever. The reason for this is simple. The Catholic Church has always claimed that one of the primary reasons it was established by Jesus Christ was to act as a sure and unfailing guide to all men through all time as to what they must believe concerning God and the moral law. If it ever substantially changed anything that it had already dogmatically taught over the course of past centuries, that could only mean either that it had been wrong in the past, or that it was wrong now to make the change. If it were wrong in the past, then it was never the unfailing guide that it claimed to be, and therefore it was never the true Church of Christ. If it has never been the true Church of Christ, then the change it makes now in doctrine is completely unreliable. Substantial changes in settled Church doctrine therefore come not from the Church at all, but only from wayward members of Her hierarchy.

Fortunately, there is nothing entirely new under the sun, and in the vast majority of cases it will not be difficult to apply the Tradition of Catholic social and moral teaching to present circumstances, even when some details of those circumstances may never have been encountered before.[75] An example may be helpful here also: That capital punishment is, at least in some cases, both just and necessary, and that the State has therefore both the right and duty to use it on occasion, is unquestionably a Traditional teaching of the Church. It has been consistently and clearly taught, even since the time of the Apostles (cf. Rom. 13:1-4). Therefore, if any authority whatsoever were to teach or demand that capital punishment is in no case advisable, its teaching and ruling would be entirely invalid; it would not be coming from the Church, but from the error of man.

> **PRINCIPLE 34:** Those who wield power in a Catholic State must refrain from making or approving laws that are, either directly or in their logical consequences, contrary or inimical to Traditional Catholic doctrine and morals. If such a law is made, it is null and void, and must be disregarded.

And on the other hand:

> **PRINCIPLE 35:** The State, in defense of Traditional Catholic morality and social order, may, if necessary, prosecute and punish

---

75 It will of course be necessary for civil rulers to be confident in discerning what among Catholic teachings is of Tradition. Again, the "old" *Catholic Encyclopedia*, 1910-1914, treats well of this subject. See the articles Infallibility, and Tradition and Magisterium. Also of great use is the *Commonitórium* of St. Vincent of Lerins, especially chapters 2 and 23. Part of the *Commonitórium* has even been *infallibly* endorsed by the Church at Vatican Council I. It is used in Dz 1800, and dogmatically affirmed in Dz 1818.

crimes against Natural and Divine Law, even those committed by clerics and religious, if the Church authorities themselves fail to do so. Before acting against clerics and religious, the civil authority must notify appropriate Ecclesiastical authority of the alleged crimes, and a reasonable period of time must be allowed to the Ecclesiastical authority to do justice against these wrongdoers through the Church's own courts, if such courts exist at that time.[76]

DOMAINS OF AUTHORITY RESERVED TO THE STATE : IN GENERAL

4.24 – First it should be noted that the Catholic Church throughout history, and especially in modern times, has naturally been more concerned to defend her own rights in Church-State relations. She has made few positive declarations on the rights of rulers of States. Beyond this, we can assume that, in her negative declarations (her declarations as to what rights the State does *not* have), she is allowing to the State authority whatever is not excluded, within reason. From all this, and the principles of such relations that we have already proposed, as well as such other sources as seem useful, we can infer a set of positive rights.

> One of the two [powers – i.e. the State] has for its proximate [immediate] and chief object the well-being of this mortal life.[77]

In previous Chapters, this purpose of the State has already been explained. A subdivision of this general domain of State authority seems unnecessary. We can then state a principle:

PRINCIPLE 36: Insofar as its Human Law is in conformity with Natural and Divine Law, the State has authority to order secular affairs for the well-being of this mortal life, and in this has a right to the obedience of the citizens.

DOMAINS OF AUTHORITY RESERVED TO THE STATE : IN PARTICULAR

4.25 – The well-being of this mortal life, as was said in Chapter 2, is the perfection of human nature via the practice of virtue, and the contemplation of truth. Again, this is the remote purpose of the State, and this well-being is achieved by first realizing some immediate purposes. These immediate purposes, and the remote purpose (No. 5), are once more listed:

1. Achieving peace and order through Human Law.

2. Providing for protection, both internal and external.

3. Promotion of economic stability and prosperity.

4. Promotion of institutions for education, health, and the arts.

5. Recognition, protection and advancement of truth and virtue.

---

76 Cf. Dz 439 (cited above, 4.14). Also 4.16 (last entry), Dz 401, 499, 1504, 1505, 1697, 1724, 1731.
77 Pope Leo XIII, *Immortále Dei*, §14 (Dz 1866)

These purposes are obviously also duties, for everyone has the duty to fulfill his purpose(s) in life. This the State cannot do without the authority to do so, hence these immediate and remote purposes are one and the same as the particular domains of authority of the State.

The reservation of these domains to the State cannot, of course, be absolute, given the restrictions of Principles 33 and 34, which are of universal application. Outside of these, however, the State authority has free scope.

4.26 – Now, in the list above was formerly a sixth duty: to promote and defend the mission of the Catholic Church. We must exclude it here as a domain of State *authority*, however, because while this remains indeed a duty of the State, the State shares this duty subordinate to the Church Herself, thus does not have principal authority in its execution. How this should be done is a direct concern of the purpose of the Church, and is neither the immediate nor remote purpose of civil government. Nevertheless, the State authority must have some say in the matter, for it has knowledge and competence as to the availability and marshalling of resources, and may be charged in part with the practical execution of plans in this area. We must say then that this domain is shared by both Church and State, with the Church having final say in any plans that are formulated, since her own promotion and defense are concerned. In regard of such mixed jurisdiction:

> [The Church] advises princes to follow justice and in nothing to err from duty; and at the same time she strengthens and aids their authority in many ways. Whatever takes place in the field of civil affairs, she recognizes and declares to be in their power and supreme control; in those matters whose judgment, although for different reasons, pertains to sacred and civil power, she wishes that there exist concord between both, by benefit of which lamentable contentions are avoided for both.[78]

The delineation we have given of the domains of Church and State authority, if observed, will very often prevent the said contentions. But where there is indeed overlap of domains of authority, the above injunction of Pope Leo XIII especially applies. (See also 4.13, ph. 4)

4.27 – A few more authoritative statements in support of or in addition to these details are perhaps useful.

Dz 1841, 1842: All Catholics, even bishops, must obey civil leaders in things falling under secular affairs, so far as their commands are not against Natural, Divine, or Church law. (Cf. 4.16, at the end)

Dz 2190: The Church should not mingle without reason in the mere controlling of politics.

Dz 1936a: The Natural Law enjoins us to love devotedly and to defend the country in which we had birth, and in which we were brought up, so that every good citizen hesitates not to face death for his native land.

Dz 1763, 1850, 1878, 2278: Sedition and rebellion against the State are against both Divine and Natural Law. Thus State leaders have a grave right and duty to suppress these. This right and duty, however, is contingent on another duty of State

---

[78] Pope Leo XIII, Encyclical *Diutúrnum Illud*, §26 (quoted from Dz 1858)

leaders: to avoid grave and continuous injustices against their own citizens. Resistance to such severe injustice is not sedition or rebellion against the State, but rather patriotic reaction to usurpation and treason in high places, provided it proceeds from correct moral principles.

Dz 595, 597: State leaders (also ecclesiastical ones) may be sinners, but must still be obeyed, except if they command sin.

Dz 1938c, 2256: The State authority has the right to impose taxes (without which it cannot carry out its duties), provided they are just and fair. See also Leo XIII, Encyclical *Rerum Novárum*, 1891, §§32 & 47.

4.28 – Now, following upon our exposition of the domains of authority of the State, the fact that our Principle 36 holds that the State government has a right to the obedience of the citizens, but that this is "insofar as its Human Law is in conformity with Natural and Divine Law", it may be asked if it is ever permitted (or even obligatory) to rebel against the State.

Given our synthesis of Catholic Church teaching – Dz 1763, 1850, 1878 and 2278 stated just above – this question is easily answered:

> **PRINCIPLE 37: Sedition and rebellion against State authority is against both Natural and Divine Law. Thus, State leaders have a grave right and duty to suppress these. This right and duty, however, is contingent on another duty of State leaders: to avoid grave and continuous injustices against their own citizens. Resistance to such severe injustice is not sedition or rebellion against the State, but rather patriotic reaction to usurpation and treason in high places, provided it proceeds from correct moral principles.**

Since, of course, the question of exactly when such resistance is legitimate requires a very difficult prudential decision which depends very much upon circumstances, it was thought useful to state the "correct moral principles" one would have to apply in making such a decision. As the matter is quite complex, we have not done so here, but in Appendix 2.

FURTHER CONSIDERATIONS ON PUBLIC SPEECH AND PUBLIC WORSHIP

In our enumeration of the particular domains of Catholic Church authority given above, there are two areas that, because of their importance and controversiality, seem to us worthy of further treatment. These are the questions of public speech and public worship.

Public Speech In A Catholic State

4.29 – Absolute "freedom of speech" does not exist in any society today, nor has it ever existed at any time in any society. In Chapter 2, 'society' was defined thus: *A society is a stable union of a number of persons in fellowship and cooperation for a common purpose of benefit to all* (2.11). In every society, therefore, certain types of speech and expression of ideas which tend to destroy the society's "fellowship and cooperation" or are inimical to its "common purpose" are limited, prohibited, and even punished. For example, expressions of constant criticism and of bitter hatred for one's spouse are incompatible with cooperation in, and the purpose of, the society called marriage. Either such forms of "free" speech will be voluntarily or involuntarily suppressed, or the union will fail.

Examples of speech that is routinely punished in contemporary liberal democracies, by loss of employment, fines, arrest and imprisonment, include: questioning the truth of the claim that six million Jews were killed in Nazi Germany; criticizing sodomite "marriages" and denouncing sodomy itself as a perversion; pointing out differences in behavior and abilities between different races; and expressing doubts about Darwinian evolution while teaching in a public institution. These questionings are a threat to the prevailing pseudo-religion of Secular Humanism, and all its dogmas, because they undermine the unity of belief in those dogmas which the Secular Humanist State recognizes are necessary to its rule – even as it hypocritically and lyingly claims that limitless "freedom" of speech is an absolute right of man.

Enemies of the Catholic Faith promoted unrestricted freedom of speech and freedom of the press during times when Catholic ideas (or even conservative Protestant ideas) were dominant. But now that such Christians are in a minority in Europe and North America, even public expressions of Christian faith, such as Christmas nativity scenes and the Ten Commandments, are persecuted.

Pope Leo XIII, seconding his predecessor, declared:

> Gregory XVI, by the encyclical letter beginning *Mirári Vos*,...struck at those teachings... that it is lawful for everyone to publish what[ever] he thinks, and likewise to stir up revolution within the State.[79]

Pope Leo XIII also stated that:

> ...[T]he unrestricted power of thinking and publicly expressing one's opinions is not among the rights of citizens, and is by no means to be placed among matters worthy of favor and support.[80]

The same Pope Leo XIII said also:

> ...[I]t is by no means lawful to demand, to defend, and to grant indiscriminate freedom of thought, writing, teaching, and likewise of belief, as if so many rights which nature has given to man. For if nature had truly given these, it would be right to reject God's power, and human liberty could be restrained by no law. Similarly it follows that these kinds of freedom can indeed be tolerated, if there are just reasons, yet with definite moderation, lest they degenerate into caprice and indulgence.[81]

In sum, every society has found it necessary to restrict the expression of ideas which tend to destroy the cooperation and common purpose of that society. Thus we may distill the following principle:

---

79 Encyclical *Immortále Dei*, §34 (quoted from Dz 1867)
80 Ibid., §35 (quoted from Dz 1868)
81 Encyclical *Libértas Praestantíssimum*, §42 (quoted from Dz 1932)

PRINCIPLE 38: Unrestricted freedom of speech is not a right in Natural or Divine Law. A State may limit or prohibit public speech, assemblies, images, teaching or entertainment which oppose the common good.

Public Worship In A Catholic State: Status Of Non-Catholic Religions

4.30 – A Catholic ruler who truly believes that the Church is the Bride of Christ, and the one true guide to everlasting salvation for all men, will not desire to foster the spread of error in the society for which he is responsible. In fact, fostering such spread of falsehood would be a sin against charity. The ruler who truly seeks the well-being of the people over whom he has authority wishes both their spiritual good and their temporal peace and prosperity. Because non-Catholic and anti-Catholic faiths, not to mention the pseudo-religions atheism, secularism, and humanism, are inimical to the true worship of God and the pursuit of justice throughout society, the Catholic ruler will most truly serve the citizens of his land by promoting the Catholic faith and strengthening its influence in every way possible.

Catholic authorities prior to Vatican II have repeatedly condemned the idea of equality of all religions. An example is Pope Pius IX's condemnation of the following two liberal propositions:

> In this age of ours it is no longer expedient that the Catholic religion should be the only religion of the State, to the exclusion of all other cults whatsoever.[82]

> Hence in certain regions of Catholic name, it has been laudably sanctioned [permitted] by law that men immigrating there be allowed to have public exercises of any form of worship of their own.[83]

Since these two propositions are false, it follows that the ideal is that the Catholic religion be the only religion of the State.

Pope Pius IX also condemned the

> ...erroneous opinion, especially fatal to the Catholic Church and to the salvation of souls, called by Our predecessor of recent memory, Gregory XVI, insanity; namely, that "liberty of conscience and of worship is the proper right of every man, and should be proclaimed and asserted by law in every correctly established society; that the right to all manner of liberty rests in the citizens, not to be restrained by either ecclesiastical or civil authority."[84]

Pope Gregory XVI in 1832 condemned the error of indifferentism; the idea that all religions are more or less valid:

> Now we examine another prolific cause of evils by which, we lament, the Church is at present afflicted, namely indifferentism, or that base

---

82 *Syllabus of Errors,* §77, originally from the Allocution *Nemo Vestrum.* (quoted from Dz 1777)
83 *Syllabus of Errors,* §78, originally from the Allocution *Acerbissimum.* (quoted from Dz 1778)
84 Encyclical *Quanta Cura,* §3. (quoted from Dz 1690)

opinion which has become prevalent everywhere through the deceit of wicked men, that eternal salvation of the soul can be acquired by any profession of faith whatsoever... For, since all restraint has been removed by which men are kept on the paths of truth, since their nature inclined to evil is now plunging headlong, we say that the "bottom of the pit" has truly been opened, from which John (Apoc. 9:3) saw "smoke arising by which the sun was darkened, with locusts coming out of it to devastate the earth."[85]

Those who advocate the principle of "freedom of religion" depart from the Catholic faith, and oppose solemn pronouncements of the Church, such as the following from the Lateran Council IV of A.D. 1215:

> One indeed is the universal Church of the faithful, outside of which no one at all is saved...(Dz 430)

"Freedom of religion" is also contradicted by Pope Boniface VIII in the Papal Bull *Unam Sanctam* of A.D. 1302:

> With Faith urging us, we are forced to believe and to hold the one, holy Catholic Church, and that apostolic, and we firmly believe and simply confess this (Church), outside of which there is no salvation nor remission of sin...(Dz 468)

4.31 – At the same time, the Catholic Church has decreed that no person may be coerced into entering the Church, or receiving Her sacraments.

> This is contrary to the Christian religion, that anyone, always unwilling and interiorly objecting, be compelled to receive and to observe Christianity. (Dz 411)

> And this also the Church especially guards against, that anyone against his will be forced to embrace the Catholic faith, for, as St. Augustine wisely advises: "Man cannot believe except of his free will." (Dz 1875)

4.32 – Lastly, the Church recognizes that there may occur circumstances in which it is prudent for the civil rulers to tolerate – not encourage or embrace – the public exercise of some non-Catholic religions. Pope Leo XIII stated:

> Indeed, if the Church judges that certain forms of divine worship should not be on the same footing as the true religion, yet she does not therefore condemn governors of States, who, to obtain some great blessing or to prevent an evil, patiently tolerate custom and usage so that individually they each have a place in the State.[86]

From these and similar exhortations we are led to the following principle to guide Catholic rulers:

---

85 Encyclical *Mirári Vos*, §14 (quoted from Dz 1613 & 1614)
86 Encyclical *Immortále Dei*, §36 (quoted from Dz 1874)

PRINCIPLE 39: While considerations of prudence may lead a State ruler to tolerate, at least for a time, public expressions of contrary religions, and while no force should be used to compel any person to embrace the Catholic Faith, no other religion than the Catholic faith should be promoted or encouraged. Catholic rulers should recognize no "right" to practice false religions, and no right for them to proselytize.[87]

Summary

4.33 – The Catholic Church and the State are two distinct societies, with distinct purposes, and distinct domains of authority within which to operate to achieve those purposes. The purpose of the Church concerns the everlasting and supernatural happiness of man (i.e. salvation), whereas that of the State directly concerns his mortal and natural happiness, yet with recognition that mortal happiness has value only insofar as it leads to immortal happiness. On account of its infinitely higher purpose, the Church as a society is of an infinitely higher dignity, and her authority is accordingly vastly superior. Nevertheless, the State, because it has such great power and influence on the conditions of this world, also has great influence on man's salvation.

The Catholic Church and the State therefore, although distinct, ought not be separated. On the contrary, they should be as closely united as possible. Each should work for the same ultimate goal, which is salvation. Where their respective domains of authority overlap, a smooth cooperation should occur, as a natural result of this unity of ultimate purpose, joined to the practice of the principles of subsidiarity and solidarity.

In the ideal Catholic State, besides the common people, the leaders thereof should be dedicated Catholics, and act habitually in accord with the Tradition of the Faith and morals of the Church, being disposed to accept also specific directives falling under the Church's domain of authority.

In such manner, Church and State will live in peace, order and harmony, being *cor unum et anima una* (one heart and one soul).

> When once men recognize, both in private and in public life, that Christ is King, society will at last receive the great blessings of real liberty, well-ordered discipline, peace and harmony. Our Lord's regal office invests the human authority of princes and rulers with a religious significance; it ennobles the citizen's duty of obedience. It is for this reason that St. Paul, while bidding wives revere Christ in their husbands, and slaves respect Christ in their masters, warns them to give obedience to them not as men, but as the vicegerents of Christ; for it is not meet that men redeemed by Christ should serve their fellow men. *You are bought with a price; be not made the bondslaves of men.* If princes and magistrates, duly elected, are filled with the persuasion that they rule, not by their own right, but by the mandate and in the place of the Divine King, they will exercise their authority piously and wisely, and they will make laws and administer

---

87 Cf. the discussion of 'rights' in Chapter 2 (2.29)

them, having in view the common good and also the human dignity of their subjects. The result will be a stable peace and tranquility, for there will be no longer any cause of discontent. Men will see in their king or in their rulers men like themselves, perhaps unworthy, or open to criticism, but they will not on that account refuse obedience if they see reflected in them the authority of Christ, God and Man. Peace and harmony, too, will result; for with the spread and the universal extent of the kingdom of Christ, men will become more and more conscious of the link that binds them together, and thus many conflicts will be either prevented entirely or at least their bitterness will be diminished. (Pius XI, Encyclical *Quas Primas,* §19)

CHAPTER 5

FORMS OF STATE GOVERNMENT

Review And Preview

5.1 – A brief look at history shows that there are many forms of government. The Hebrews had their theocracy, and then monarchy. The Greeks had monarchy and democracy. It was a Greek, Aristotle, who wrote the first comprehensive treatment of forms of government: the *Politics*.[88] Rome had a kingdom, then a republic, and finally an empire. Christendom largely adopted monarchy but accepted other forms, such as the republic of Venice.

Government of the One, the Few, and the Many; these are the fundamental possibilities for forms of government. These possibilities come in various organizational styles, but the purpose should always be the same: a just rule for the common good. Any government has the same basic role as stated in Principle 36: *Insofar as its Human Law is in conformity with Natural and Divine Law, the State has authority to order secular affairs for the well-being of this mortal life, and in this has a right to the obedience of the citizens.*

And as shown in Chapter 3, this authority is given so that the State can fulfill its primary duty of dispensing justice, which shows up in detail as we have given in 4.2.

In the measure it becomes derelict in these duties, the government becomes self-serving.

Recognizing an ever-present tendency toward selfishness, Aristotle's classic division into One, Few and Many contains a subdivision into Just and Unjust forms. St. Thomas Aquinas quotes Aristotle explaining how, at first, men wish to serve the State and therefore are content to rule for shorter periods of time, but later they wish to rule permanently: "Thus men seem to desire rulership as the sick desire health."[89]

Of course, a permanent rule is stable, and as such is therefore good (cf. 5.30), but the motive for this stability is too often love of power rather than the benefit of the people. The explanation of this is of course original sin (cf. Principle 8).

As St. Thomas quotes Aristotle again:

> In a city, either one, or a few, or the many rule; and any one of these three cases can come about in two ways: in one way, when they rule for the common benefit, and in this case we shall have just regimes; in the other, when they rule for the private benefit of those who are in power, whether that be one man, or a few, or many, and in this case we have perversions of regimes... (ibid. Bk. 3, Less. 6, 392)

---

[88] Although his teacher, Plato, had treated extensively of government in his *Republic*, this was mainly to promote his own rather unique views as to its best form. Aristotle's work was an analytical treatment of government as such.

[89] *Commentary on Aristotle's Politics*, Book 3, Lesson 5, 389 (online edition, trans. Ernest Fortin and Peter O'Neill: https://isidore.co/aquinas/Politics.htm – accessed 11 Nov. 2025)

Classical Forms Of Government

THEOCRACY

5.2 – The *Catholic Encyclopedia*, 1910-1914, in the article Theocracy, says this:

> *Theocracy is a form of civil government in which God Himself is recognized as the head.*

The Deity may be real or supposed. In such a government, the laws of the nation are the commandments of God (or gods) and the representatives are generally priests. The Israelites for some time were ruled by such a form, through the Judges. However, even after kings ruled the Hebrews, prophets still communicated directly with God for the good of the nation.

Common thought today, however, makes theocracy broader, and it includes the Vatican as a theocracy, at least in part. Thus, the Papal States were a theocracy. The Islamic State is also considered a theocracy wherever Sharia law is in place. These States, however, have within them the forms that will be described below: rule either of One, Few, or Many.

RULE BY ONE MAN

The Just Form : Monarchy

> **5.3** – *Monarchy is the concentration of the political power of a State in one person, who rules for the benefit of all the subjects of a State.*[90]

The monarch delegates the exercise of his authority to various officials, in order to carry out State functions in various geographical regions and in various fields of endeavor. These officials are accountable to, and obey, the monarch.

When looking at the history of Christendom, we see that monarchs ruled nearly every nation of Europe. At times one man ruled most of Europe (or large parts of the East and West), as with Constantine, Theodosius and Justinian. These men were able to accomplish a great deal for the Church. They built churches and supported the Church, and they fought heresy. On the other hand, sometimes monarchs supported heresy when they meddled with affairs of the Church. The ensuing centuries likewise are filled with Catholic monarchs who did a great deal for Christendom, such as Charlemagne and the Holy Roman Emperors that followed. Some monarchs are saints, such as St. Edward the Confessor of England, St. Henry II the Holy Roman Emperor, and St. Louis IX of France. These men certainly ruled with justice at the forefront of their actions. Other monarchs used their power poorly, such as Holy

---

90 The word 'monarch' comes from the Greek *monos* and *archein,* which means simply 'to rule alone'. In most Western languages, the word has come to mean a lone ruler that is either hereditary or elected. We use the term the same way, but, following Aristotle and Aquinas, for us the word 'monarch' (as also the word 'king') will connote not only a single ruler but a just one. As Aquinas says in his *Commentary on the Politics:* "If there is a rule of one man, it is usually called kingly rule if it seeks the common benefit." (Bk. 3, less. 6, 393) Regardless of how they are chosen, unjust single rulers will be designated by such terms as 'dictator', 'autocrat', 'tyrant'. Thus a king/monarch who "goes bad" and does not fulfill his true purpose will no longer be a true monarch, but a tyrant.

Roman Emperor Frederick II, King Henry VIII of England, and Napoleon. We would call these tyrants rather than monarchs.

5.4 – To ensure a just rule, St. Robert Bellarmine shows that laws are necessary:

> Moreover, Aristotle states that it is better for a people to be ruled by laws than solely by the will of the ruler, and, indeed, that this is to a certain extent necessary. And this is proved, first, because it is easier to find one or two good and wise men, than to find many. If the State is to be ruled by the will of a wise prince, this would require an endless number of good princes, one in succession to the other, but if it is ruled by laws, it is sufficient that there should have been at some time a few wise men, or even one wise man, to make the law. Secondly, those who make laws are many, and they consider the laws carefully; but the ruler is only one, and frequently has to judge without due consideration.[91]

He adds this:

> ...[G]overnment by law can be reduced to a system and the more easily carried out; not so with government according to the will of a man. (ibid.)

The Unjust Form : One-Man Tyranny

5.5 – *A Tyranny is a one-man rule where the ruler seeks his own private good rather than that of the nation.*

Some tyrants are better than others. In ancient Greece a tyrant did not necessarily have to be seeking his own private gain to be called 'tyrant', and might have accomplished a great deal of good. Athens had such tyrants as Pericles, under whom the city flourished in its Golden Age. In that State, which did not normally have a king, a one-man ruler was called a tyrant no matter how well he ruled. Later the word 'tyrant' came to be used only in the pejorative sense. In modern times one-man rule *as such* is falsely viewed as evil, just as how the ancient Romans detested kings during the age of the Republic. This is in large part because we have seen so many dictators or tyrants in our day, just as the Romans did in theirs. Nowadays, people generally speak of a tyrant as any one-man ruler, whether he be just, or lords it over a nation for his own selfish gain. Thus, today a king is called a tyrant, and a dictator is likewise called a tyrant. The early Caesars understood the need to manipulate language in order to avoid negative reactions to their power, thus they did not use the terms 'king', or 'monarch', but used other terms such as 'Princeps' (Leader), 'Imperator' (General), 'Augustus' (Revered One), etc. But their position in society was equivalent to that of a king. In a similar manner, some dictators of the 20th century (e.g. Hitler, Mussolini) ruled with a power equal to or greater than that of some kings, but chose to be called Leader, or chose some other title.

With Franco of Spain, Salazar of Portugal, Dollfus of Austria, and even going back to Moreno of Ecuador, we find examples of one-man rule nearing kingly power.

---

91 *De Láicis*, or *Treatise on Civil Government*, Bk. III, ch. 10, ph. 3

But these men ruled as true monarchs; that is to say, as good one-man rulers. Today, however, the push toward democracy has ensured that these types of rulers no longer exist, and they are discredited as tyrants in the worst sense simply because they held power as one man; they have been painted with the same brush as true tyrants such as Hitler, Mussolini or Lenin.

Recognizing that one-man rule can be good, we will henceforth restrict the terms 'tyrant', 'dictator' or 'autocrat' to those rulers who are not good, and 'king' or 'monarch' to those that are.[92]

RULE BY FEW

The Just Form : Aristocracy

5.6 – *Aristocracy is the rule of the best for the sake of the common good.*

In this case the aristocracy or nobility are considered the best citizens of the nation and most able to rule. They are generally wealthy, but need not be. In the aristocracy, however, the rulers do not use their position for their own selfish gain but for the common welfare of all citizens of the nation.

This form is not so efficient as a monarchy due to the fact that it is made up of several rulers who might disagree with each other in making decisions. Nevertheless, since they should be the best citizens, they should have the virtue to make just decisions. On the other hand, aristocracy is considered better in this respect than rule by democracy, because in the latter the decision-making process is even slower due to the difficulty of making so many agree. Aristocracy, however, has no less legitimacy than other forms of government, as Bellarmine shows in relating which governments have the right to declare war:

> ...[A]uthority for declaring war resides, according to common opinion, in all rulers who in temporal affairs have no superior, such as are all kings, likewise the Republic of Venice and similar States, and likewise some Dukes and Counts who are subject to no one in secular matters. (*De Láicis*, ch. 15, ph. 3)

The Unjust Form : Plutocracy[93]

5.7 – *Plutocracy is the rule of a few rich men for the sake of themselves at the expense of others.*

Because it seeks the good of the rich, a plutocracy seeks the good of more citizens than does a dictatorship, but of fewer citizens than does an unjust demo-

---

92 Though it should be evident from our previous Principles (e.g. subsidiarity, and that laws must be reasonable and in accord with Natural and Divine Law in order to be real laws), we should emphasize here that we repudiate the so-called Divine Right of Kings, if it is taken in the perverse sense proposed by its most famous advocate, James I.

93 *Plutocracy* means rule by the wealthy. *Oligarchy* is a general term meaning rule by the few; rule by any dominant clique of whatever character, and so would of itself include both aristocracy and plutocracy. In modern times *oligarchy* is moving toward becoming nearly synonymous with *plutocracy*. This is incorrect. Sometimes also *oligarchy* is used to refer to rule by a few. The word itself, however, means multiple rulers, and suggests more than a few.

cratic rule, and so, among the worse kinds of governments, democracy is better. Plutocrats can easily tend toward discord due to the selfish nature of their rule.

RULE BY MANY

The Just Form : Democracy Or Republic[94]

> **5.8 –** *A Democracy or Republic is the wielding of the State's political power by a relatively large portion of the citizens, in particular by a portion of the citizenry much larger than an aristocracy.*

The privilege of formal participation or voting may be extended to all adults, or may be restricted according to property ownership, gender, race, wealth, legal status, or other criteria. When all participants wield direct power, it is a pure democracy. When the participants choose a few among themselves to represent the rest in wielding power, it is variously called a representative democracy, a democratic republic, or simply a republic.

In brief, this form of government is the just rule by many for the common good of all. Notice that it is not called the rule of all, but the many. St. Thomas gives one example of "the many" as a group of warriors who rule the State.[95] Perhaps in our own day it could be a class of businessmen and statesmen, so long as they govern with justice for the common good.

If a person's nation is a democracy he should participate as he is able. This is clear from the teachings of the Church and has already been addressed in the supporting arguments for Principle 30, which concludes: *Citizens must take an active interest in the commonweal and participate according to their station in life.*

The Unjust Form : Popular Tyranny

> **5.9 –** *Popular Tyranny is a democracy where the people rule, but for the sake of a real or supposed downtrodden class, so that they oppress the rich, or others they view as enemies.*

St. Thomas explains in the following way:

> If...a bad government is carried on by the multitude, it is called a democracy, i.e. control by the populace, which comes about when the plebeian people by force of numbers oppress the rich. In this way the whole people will be as one tyrant.[96]

This, however, is the least oppressive of the unjust governments because it seeks the private good of the largest multitude. Still, it does not seek their truest and best good, which is the common good. Pope Leo XIII also warned against a godless democracy:

---

94 *Democracy* is from the Greek *demos* (people) and *krateein* (to rule).
95 *De Regno,* Bk. 1, ch. 2, 12
96 *De Regno,* Bk. 1, ch. 2, 11. Here we see the word 'tyranny', by a natural transferal of meaning, being applied to a popular government. Although a tyrant was historically one man, the tyran*nical* nature of his rule is possible in any form of government.

> ... a State becomes nothing but a multitude which is its own master and ruler. And since the people is declared to contain within itself the spring-head of all rights and of all power, it follows that the State does not consider itself bound by any kind of duty toward God.[97]

Today this form of government abounds, especially due to the influence of Communism. This, however, is nothing new, as centuries ago Aristotle outlined the reasons for class division, as found in St. Thomas' *Commentary*:

> For those who abound in riches are few, but all share in freedom [free will]; and for this reason these two elements fight with each other. The few wish to be set over the others on account of their excess of riches, and the many wish to prevail over the few, being as it were their equals on account of freedom.[98]

Although St. Thomas wrote the following about single tyrants, the similarity between the effects of the tyrant on his nation, and class or race strife stirred up in our democratic society by special interest groups, is startling.

> They [tyrants] sow discords among the people, foster any that have arisen, and forbid anything which furthers society and cooperation among men, such as marriage, company at table and anything of like character, through which familiarity and confidence are engendered among men. They moreover strive to prevent their subjects from becoming powerful and rich since, suspecting these to be as wicked as themselves, they fear their power and wealth; for the subjects might become harmful to them just as they are accustomed to use power and wealth to harm others. (*De Regno*, Bk. 1, ch. 4, 27)

Modern Political Systems

5.10 – These are Totalitarian, Communist, Socialist, Democratic Socialist, Fascist.

These technically are not *forms* of government different from the traditional view of the three basic forms: rule by One, Few or Many. They are systems of social, political, and economic order that involve varying, but excessive, levels of government control. This excessive control may extend into the areas of production, distribution and exchange of goods, property ownership, transportation, and communication. It may also involve extreme nationalism or other aberrations.

TOTALITARIAN SYSTEMS

5.11 – *Totalitarian* is a generic term that refers to any kind of government which takes more or less total control of the people. These governments are unjust and tyrannical by nature, for not only do they grossly violate the principle of subsidiarity, but they govern for the selfish good of the rulers, certainly serving at least their sheer love of power and their own ideas, and usually also their own material benefit.

---

97 Leo XIII, Encyclical *Immortále Dei*, §25
98 St. Thomas Aquinas, *Commentary on Aristotle's Politics*, Bk 3, Less. 6, 398

COMMUNIST SYSTEMS

5.12 – *Communism is a social system in which class distinctions and private property are abolished, and all goods are shared in common.*

This is according to the dictum *from each according to his ability, to each according to his needs.*[99] In its pure form it even seeks to do away with all authority, and thus the government as such. In this case it becomes identical to anarchy (see 5.20 below). Its fundamental tenets are evolutionistic materialism, egalitarianism, and the denial of original sin. These theoretical principles are errors concerning the nature of man, and in practice they lead primarily to an *economic* system. But an economic system cannot be imposed without political power. Therefore, politically speaking, Communism is simply the system that results from attempting to impose an economic system consonant with these errors.

5.13 – Like most other ideas, Communism is not really modern. It is not within the scope of this work to descend to historical details on this point, but the basic elements of Communism have been seen among the Pythagoreans, in ancient Sparta, perhaps among the Essenes, among the Zandiks of Persia, the Taborite sect of the Hussites, some of the Anabaptists, the Digger movement in England, and others. It is said by some that the early Christians also practiced Communism. This is totally false, because the Catholic Church has always supported the right to private property, which real Communism always denies. While the slogan *from each according to his ability, to each according to his needs* was certainly influenced by Scripture (Acts 4:32ff), it is just as certainly true that Scripture also declares that, though donation of one's personal property to the common good is virtuous (Acts 4:34f), it nevertheless remains one's personal property *until* surrendered, and one has a *right* to retain it if desired (Acts 5:4).

5.14 – Although Communism has had temporary successes in history, these have always been in small, tightly-knit communities. The only place where its success has been persevering is also within this context, and that is, ironically, in Catholic monasteries, where the members make a vow of poverty, work without pay, and have all their needs provided by the common resources. Even here, there is no one-to-one correspondence between monastic life and Communist principles. Firstly, man's *right* to private property as such is by no means denied; its exercise is merely voluntarily suspended by the vow of poverty. A person entering a monastery is free to dispose of his goods beforehand as he or she sees fit; there is no requirement that they be handed over to the community. Further, even if one's class status before entering is normally ignored in a monastery, there is always a very clear structure of authority, and thus there is at least a class of leaders and a class of subjects. We must say then that monasteries *practice* much of the Communist ideal, but for different reasons, and they deny its *theory* of a classless and propertyless society.

5.15 – In sum: The Communist rejection of the Natural Law principles of class distinction and individual property rights completely disqualifies this system as a possibility for any Catholic government. Indeed, Communism is so radically contrary

---

99 This dictum is ostensibly from Karl Marx's *Critique of the Gotha Program*, 1875, but was borrowed by him from earlier commentators, and actually originates in the New Testament (Acts 4:32ff).

to Natural Law that it is not possible that *any* State of any reasonable size could be successful using this system (cf. Principle 13), and history shows that this has in fact been the case. If it is argued that the Soviet Union and China (or others) have been successful, we deny this on two irrefutable counts. Firstly, these States have not been truly Communistic, and the founders and leaders thereof even admit this. Marxism-Leninism and Maoism, for instance, were recognized from the beginning as transitional governmental styles; they were systems designed to train the people toward acceptance of a *true* Communist State that would develop later. That development has never occurred.[100] Russia and China in fact transitioned not to Communism but to Socialist Plutocracy. Secondly, even if this fact were refused, the mere continued existence of these States is not an indicator of success. We have fully covered the purposes of a State (cf. 4.2), and simple survival is only the first indispensable part of them. These States have not been successful by any rational standard of human happiness, even merely natural happiness. As for supernatural happiness, since these States have been atheist, there is no need to say more. (For further support of this section, see 8.2 and following).

SOCIALIST SYSTEMS

5.16 – Socialism seems very difficult to define. We can safely say it has a strong affinity to Communism, especially in regard to its egalitarianism and denial of original sin. But there are many different "flavors" of Socialism; different degrees, different emphases, and methods of applying it.

It will be an initial and easy clarification to say what socialism is *not*:

> Socialism is not "the government should provide healthcare" or "the rich should be taxed more", nor any of the other watery social-democratic positions that the American right likes to demonize by calling them "socialist". (*The Economist*, Jan. 6, 2012)

Leo XIII said that the main tenet of Socialism is community of goods (*Rerum Novárum*, §15). Pius XI confirmed this (*Quadragésimo Anno*, §§111ff).

It is interesting to see what the common consensus of the day is concerning this. A look at the Wikipedia article *Socialism* shows twenty-two definitions offered by various sources, and about seventeen state that social ownership of the *means* of production was essential to socialism. Not all agreed that social ownership of land or capital was *also* required, or social *control* of the production or allocation of these resources.

But since we are concerned only with types of government that apply to the highest level, which is the State, we can eliminate lower level types, so our definition need not include them in its comprehension. And given this, we have to consider the consequences of State government ownership even if only of the *means* of production. It is evident that he who owns the means of production will have owned the capital that pays for it. Owning the means of production also means controlling

---

[100] Nor *can* it occur. Since pure Communism is a classless, propertyless, Stateless "society" – which is to say in reality an anarchy – it is not a society at all. The term 'Communist State' is an oxymoron. But even assuming it could exist, a nation adopting it would be completely at the mercy of any other nation with a strong central government that wished to annex or destroy it. The Communist "society" by definition would have no authority that could enforce the raising of an army.

the production. Finally, the government has the power to legislate concerning the use of what is produced. In fine then, the teaching of the above cited popes is confirmed. As a form of government then,

> **5.17 – Socialism is State ownership and control of the means of production, and control of the distribution of products.**[101]

In comparing this definition to that for Communism given above (5.12), we see that, while the words are different, the meaning is nearly the same, for although Socialism in itself makes no demand for the elimination of class distinctions and private property, and the sharing of goods in common, these things are going to be the result of government distribution of goods anyway, for by what criteria could it justify giving more to some and less to others? A supposed equality between all men, and the need to cure the drastic disparity between rich and poor, was the very reason for the rise of the Socialist Idea in the first place.

Pius XI explicitly condemns Socialism in government in *Quadragésimo Anno*, §§111-120. He does this because, like Communism, it violates the Natural Law by denying the right to private property (*QA* §44).

This said, it must be remembered that private property is not an end in itself, and that there are certain social obligations involved in its possession. There is also such a thing as social or communal property. We will treat more fully of these things in later Chapters.

DEMOCRATIC SOCIALIST SYSTEMS

> **5.18 – Democratic Socialism is a combination of a socialist economic system with a democratic political system of government.**

Democratic Socialism calls for the government to engage in socialist economic policies and programs, but through the democratic process. The voters are encouraged to decide whether policies are beneficial or not – even if they violate some fundamental individual rights. In the name of social justice and equality it becomes entirely acceptable to take property from those who have more than others. Although a great number of people understand the inherent shortcomings and errors of socialism, Democratic Socialism is presently popular because its democratic aspect seems to be a solution to the excesses that history has shown us in previous socialistic governments, which were dictatorial. The public, however, is still led to believe that someone else will pay the costs of education, that there will be guaranteed income (Universal Basic Income), housing, health care, or other social programs, and the rich will seemingly be stripped of their perceived monopolistic power over the wealth of the nation. Thus Democratic Socialism still feeds off the concept of class warfare, and still denies the right to private property. Moreover, it is doomed eventually to the same tyranny it hopes to avoid.

---

101 See the discussion of the difficulty of defining Socialism in the publisher's preface of G. R. Stirling-Taylor's *The Guild State* (IHS Press, 2006). A salient point is that *Quadragésimo Anno* really settled the question for Catholics, reducing the essence of Socialism to the community possession of goods. Fr. Edward Cahill, in *The Framework Of A Christian State*, p. 163f (M. H. Gill & Son, Dublin, 1932), also mentions the vagueness attached to the term 'Socialism' in his day, and gives a definition, which though more verbose, is essentially the same as ours.

> A democracy cannot exist as a permanent form of government. It can exist only until the voters discover that they can vote themselves largesse from the public treasury. From that moment on, the majority always votes for the candidate promising the most benefits from the public treasury, with the result that a democracy always collapses over loose fiscal policy, always followed by a dictatorship. (*adapt. from* Alexander Fraser Tytler)

In the end, the tyranny of a mob is still a tyranny. That of a dictator may be worse at times, but both are unjust, and should not be accepted.

FASCIST SYSTEMS

5.19 – Fascism seems just as difficult to define as Socialism. This is not so much because there are many flavors of Fascism, but rather because it is strongly identified with cultural currents present in Europe during the time of its ascendancy, and these currents colored its formation. They include political, philosophical, and even scientific ideas. These ideas were influential from World War I until the end of World War II, and manifested themselves in fascist governments of the time. Thus Fascism is sometimes defined largely by the governments of Nazi Germany and Fascist Italy. In forming a true definition, however, we will have to abstract from these colorations, and reduce Fascism to its essence. The influences we must eliminate are: Social Darwinism (with its doctrines of eugenics, survival of the fittest, and racism), advocacy of political violence, hypernationalism, militant imperialism, heroism, modernism and futurism, secularism, anti-Marxism, and Nietzschean anti-egalitarianism. What is left as the essence of Fascism?

> ***Fascism is a government under one party and one principal leader that divinizes the nation, and seeks to strongly unify and subordinate both individuals and industry to the goals it sets.***[102]

Fascism then is a quasi-dictatorship (see 5.5), and one tending to totalitarianism, but which aims not at the mere aggrandizement of the dictator, but at whatever the dictator and his party see as the good of the nation. Of course, if the *true* good of the nation (see 3.4 & following) were adopted as the goal, a Fascist government would in reality be a monarchy, although possibly an excessively controlling one. *But fascist governments are completely unacceptable on at least one count: divinization of the State.* The resultant tendency toward totalitarianism is also a negative, since it fails to account for the reality of free will, and makes demands for a lockstep unity that is outside the domain of practicality and will necessarily lead to problems, even if the

---

[102] It will be noted that concepts of political "left" and "right" do not enter into this definition. Regarding divinization of the State as an essential note of fascism, see Pius XI, *Mit Brennender Sorge*, 1937, §§ 8, 11, 34. For a discussion of the difficulty of defining 'fascism', with examples of attempts by intellectuals to do so, see https://en.wikipedia.org/wiki/Definitions_of_fascism. As far as popular notions are concerned, already in 1944, George Orwell perhaps said it best: "...[A]s used, the word 'Fascism' is almost entirely meaningless. In conversation, of course, it is used even more wildly than in print. I have heard it applied to farmers, shopkeepers, Social Credit, corporal punishment, fox-hunting, bull-fighting, Kipling, Gandhi, Chiang Kai-Shek, homosexuality... astrology, women, dogs and I do not know what else. ... [T]he people who recklessly fling the word 'Fascist' in every direction attach at any rate an emotional significance to it... [A]lmost any English person would accept 'bully' as a synonym for 'Fascist'. That is about as near to a [popular] definition as this much-abused word has come." (https://en.wikipedia.org/wiki/Fascist_(insult) URLs accessed 11 Nov. 2025.

national goals are the best possible. Also, while Fascism in itself does not require government ownership of industry, it does have the core principle of subordinating industry to the national goals, and this is difficult to achieve without ownership. In this respect then, Fascism also tends toward a violation of private property rights.

For further clarity, it is important to note that the government of Spain under Franco (1939-1975) was never a fascist government,[103] for it never, either in theory or in practice, actually divinized the State. Franco's government was a military dictatorship, and it can be argued that it was simply a necessity of the time, as being the only way to reverse the Communist and Anarchist insurrection which had gained much power in the country.

A SPECIAL QUESTION : ANARCHY

5.20 – Anarchy is not government at all, but the absence of government.[104] This is not only an unnatural state of being for civil society, but in reality is totally incompatible with it (see 2.11). There has never been an anarchic "society" of any size or kind. What people call anarchy is, at best, a more or less successful attempt at pure Communism (see 5.12 above).[105] Nature tends away from anarchy and toward government:

> While many dislike the authority under which they live, no man wishes for anarchy. What malcontents aim at is a *change* of government; to get authority into their own hands and govern those who now govern them. Even the professed anarchist regards anarchy as a temporary expedient, a preparation for his own advent to power.[106]

But today one sees people seriously using the term 'anarchic society', not realizing that it is an oxymoron. The key and irredeemable error of such people is the denial of original sin; an assumption that people will do justice to one another, at least at a minimum level, without force ever being needed. Certainly the anarchist might tend toward his position with the idea that leaders are all bad and therefore they should all be gotten rid of. But if all leaders were bad, that would only be because power always corrupts, but if power always corrupts, that would only happen because of original sin, which would be in everyone, wherefore the force of some government would still be needed. The solution is not anarchy, but to establish effective laws or societal or moral motivations that will keep the leaders themselves in line.

The Anabaptists held anarchic ideas, and Bellarmine wrote against them. He addressed the issue of bad rulers in *De Láicis*:

---

103 Even secular sources admit this. For example, see the Wiki article on Franco (accessed 16 May 2021), where it is stated: "...[M]ost historians agree that although Franco, and Spain under his rule, adopted some trappings of fascism [e.g. uniforms, special salutes, etc.] they are generally not considered to be fascist, at most describing the early totalitarian phase of his rule as a 'fascistized dictatorship', or a 'semi-fascist regime'."
104 Greek *an* + *archos* = without a leader.
105 Some would take umbrage at the comparison to Communism, but that would be because of an incorrect understanding of either the term 'Communism' or the term 'anarchy'. There are many "anarchic" movements today. Almost none of them are truly anarchic.
106 *Catholic Encyclopedia*, 1910-1914, art. Authority, Civil.

> I say: Firstly, it is false to state that most rulers are evil, for here we are not speaking of royalty in particular, but of political power in general,...if, therefore, there were wicked rulers: Cain, Nimrod, Ninus, Pharaoh, Saul, Jeroboam, and other Kings of Israel, so, on the other hand, there were good rulers: Adam, Noe, Abraham, Isaac, Jacob, Joseph, Moses, Josue, almost all the Judges, and many kings of Juda.
>
> Secondly, I say that the examples of evil rulers do not prove that authority is evil, for evil men frequently abuse good things, but the examples of good rulers rightly prove that authority is good, since good men do not make use of evil things. Besides, even evil rulers often do more good than harm, as is evident in the cases of Saul, of Solomon, and of others. Finally, it is better for a State to have an evil ruler than none at all, for where there is no ruler the State cannot long endure, as Solomon says: *Where there is no governor, the people shall fall.* And where there is a ruler, though he be evil, the unity of the nation is preserved.[107]

Anarchy, or pure Communism, has actually been applied with some success, but only in a few small communities. In these cases, peace and order are maintained simply by a strong commonality of fundamental life principles and interests, where people most often agree by mutual discussion, without the need for formal, *appointed* leadership. Otherwise, anarchy is a crass stupidity, and completely unworkable.[108]

5.21 – In all our discussion of forms of government above, we see one thing that all unjust governments have in common: they seek a supposed benefit of one person or group in society at the expense of others. That is exactly the cause of their injustice.

> **PRINCIPLE 40: Any form of government which seeks only the private good of one part of society is unjust.**

How Governments Are Formed

GOVERNMENT IS OF THE NATURAL ORDER

5.22 – As Chapter 1 (1.8) acknowledges, man has the free will to choose between goods.

Government exists due to man's social nature as stated in Principle 12: *That man live in society is a precept of the Natural Law, and admits of no exceptions. Those few who do not do so are spiritually perverted or psychologically ill...*

The movement toward modern democracy is fundamentally a shift from viewing man's true nature as created by God toward viewing it from an atheistic standpoint

---

107 *De Láicis*, or *Treatise on Civil Government*, Bk. III, ch. 4, ph. 5f
108 An examination of "anarchist" communities given by the Wiki article List of Anarchist Communities, clearly shows that, of these, there is only one (the squatter movement of Barcelona) that is *perhaps* truly anarchistic. The rest are clearly either simply rebellions against a larger authority, or socialist governments, or, at best, examples of pure democracy as we have defined it above (see 5.8).

and trying to figure out speculatively how man might have been in his "natural state", prior to contact with other human beings, which caused an "evolution" into societal groupings. Thus, the ideas of Hobbes and Rousseau led to the liberal democracy of today. But their ideas are nothing new to humanity, since Cicero of ancient Rome said similar things:

> There was a time when men wandered about in the fields in the manner of beasts...when some great and wise man learned what...great things lay in the souls of men...who...by some reasoning or other, herded and gathered them into one place.[109]

But this evolutionary idea is false; civil authority has always been part of the natural order, therefore government is natural, and it is by nature that men must be ruled for the sake of the common good, and to ensure justice. Church writers are in accord with this point, as Bellarmine states:

> Political rule is so natural and necessary to the human race that it cannot be withdrawn without destroying nature itself; for the nature of man is such that he is a social animal.[110]

Likewise, the *Catholic Encyclopedia* of 1910-1914 puts it very clearly:

> Authority, though varying in amount, is as universal as man is everywhere. Man cannot live except under authority, as he cannot live outside of civil society. It is by no convention, compact, or contract, that authority takes hold of him. It is a necessity of his nature. (art. Authority, Civil).

WHO CHOOSES THE FORM OF GOVERNMENT

5.23 – The citizens themselves normally choose the form of government, or at least give tacit approval by allowing a government to rule over them. It is they who designate the ruler who is to wield political power.[111]

> Political power considered in general, not descending in particular to Monarchy, Aristocracy or Democracy, comes immediately from God alone...and this seems to be what the Apostle properly means when he says: 'He who resists the [government] power resists the ordinance of God' (Rom. 13:2). This power is, as in its subject, immediately in the whole multitude, for this power is by Divine Law, but Divine Law gives this power to no particular man, therefore Divine Law gives this power to the multitude.[112]

---

109 *De Inventióne*, Bk. I, §2 (www.thelatinlibrary.com/cicero/inventione1.shtml – accessed 1 Nov. 2025). Our translation.
110 *De Láicis,* Bk. III, ch. 5, ph. 1; cf. St. Thomas, *Summa Theol.* I Q.96, a4
111 Of course, this designation does not need to be *renewed* in a hereditary monarchy or other government in which the succession of power is established according to custom.
112 Bellarmine, *De Láicis,* Bk. III, ch. 6, ph. 2f. Bellarmine does *not* mean here that the people actually *possess* authoritative power over themselves, for if that were the case, since each individual shares human nature equally with all other individuals, each individual would have equal authority over all other individuals, but this would in effect mean also a mutual *cancellation* of authority of any individual over any other. Thus when Bellarmine says, "This power is, as in its subject, immediately in

We refer the reader also to the arguments leading to our Principle 29. That Principle again is: *Political leaders of a State derive their authority from God, not from the people over which they rule.*

Thus while the people choose the form of government, they are not the source of government power.

Since a political regime (i.e. civil authority or government) finds its basis in the people of the State, it is important that the people be of similar mind with regard to government. (cf. Principle 18)

The Best Form Of Government

5.24 – Firstly, the choice of form simply depends upon the customs and dispositions of a people. According to Aristotle, the virtues of the citizens play a role in the choice of form:

> Since there are many regimes differing in species, and since one speaks of a citizen in relation to a regime,...there must also necessarily be several species of citizens. This difference is best seen with reference to the subjects among the citizens, who are diversely related to the rulers under different regimes. Now those who are set over the others are the rulers under any regime. Hence, because of the diversity of regimes and consequently of citizens, it is necessary that under a certain regime – for instance, the popular State, in which only freedom is sought – laborers be citizens; for, since they are free, they will have the possibility of being promoted to the government. Under other regimes, however, this is impossible, as is especially the case in the rule of the Best, where honors are granted to those who are worthy of them by reason of their virtue. Those who live the life of laborers cannot, as rulers, provide the city with the things that pertain to virtue since they are not practiced in such things.[113]

Bellarmine on this point says:

> Individual forms of government in specific instances derive from the Law of Nations, not from the Natural Law, for, as is evident, it depends on the consent of the people to decide whether kings, or consuls, or other magistrates, are to be established in authority over them; and, if there be legitimate cause, the people can change a

---

the whole multitude", this power has to be understood as designatory, not executive. This is clear from what he says in the following paragraphs of the same chapter, and especially: "Fifthly, note that it follows from the aforesaid that this power is in particular indeed from God, but by means of counsel and human election, as are all other things which pertain to the Law of Nations."
Bellarmine's fellow Jesuit, Suárez, asserts the same in *De Légibus*, Bk. III, ch. 3, §§2-6, where he argues that the power itself is from God alone, and that human governing power arises "by force of natural reason" the moment that men decide to live in community, and "thus this power is given to a community of men by the Author of nature, but not without the intervention of the will and consent of men".

113 St. Thomas Aquinas, *Commentary on Aristotle's Politics*, Bk. 3, Lesson 4, 381. https://isidore.co/aquinas/Politics.htm (accessed 9 Nov. 2025)

kingdom into an aristocracy, or an aristocracy into a democracy, and vice versa, as we read was done in Rome.[114]

And the *Catholic Encyclopedia* says:

> ...[T]he distribution of authority, otherwise called the form of government, or the constitution of the State, is a human convention, varying in various countries, and in the same country at different periods of its history. (art. Authority, Civil)

Pope Leo XIII also explained this very clearly in his encyclical *Diutúrnum Illud*:

> ...[R]especting forms of government,...there is no reason why the Church should not approve of the chief power being held by one man or by more, provided only it be just, and that it tend to the common advantage. Wherefore, so long as justice be respected, the people are not hindered from choosing for themselves that form of government which suits best either their own disposition, or the institutions and customs of their ancestors. (*Diutúrnum*, §7)

And so we can say that, subjectively or relatively; that is, for a particular nation at a particular time in history, the best form of government will be that which best helps to achieve the temporal goals which are the very purpose of government.

> **PRINCIPLE 41: Any just form of government is acceptable and can be right for a nation to have. This includes variations of monarchy, aristocracy, and democracy.**
>
> **PRINCIPLE 42: For a specific people, the best form of government will be the form that they choose, provided that it suits their dispositions, institutions and customs, and provided that it is just and rules for the common good to ensure the peace and happiness of its citizens.**

5.25 – Absolutely and objectively speaking, St. Thomas Aquinas, both in *De Regno* and in the *Summa Theologiae*, teaches that the kingdom (monarchy) is the best form of government. In *De Regno* he states this over and over again:

> Therefore the rule of one man is more useful than the rule of many...
>
> So one man rules better than several [aristocrats], who come near being one [but are not one]...
>
> Whatever is in accord with nature is best, for in all things nature does what is best. Now, every natural governance is governance by one...it follows that it is best for a human multitude to be ruled by one person. This is also evident from experience. For provinces or cities which are not ruled by one person are torn with dissensions and tossed about without peace. (*De Regno*, Bk. 1, ch. 3, 17-20)

---

[114] *De Láicis*, Bk. III, ch. 6, ph. 5

In the *Summa Theologiae* he adds that the best nobles should also govern under the ruler and that the people should choose their ruler:

> For whereas these [forms] differ in kind, as the Philosopher states (*Polit*. III, 5), nevertheless the outstanding ones are the Kingdom, in which one man of virtue leads, and Aristocracy; that is, rule of the best, in which some few men of virtue lead.
>
> Hence, the best form of government is in some State or Kingdom where one man is put in charge to preside over all because of his virtue; while under him are others, also leaders because of their virtue, and yet a government of this kind is shared by all, whether because the leaders are able to be elected from among all, or also because they are chosen by all. For this is the best form of polity, well composed; from a Kingdom, since there is one at the head of all, and from Aristocracy, insofar as many also lead [under him] because of their virtue, and from Democracy, i.e. government of the people, in so far as the rulers can be chosen from the people, and/or the election of leaders belongs to the people.
>
> And this was the institution according to the Divine Law. For Moses and his successors governed the people as if they were rulers over all; so that there was a kind of Kingdom. But seventy-two elders were chosen, because of their virtue: for it is written: "I took out of your tribes wise and noble men, and appointed them rulers" (Dt. 1:15): so that there was an element of Aristocracy. But it was a democratical government [also] because these men were chosen from all the people; for it is said: "Provide out of all the people wise [Vulg.: able] men", etc. (Ex. 18:21) Consequently, it is evident that the order of rulers which the Law instituted was the best.[115]

Thus, as an ideal, St. Thomas advocates a form of civil society whereby all the citizens participate in government in this way. This is the most equitable situation, and one in which most of the citizens will be content with their participation in civil society.

> **PRINCIPLE 43: Objectively, the best form of government is a monarchy. For a Catholic confessional State, the monarch would be a convinced Catholic, and would be crowned by a representative of the Catholic Church. The monarchy could be purely hereditary, or the monarch could be elected by a body of aristocrats, or could be elected in a way that gives a larger part of society a vote.**

---

115 *Summa Theol.* I-II Q.105, a1, resp.

The Worst Form Of Government

TYRANNY OF THE PEOPLE IS BAD

5.26 – It is expedient therefore that a just government be that of one man only in order that it may be stronger; however, if the government should turn away from justice, it is more expedient that it be a government by many, so that it may be weaker and the many may mutually hinder one another. Among unjust regimes, therefore, tyrannical democracy is the most tolerable, but the worst is [one-man] tyranny. (*De Regno,* Bk. 1, ch. 4)

PLUTOCRACY IS *USUALLY* THE WORST

5.27 – Concerning this, it is said in *De Regno,* Bk. 1, ch. 6:

> Group government most *frequently* breeds dissension. This dissension runs counter to the good of peace which is the *principal* social good. A tyrant, on the other hand, does not destroy this good, rather he obstructs one or the other individual interests of his subjects – unless, of course, there be an excess of tyranny and the tyrant rages against the whole community. Monarchy is therefore to be preferred to polyarchy, although either form of government might become dangerous.
>
> Further, that from which great dangers may follow *more frequently* is, it would seem, the more to be avoided. Now, considerable dangers to the multitude follow more frequently from polyarchy than from monarchy. There is a greater chance that, where there are many rulers, one of them will abandon the intention of the common good than that it will be abandoned when there is but one ruler. When any one among several rulers turns aside from the pursuit of the common good, danger of internal strife threatens the multitude because, when the chiefs quarrel, dissension will follow in the people. When, on the other hand, one man is in command, he more often keeps to governing for the sake of the common good. Should he not do so, it does not immediately follow that he also proceeds to the *total* oppression of his subjects. This, of course, would be the excess of tyranny and the worst wickedness in government, as has been shown above. The dangers, then, arising from a polyarchy are more to be guarded against than those arising from a monarchy.
>
> Moreover, in point of fact, a polyarchy deviates into tyranny not less but perhaps more frequently than a monarchy. When, on account of there being many rulers, dissensions arise in such a government, it often happens that the power of one preponderates and he then usurps the government of the multitude for himself. This indeed may be clearly seen from history. There has hardly ever been a polyarchy that did not end in tyranny.

ONE-MAN TYRANNY IS SOMETIMES WORSE THAN PLUTOCRACY

5.28 – Again, *De Regno*, in Bk. 1, ch. 4:

> Just as the government of a king is the best, so the government of a tyrant is the worst...Now, as has been shown above, monarchy is the best government. If, therefore, "it is the contrary of the best that is worst", it follows that [one-man] tyranny is the worst kind of government.
>
> Further, a united force is more efficacious in producing its effect than a force which is scattered or divided...so the contrary will be true of an unjust government, namely, that the ruling power will be more harmful in proportion as it is more unitary.

And the *Summa Theol.* I-II Q.105, a1, ad2:

> A kingdom is the best form of government of the people, so long as it is not corrupt. But since the power granted to a king is so great, it easily degenerates into tyranny, unless he to whom this power is given be a very virtuous man: for it is only the virtuous man that conducts himself well in the midst of prosperity.

No Government Can Long Endure Unless Based On Immutable Fundamental Laws

5.29 – The best possible governmental system, conceived and established by the greatest genius and virtue of man, is still doomed to decay and destruction. Original sin assures this. It is no part of the Eternal Divine Plan that any nation live in an everlastingly perfect earthly regime. Rather, man must pass through trials, often great ones, in order to earn and be worthy of the privilege of living in the only perfect and everlasting government that exists: the Kingdom of Heaven.

Still, one of man's trials is to strive to do the best he *can* do for this earthly society he lives in, and there is arguably no higher good he can do for it than to work for the institution and maintenance of the best government possible. Having spoken above about the best kinds of government, we should say a word about how such governments can best be maintained. As Cicero has said:

> "...[F]or in the nature of things, it is by far of best counsel to construct a State such that it may be everlasting. If we were to number each [great] man in each such State, what a great multitude of excellent men would now be found!"[116]

It is said also in *De Regno*:

> When virtuous living is set up in the multitude by the efforts of the king, it then remains for him to look to its conservation...The good of

---

[116] *De República,* or *On The Commonwealth*, Bk. 3, §7. Our translation.
https://www.thelatinlibrary.com/cicero/repub3.shtml (accessed 2 Nov. 2025)

the multitude should not be established for one time only; it should be in a sense perpetual. (Bk. 1, ch. 16, 119)

STABILITY IS A PROPERTY OF GOVERNMENT AS SUCH

5.30 – Stability is so important that, among students of government, it is considered to be the main factor of a successful political system. In fact, stability in government is a property of its nature, for authority and law are essential to the very notion of government. If laws were to change constantly, the people would eventually despair of keeping up with the changes, and end by simply ignoring the laws, and the authority behind them. Hence lack of stability in laws inevitably results in anarchy, which is precisely absence of government. Hence government ceases to *be* government to the extent that it lacks stability.

THE PREREQUISITES FOR A STABLE GOVERNMENT

5.31 – The first prerequisite for a stable government is agreement by a strong majority of citizens on the reason for man's existence. In other words, a national religion must be the First Law of the nation. We have said enough on this already, and need only refer the reader to 2.11, 4.8, 4.9, and footnotes 45, 65, 100, with their associated body text.[117] It should be stressed here, however, that this majority consensus on man's *raison d'être* must be maintained at all costs. If it begins to fail, the decline must be stopped, or the death of the nation will inevitably follow, sooner or later depending on how rapid the decline is. Also, again, the State religion should be the Catholic religion. (Principle 32)

The second prerequisite for a stable government has also already been stated, in Principle 13: *No society can hope to* **maintain** *order or achieve any sort of happiness without substantially conforming to Natural Law.* In practice, this means that governments must hold the Ten Commandments as an immutable legal foundation of the nation. These precepts must be held without exception, and must absolutely overrule any merely Human Laws. Any attempt to propose a Human Law that would contradict the Commandments should be viewed as a crime, and any legislation that actually does so will be held as completely null and void. This principle of the inviolability of the Ten Commandments should be enshrined in the Constitution of the State, and irrevocably so.

The third prerequisite is adherence to the Law of Nations.

The fourth prerequisite is a body of written or at least customary law that establishes the Constitution of the government; that is, its basic structure and operations. It should not be possible to change this without great difficulty.

On The Third Prerequisite For A Stable Government : The Law Of Nations

Chapter 2 introduced the basic concept of Law, and the basic kinds of Law, but although the Law of Nations is among the basic kinds of Law, we did not treat of it there, as it was not going to be relevant for some time in our discussions. It is now relevant, so we explain it here.

---

117 Here let us recall that, while any religion, even a pseudo-religion, provides the needed unity of purpose, this unity is not by itself beneficial except in the measure that the religion is true.

WHAT IS THE LAW OF NATIONS?

5.32 – The Law of Nations lies midway between Natural Law (see 2.3) and Human Positive Law (see 2.25f). Recall that Natural Law is *the natural inclinations in creatures to do certain things and tend toward certain ends*, and that Human Positive Law is *an ordinance of reason for the common good, promulgated by him who has charge of a community*. Now Natural Law does not need to be promulgated, declared or published, as Human Law does, for all know the Natural Law by nature itself. But there is a category of laws that are sometimes not explicitly promulgated (at least originally), and yet are not given directly by nature either. They are given by long-standing custom. If this custom is one shared by nearly all nations since time immemorial, it is safe to say that, while it is a law discovered by human reason, the reasons that do establish it are so obvious and commonly known that they must be logically and directly connected to realities that at least concern or surround human nature.

> ***The Law of Nations is that body of law containing the universal rational customs of men, derived from Natural Law.***

Or as Gaius puts it: "What natural reason has constituted among all men and nations is called the Law of Nations."[118]

In modern times, many people have come to equate the term 'Law of Nations' with International Law. We must make clear at the outset that these terms are *not* synonymous. We insist on the meaning of 'Law of Nations' in its classical sense. As Sterling Edmunds points out, the Law of Nations, coming as it does from Natural Law, is a body of law that is *above* nations.[119] Thus all nations are subject to it by nature. Even though he came from an early modern tradition, it is with this classical understanding that Blackstone observed that sovereign States, in setting rules between themselves, have "no judge to resort to, but the law of nature and reason", so that the Law of Nations must be "adopted in its full extent" as part of the fundamental law of a State, if that State is to be counted as "part of the civilized world".[120]

5.33 – One way International Law is different from the Law of Nations is that International Law's source of authority is *entirely* human; it does not have a direct logical connection to the Natural Law established by God. International Law then is strictly a branch of Human Positive Law. As such it is legitimate and necessary whenever Human Positive Law is legitimate and necessary; that is, whenever a legitimate human authority adds a detail of law (not already contained in Natural or Divine Law but not contrary to it) that will truly contribute to the common good by increasing order and peace.[121]

---

118 *Summa Theol.* I-II Q.95, a4; II-II Q.57, a3. Gaius was a noted Roman jurist (d. ca. A.D. 180)
119 Sterling Edmunds, *The Lawless Law of Nations*, Washington Law Review, 1925
120 *Commentaries*, V.4, ch. 5 (*67), William Blackstone, 1769
121 A good example of the necessary distinctions is a provision of Mexico's International Law, whereby it forbids the extradition of *both* Mexican nationals *and* foreigners within its borders to other nations whenever those other nations may seek capital punishment upon the alleged offender. This law is contrary to the Natural Law, and thus the Law of Nations, because the Natural Law recommends capital punishment in certain cases. There could be a reason why Mexican nationals should be exempted from being subject to capital punishment by *foreign* nations. For instance, certain foreign nations might deal with Mexicans in an excessively harsh way, or it might be that Mexico simply wished to reserve to itself the decision of imposing capital punishment on its own citizens. But in

5.34 – It is worth noting that modern International Law is based on a principle of legal positivism, which is the false idea that *all* law is merely what man says it is; all law is Human Positive Law. Our present International Law then is law *between* nations, not above them; it recognizes no higher authority than the nations themselves. In fact it takes the old and false Divine Right of Kings, applies it to the judicial power of the State (of whatever form the State may be), and then raises the State to a new level of arrogance, whereby God is ignored entirely, and the man or men who run the State can do *whatever* they deem right. Each State is above any law, and ultimately can "legally" do anything it has the power and will to do. Modern International Law can therefore be arbitrary, and when it is, it is not real law at all. We mention this so that the Catholic statesman can recognize that, while the Catholic State must have International Law, the present body of International Law is not a reliable reference point for forming a specific body of International Law to be adopted by a Catholic State. The Law of Nations should be that reference point.

5.35 – There is another distinction that must be made between the Law of Nations and International Law. As is clear by definition, the Law of Nations does not apply only to international affairs. Much of it applies also to mankind *within* societies (even small ones), and hence to the *internal* affairs of a nation. In this way too it differs from modern International Law, which concerns itself only with legal matters between States. The internal affairs of a nation are, understandably, even more important to its stability than its external relations.

> **Principle 44: States ought to take the Law of Nations; that is, the universal rational customs of men which flow from Natural Law, as part of their immutable and foundational law, and should practice the Law of Nations in both their internal and external affairs.**

In other words, nations ought to practice the Tradition of the Ten Commandments, both within and without their borders.[122] By keeping this simple policy, a State will become internally stable, and will foster international goodwill toward itself, minimizing the danger of external destabilizing forces, which ultimately could result in the State being subjugated or destroyed by annoyed foreign powers. On another level, the world of nations ideally ought to be a society of nations just as the individuals within a nation ought to be a society of individuals. This of course cannot happen except to the extent that the individual nations share the same conviction on the meaning of life (as per our first prerequisite), just as the majority of individuals within a nation must do so in order to have a true society among themselves.

---

forbidding extradition of *foreigners* when that might result in capital punishment, Mexico is clearly stating that capital punishment is *in itself*, unjust, and this is entirely false. See https://en.wikipedia.org/wiki/Capital_punishment_in_Mexico (accessed 11 Nov. 2025)

122 An even simpler statement would have been to say that nations ought to practice the Golden Rule. Unfortunately, our age is so irrational and morally corrupt that doing unto others as you would have them do unto you does not always work anymore. For instance, to apply such a policy these days would result in many people condoning such harmful behavior as homosexuality and transgenderism.

HOW TO INTEGRATE THE LAW OF NATIONS INTO A GOVERNMENT

5.36 – In no particular order, some concrete examples of international rules coming from the Law of Nations are: the privileges of ambassadors (immunity, safe conduct, etc.), the punishing of piracy, laws concerning common use of the seas, privileges of international trade and legitimate cross-border travel, granting equal protection against crime to foreigners as to citizens, and the rules of a just war, including refraining from militaristic meddling in the affairs of other countries.

Some concrete examples of *intra*-national rules of the Law of Nations are: monogamous marriage between one man and one woman (see 6.3 below), the right to private property (8.6), and the right to a fair trial.

5.37 – There are many more laws included within the Law of Nations, and every nation needs a full complement of these laws to help govern its internal and external affairs. Consonant with this, International Law can then be added, tailored in its details to suit the differences in forms of government among nations, their varying cultures, and the geopolitical realities of the time. When new nations have been formed, they have usually acted thus. For example, the United States used English common law at first, then began adapting it, even during colonial times. Lawmakers charged with forging these laws should know, firstly and clearly, what the Law of Nations *is*, as defined above, then study its historical development and the body of individual laws that has arisen over time. Then they must choose or adapt laws for their own nation in light of Catholic principles. Nearly all nations that are already established could also benefit from a review and revision of their current body of law in this same light. Helpful in this will be such classic works as Francisco de Vitoria's *On the Indians Lately Discovered* and *On the Law of War* (1532), Suárez's *Tract Concerning Laws and God as Legislator* (1612), Hugo Grotius' *On the Law of War and Peace* (1625), and Emer de Vattel's *The Law of Nations* (1758). Of more modern authors we could mention James Brown Scott's *The Catholic Conception of International Law* (1934), and John Eppstein's *The Catholic Tradition of the Law of Nations* (1935). There are of course many other authors who could be usefully consulted. In all this it must be noted that some of these authors are not Catholic, and that even the Catholic authors cannot be blindly trusted to be correct in everything. A good rule to follow in such a study would be to hold St. Thomas Aquinas' definitions and fundamental ideas as the standard of judgment, for he is officially *the* Doctor of both philosophy and theology in the Church.[123]

---

123 For a sobering example of the need for caution, in *De Legibus*, V. 1, ch. 1, Suárez makes some criticisms of St. Thomas' definition of law given in the *Summa Theol.* I-II Q.90, a1, saying that Thomas' definition is too broad, and does not accurately describe law, and in particular its moral nature. It would seem that Suárez failed to note the key significance of the word *áliquis* in Thomas' definition, but also the fact that Thomas here was not even attempting to give a definition of *political* law at all, but disposing of preliminary notions so as to work toward one, which he *does* give later in article 4 of the same question (see 2.25 above, where we give that definition). However, Suárez is aware of, and also disagrees with, that latter definition, claiming that a law is primarily an act of will rather than reason. This Suarezian principle, if logically followed, would destroy all law at its essence, for it would change the final cause (purpose) of law, from *order* in the community (the common good) to enforcement of the arbitrary will of the ruler. However useful Suárez' work may potentially be otherwise, it must be studied with an awareness of this fundamental error, and a proper caution in general.

On The Fourth Prerequisite For A Stable Government: Constitutional Law

> **5.38 –** *Constitutional Law is any set of fundamental rules for the structure and practical operation of a State.*

These rules could be simply handed down by oral tradition or preserved for posterity by writing them down.

Political philosophers have persuasively argued the need for rule by precedent of law vs. rule by on-the-spot decrees, and their arguments obviously hold the more for decisions affecting the very structure and workings of the State.

Aristotle

> The discussion of the...question shows nothing so clearly as that laws, when good, should be supreme, and that the magistrate(s) should regulate those matters only on which the laws are unable to speak with precision owing to the difficulty of any general principle embracing all particulars.[124]

> We thus arrive at law; for an order of succession implies law. And the rule of law, it is argued, is preferable to that of any individual... Therefore, he who bids that law rule may be deemed to bid God and Reason alone rule, but he who bids that man rule adds an element of the beast; for desire is a wild beast, and passion perverts the minds of rulers, even when they are the best of men. The law is reason unaffected by desire.[125]

Bellarmine

> [C]hristians, by the mere fact that they are Christians, do not cease to be men and citizens, and hence members of a temporal State... [T]herefore, some...human rule is necessary, the will, surely, of the ruler, or some law drawn up by the authority of the ruler. And although the will of the ruler suffices to some degree when the ruler is wise and the nation is small, yet it is absolutely necessary that the nation, if it is to be ruled rightly, must be ruled by laws, not merely by the will of the ruler. It is clear that in the meantime the will of the ruler suffices, since kingdoms are older than laws. Justinus says that formerly it was customary for the people to be governed by the will of the ruler, without any laws (History, Book I); and from Livy, it is plain that the Republic of Rome was governed for three hundred years without any laws (Book III).

> Finally, the first law-giver is either Moses, as Josephus claims (Book II) against Appio, or even Pharoneus, who lived three hundred years before Moses, as Eusebius (*Chron.*) and St. Augustine (*Cívitas Dei*,

---

124 Aristotle, *Politics*, Bk. 3, ch. 11.
125 Ibid., Bk. 3, ch. 16.

Book XVIII, ch. 3) teach. But before the time of Pharoneus, the Kingdoms of Assyria, of Greece, of Egypt, and others, were founded. Moreover, Aristotle states (Book III, ch. 11) that it is better for a people to be ruled by laws than solely by the will of the ruler, and, indeed, that this is to a certain extent necessary. And this is proved:

Firstly, because it is easier to find one or two good and wise men, than to find many. If the State is to be ruled by the will of a wise prince, this would require an endless number of good princes, one in succession to the other, but if it is ruled by laws, it is sufficient that there should have been at some time a few wise men, or even one wise man, to make the law.

Secondly, those who make laws are many, and they consider the laws carefully; but the ruler is only one, and frequently has to judge without due consideration.

Thirdly, those who made the laws did so without love or hatred, for they passed judgment concerning things distant from themselves. A ruler judges of present matters in which friends, relations, gifts, fears, etc., have an influence. Hence, judgment by law is the judgment of reason alone; the judgment of a man is a judgment of reason and passion, that is, of the man and of the beast.

Fourthly, even if the decision of a ruler be most upright, it is scarcely ever free from suspicion, envy, complaints, and abusive words; but decision by law is free from all these, because, indeed, it is known that the law cannot be corrupted by bribes.

Fifthly, legal decisions can remain the same for a long time, but the judgments of men are often changed.

Sixthly, government by law can be reduced to a system and the more easily carried out; not so with government according to the will of a man.

Seventhly, it is better for a ruler to govern personally than by deputies, but government without laws necessarily requires many deputies, who are all to judge [presumably] according to the will of the ruler; but when a nation is governed by laws, the ruler is held to judge all cases personally, since judgments are given according to his laws.[126]

It seems to us that Bellarmine's argument for Constitutional Law is conclusive.

---

126 Bellarmine, *De Láicis*, Bk. 3, ch. 10, ph. 2ff

Is *Written* Constitutional Law Required For A Stable And Successful State?

5.39 – At this point another question interposes itself: *Given that fundamental and stable rules for the structure and practical operation of a State (i.e. a Constitution) are required for a State to be successful, is it necessary that this Constitution be written down? Is it not sufficient if these fundamental rules are established by custom or tradition?*

It can be said in favor of a Constitution of tradition that the moment a State comes into being – or indeed any society comes into being – it already has at least a rudimentary Constitution. As we have seen, authority is essential to any society. Therefore, no State even begins to be, without some authority being in place at the very origin, and this authority is itself a constitutional structure, even if perhaps quite crude. As Chapter 2 noted, the most natural way that States arise is that the father of some family becomes a patriarch of his progeny (and possibly other families or communities that come under his sway). He then in fact, from being king of his own family, becomes king of a nation. (Of course, the rule of a nation as such rather falls to those of his progeny who continue his role after his death). Thus the State he founds, from its very birth, is constituted as a monarchy.

5.40 – In modern times, written Constitutions have been a major tool of Liberals to impose their governmental ideas. This does not in itself mean, however, that a written Constitution is a destabilizing force. When one thinks about it, it is clear that, in the first place, a new Constitution cannot be imposed over an existing one unless that preexisting one already be destabilized. Then too, why would revolutionaries impose a written Constitution unless it afforded the very advantage we are considering? It would seem the whole idea was to make their revolution stick by force of laws that would be known to all, and into the future.

In any case, we will have to investigate the larger historical context, and apply reason to the question, to find out if they, as such, promote a stable government or not.

5.41 – Now, for Aristotle (*Politics*), a Constitution is simply a synonymous term for Form of Government; he speaks of monarchy, aristocracy, democracy, etc., as being constitutions. The very word 'constitution', in its original and most literal sense, means something made to stand together. In other words, in respect of government, it is the firm structural arrangement that we have spoken of. In order to find whether an unwritten Constitution suffices or not, let us make a historical review of the development of written constitutional law. This development may show us something about the motivations behind the adoption of written or unwritten constitutions, and whether the written kind has shown itself to be necessary or not.

5.42 – From https://en.wikipedia.org/wiki/Constitution (accessed 5 Nov. 2025)

1. The earliest known code of justice was issued by the Sumerian king Urukagina of Lagash, *ca* 2300 B.C. This was a system of written statutes, but did not define the structure of the State itself.

2. After that, many governments ruled by special codes of written laws. There was the Code of Ur-Nammu of Ur (*ca* 2050 B.C.). Later were the codes of Ushnunna (1930 B.C.), and Lipit-Ishtar of Isin (1870 B.C.).

Again, none of these were constitutional; they were not rules for the rulers, but rules for the people. *The code of Hammurabi of Babylonia (1754 B.C.) made provisions regulating judges, and so in part the government itself.*

3. The Mosaic Law made some specific rules as to how government would be structured and would operate. Exodus 18 relates Moses' acceptance of a judicial system suggested by Aaron, who further requested that the men chosen as judges be lovers of truth and haters of avarice. Deut. 16:18ff (ca. 620 B.C.) seems to refer to this. It is important to note here that, when these rules were adopted, Moses was acknowledged by all to be directly speaking for God in the matter.

When Joshua took command of Israel after Moses' death, God told him directly:

> "Take courage therefore, and be very valiant: that thou mayst observe and do all the law, which Moses my servant hath commanded thee: turn not from it to the right hand or to the left, that thou mayst understand all things which thou dost. Let not the *book* of this law depart from thy mouth: but thou shalt meditate on it day and night, that thou mayst observe and do all things that are *written* in it: then shalt thou direct thy way, and understand it." (Jos. 1:7f)

Interestingly, when Joshua was near death, and about to pass command to someone else, he repeated this Divine command nearly verbatim to the people. (Jos. 23:6)

The Mosaic system of Judges endured as written constitutional law. Joshua 8:32ff clearly shows that what Moses had handed down was considered sacrosanct:

> "And he wrote upon stones the Deuteronomy of the law of Moses, which he had ordered before the children of Israel...After this he read all the words of the blessing and the cursing, and all things that were written in the book of the law. He left out nothing of those things which Moses had commanded, but he repeated all before all the people of Israel."

The last chapter of Joshua (24:25,26) adds that he "set before the people commandments and judgments in Sichem. And he wrote all these things in the book of the law of the Lord". The book of Judges shows that this written governmental Constitution remained in place for generations.

Finally, we can see God's purpose in commanding that this Constitution be written down, for otherwise His laws would almost certainly have been corrupted by a faulty oral tradition, or even entirely lost, as for instance during times of great upheaval, such as the Babylonian captivity.

Later, the rule by Judges was changed to rule by a king. However, kings were still subject to the Ten Commandments (of course), as well as laws

already recorded in the Scriptures (Deut. 17:14-20). Since time immemorial, there has been a tradition of treating the first five books of the Bible as written law that must be followed both by individuals and States. This latter part even descends to details of structure and procedure. Thus we can fairly say that, although at times it was rudimentary, the Hebrew/Jewish nation has been under a written constitutional law nearly since its founding.
http://www.jcpa.org/dje/articles2/deut-const.htm (accessed 5 Nov. 2025)

4. As far as we know, Draco was the first among the Greeks to establish a written code of laws. He did this around 621 B.C., at the request of the citizens of Athens. They wanted to replace the prevailing system of oral law, known only to a few, by a written code to be enforced only by a court of law. By this means they hoped to prevent arbitrary interpretations and injustices. Draco's code also made substantial requirements concerning the structure of government, and those who served in it. https://en.wikipedia.org/wiki/Draco_(legislator) (accessed 5 Nov. 2025)

5. In 594 B.C. Solon abolished nearly all of the Draconian Law. He also made major revisions to the Athenian State. His law was not only written, but written in poetic form.
https://en.wikipedia.org/wiki/Solonian_Constitution (accessed 5 Nov. 2025)

6. Around 450 B.C., about 300 years after the founding of their nation, the Romans first codified their Constitution, writing it down and calling it *The Twelve Tables*. From that time forward, they operated under a written constitutional law, with additions or amendments.

7. Around 350 B.C. Aristotle, in his works *Constitution of Athens, Politics,* and *Nicomachean Ethics,* made an explicit distinction between civil law and constitutional law.

8. In A.D. 438, Roman law was reorganized into a single code under Theodosius II (*Codex Theodosiánus*). This naturally included previous (perhaps amended) constitutional law.

9. In A.D. 534, in the Eastern Empire, a revision of the Justinian Code, called the *Codex Repetítae Praelectiónis,* contained constitutional laws.

5.43 – Since the invention of the printing press, and the common availability of books, mankind has been without the need to memorize large quantities of verbal material. The skill has been lost, and is almost certain to remain so for the foreseeable future. For this reason we will say that, as Suarez points out, a written Constitution is not absolutely necessary to the stability of a State. However, it is at least helpful, and in modern times is a practical necessity. Further, in all cases where a *new* government is going to be formed, it will be absolutely necessary. A written Constitution can be passed on through generations with little chance of unintended or spurious modifications creeping in. It will also be some defense against intentional and malicious attempts to undermine the State.

Governmental Forms Can Legitimately Change

5.44 – Having argued at length the great need of stability in a governmental system, we have to admit that, by way of rare exception, there can arise an even greater need to change it.

HISTORICAL PRECEDENT

5.45 – The Hebrew nation was ruled directly by God, through the Judges, as a theocracy. After their settlement in the Promised Land, they wanted a king so that they might be powerful like other nations, so the form of government changed to a monarchy.

Another example of regime change is found in the history of Rome. According to tradition, Romulus founded Rome as a monarchy, and it continued as such until the reign of Tarquin the Proud, when the Romans decided to end monarchy in favor of a republic. Following this change, the Roman civilization flourished, but then fell into civil war and tyranny for centuries, before one-man rule returned in the first century B.C. when the Roman Empire was established.

In our own times, regime change has occurred over and over again. Sometimes the change is for the better, but most often it seems to have been for the worse. Take the French Revolution as a case study. The Revolution began in 1789; the revolutionary leaders executed King Louis XVI in 1793, then turned on each other, finally to be overcome by the arrival of Napoleon. Napoleon then went on to establish his empire and was crowned emperor of the French by the Pope in 1804. This was a confusing time for the nation, and many believed that the rightful king of France was a Bourbon and he was recognized by them as the legitimate ruling authority even if the Revolution had usurped his power. Yet, after several years, Pope Pius VII recognized Napoleon's rule for the sake of the common good.

WHEN IS REGIME CHANGE JUSTIFIED?

5.46 – There have of course been many unjust governmental usurpations and revolutions throughout history. Obviously, these are wrong when perpetrated against a just government, but we see from the above that there are conditions when a newly established government becomes legitimate, and justified in that sense, even if it began as an unjust revolution. There are two basic ways this can happen:

1. The new government is recognized by a sufficient outside authority (e.g. as Pius VII recognized Napoleon, or if a significant number of nations recognize the new government).

2. The people eventually acquiesce to the new regime.[127]

---

[127] Change of the form of government can be effected constitutionally, but, as history shows, as often as not, it is brought about unconstitutionally. When the change is complete, the new government rules by right of accomplished fact. There must be authority in the country, and theirs is the only authority available. (*Catholic Encyclopedia*, 1910-1914, art. Authority, Civil)

Regarding the second point, Bellarmine says:

> Even if at the beginning those who founded kingdoms were usurpers for the most part, yet, by the passing of time, either they or their successors became lawful rulers of these kingdoms, since the people gradually gave their consent. (*De Láicis,* ch. 6, last ph.)

Though most modern revolutions have not followed a correct path of change, there are times when a revolution can be justly carried out. Principles by which this can be decided are given in Appendix 2.

A fortiori, a government can be peacefully changed, if there are very grave and good reasons for doing so, if there is general acquiescence to it, and if the rules given above (5.29ff) for assuring its stability are followed. See also our quote of Bellarmine's *De Láicis* in 5.24 above, especially: "...if there be **legitimate** cause, the people can change a kingdom into an aristocracy, or an aristocracy into a democracy, and vice versa, as we read was done in Rome".

> **PRINCIPLE 45: A nation's form of government is not fixed in perpetuity and may be changed for very grave reason. It is best if the form is changed at the just and true request of the people, but it may be changed without their consent and be recognized as at least the *de facto* government after it is established for a period of time.**

In Practice, The Best Form Of Government Is That Which Best Aids The Church And Therefore Jesus Christ

PRECEDING PRINCIPLES CONFIRM THIS

5.47 – Principle 1 states: *God exists as a personal being,... and He has created all other things, and sustains them in being. Therefore, creatures belong to God, and exist in order to do His will.*

Principle 10 states: *The Eternal Law exists inherently in Christ, the Son of God, True God and True Man. In Christ is summarized all man's capacities, hopes, and all truth and laws governing human life.*

Principle 31 states: *In the fulfillment of its duties, the State government passes laws with moral implications. Those laws are either in accord with God's Law or reject God's Law. Therefore, it is not possible for the State to be neutral regarding matters of religion.*

Principle 32 states: *To the extent that the religion professed by the State is true, and assuming that Church and State are pursuing their purposes correctly, then the more closely they cooperate, the more functional is the nation, and the more peace and happiness for the citizens will result.*

HISTORY SHOWS THIS

5.48 – Christendom achieved the most for the temporal common good of nations, because in general the governments of that time not only sought the common good, but also aided the people in their pursuit of heaven. The Church in turn supported the Catholic monarchies and ennobled them with sacred ceremonies and blessings which increased the ruler's authority. "The king is indeed the minister of God in governing the people, as the Apostle says: 'All power is from the Lord God'." (*De Regno,* Bk. 1, ch. 9, quoting Rom 13:1) Therefore the ruler's role is a lofty one. Yet, monarchs who turned tyrannical show that the monarch can indeed do great evils to the Faith. Notwithstanding the faults and errors of those rulers, the achievements of others show that the faith united with political power achieves the greatest good for a nation. Pope Leo XIII emphasized the necessity of rulers to follow God's laws in all things:

> Rulers must ever bear in mind that God is the paramount ruler of the world, and must set Him before themselves as their exemplar and law in the administration of the State. (*Immortále Dei,* §4)

Practically speaking, the modern liberal democracies of our age have brought such astounding destruction to society and religion that it prods the question: How did they achieve this if it really is the rule of the many/the people? Is there, rather, someone directing this destruction? One thing is certain: a mass of people does not move itself; even in a "grassroots" movement there are instigators and leaders. (cf. footnote 65)

CHAPTER 6

MATRIMONY AND THE STATE

The Origin Of Matrimony

AS SHOWN IN SCRIPTURE

6.1 – "In the beginning was the Word, and the Word was with God, and the Word was God... All things were made by Him." (Jn 1:1,3)

Turning to Genesis to see what God and the Word made, we find He said:

> Let us make man to Our image and likeness:...And God created man to His own image: to the image of God He created him: male and female He created them. And God blessed them, saying: "Increase and multiply, and fill the earth, and subdue it, and rule over the fishes of the sea..." (Gen 1:26-28)

Further we see that during the time of creation God said: "It is not good for man to be alone; let us make him a help like unto himself." (Gen 2:18) It was as if He wanted us to have a pure insight into his motive for creating man and woman. The inspired narrator goes on to describe how God cast Adam into a deep sleep and created Eve from a rib (Gen 2:21-22). Then the Father of all brought her to Adam and gave her to him. Whereupon Adam, full of the supernatural wisdom infused in him by God, states: "This now is bone of my bones and flesh of my flesh... Wherefore a man shall leave father and mother and shall cleave to his wife and they shall be two in one flesh." (Gen 2:23-24) And surely at this time God imparted the simultaneous command and blessing to Adam to "...increase and multiply, and fill the earth..." (Gen 1:28)

The fact that this giving of Eve to Adam by God constituted matrimony is clear from the last verse of this ancient text: "And they were both naked: to wit, Adam and his **wife** (Lat. *uxor*)..." (Gen 2:25)

For all Christians of good faith it is abundantly clear that:

PRINCIPLE 46: God is the Author and Creator of marriage.

AS SUPPORTED BY SECULAR HISTORY

6.2 – In addition, from the earliest records of history, we see that marriage existed even outside the chosen people of Israel for the same basic purposes: close and lifelong union of one man and one woman, and the begetting of children.

1. The institution of marriage being between one man and one woman is enshrined in the laws of Hammurabi, and was considered to be primarily for procreation rather than amorous love. Although the Mesopotamians allowed concubinage, the wife had a particular place and could not be

divorced without causes. The laws in general strongly encouraged a lifelong marriage. (*Code of Hammurabi*, 129-170)

2. Marriage in ancient Rome was a monogamous institution. The begetting of children was seen as the primary purpose of the union.[128] In different periods the Roman law protected and encouraged marriage and punished those who violated the covenants of marriage through adultery. The sanctions against adultery were severe, and could include capital punishment.[129] Those who chose not to have children (or not enough) were at times subject to various penalties.[130]

3. An epic poem of ancient India is the *Ramayana*. In India, it is similar in importance to that of the *Odyssey* in western European culture. The key theme of the *Ramayana* is the virtue of the central couple, King Rama and Queen Sita. The purity and loyalty of the spouses is portrayed as being so important that when Rama doubts Sita's faithfulness to him, she responds by asking that a bonfire be lit, which will test her. She jumps into the flames, and the flames become flower petals, which do not burn her. Her purity thus proven, she is accepted by Rama and is crowned as queen.

4. Among the Israelites we see that many of the Patriarchs practiced the form of polygamy known as polygyny. However, it should be noted that the majority of the Israelites engaged in marriage between one man and one woman.

5. Marriage existed among Native American tribes in many different forms prior to their contact with Europeans, typically involving a young man or his family giving gifts to the prospective bride's parents. It was between one man and one woman, but divorce was common, though the bride not having children was generally viewed as the only completely legitimate reason. Polygyny was also common among some tribes, however, and premarital sex also.[131]

6. In ancient China, marriage was again viewed as essentially lifelong and monogamous. It was wrapped up in an ensemble of serious social duties, and marriages were pre-arranged, sometimes between a bride and groom who had never seen each other until their wedding day. Concubinage was perhaps more common than among Native Americans, but again, the wife always had higher status. Divorce was only allowed for specific and grave reasons. Widows were to some extent even expected to remain single. Polyandry was practically unknown.[132]

---

128 *Catholic Encyclopedia*, 1910-1914, art. Law, Roman.
129 *Lex Júlia de Adultériis Coercéndis*, ca. 17 B.C.
130 Mandated, for example, in Augustus' *Lex Júlia de Maritándis Ordínibus* of ca. 18 B.C., as modified later by the *Lex Pápia Poppæa*.
131 https://www.accessgenealogy.com/native/indian-marriage.htm (accessed 2 Nov. 2025)
132 Wiki art. Traditional Chinese Marriage. https://en.wikipedia.org/wiki/Traditional_Chinese_marriage (accessed 2 Nov. 2025)

Similar stories could be told of ancient civilizations in other lands. There is a correlation between respect for monogamous and permanent marriage, and the level of culture within a people.

AS SUPPORTED BY NATURAL LAW AND REASON[133]

6.3 – The parents of children should be indubitably known to each other, and dedicated to each other and the children, because:

1. Responsibility for the children must be clearly assigned to a male and female parent, otherwise, due to original sin, the children are likely to be more or less neglected by a communal upbringing. (cf. 8.4)

2. Nature requires for children both a female formative presence, and a male formative presence, and this upon children of both sexes.

3. The strong personal bond between father and mother, father with children, and mother with children, is also part of the Natural Law.

Polygyny is against Natural Law, for although the origin of children can be known, and the proper father and mother can serve as formative influences, the needed personal bond between father and mother cannot be strong enough. Also, when there are multiple wives, the right of each to the marital act is necessarily compromised.

Polyandry is still more contrary to Natural Law, since the fathers of the children cannot in practice always be known with certainty. Hence even a legal obligation of fathers to care for their children cannot always be enforced.

Polyamory, since it requires no permanence in its "unions", is even worse than polyandry. Furthermore, such promiscuity leads to widespread venereal disease.

From 6.2 and 6.3 above it is clear that a monogamous, enduring, one-man and one-woman marriage is also part of the Law of Nations.

The Five-Fold Characteristics Of Christian Marriage

6.4 – The corruption of men due to original sin produced the varieties of corrupted sexual relationships found around the world: Polygyny, Polyandry, Polyamory, etc. We have the word of the Word Incarnate, however, to set the record straight. First He says: "Have you not read, that He who made man from the beginning made them male and female?" Then He quotes Genesis, adding: "Therefore now they are not two, but one flesh. What therefore God hath joined together, let no man put asunder."

6.5 – So we come to the five-fold characteristics of Christian Marriage, as revealed to us by God Himself.

1. Perfect Unity: One man and one woman, joined for the propagation and education of children.

---

133 *Summa Theol.* Suppl. Q.41, a1, and *Summa Contra Gentiles,* Bk III, ch. 124

2. Lifelong Stability: The union, properly formed and consummated, may not be broken by any earthly power.

3. Perfect And Permanent Fidelity: Both parties have sworn the use of their body to the other for the ends of marriage. They may not lawfully give themselves to another while the contract of marriage is still in place.

4. Equality In Primary Rights: Both the man and the woman are equally persons, each possessing an immortal soul, each destined for heaven. Both have equal rights on the other's body as St Paul declares to the Corinthians. (1 Cor. 7:3f)

5. Inequality Tempered With Love In The Ruling Of The Family: Although equal in dignity and essential rights, the husband and wife form the basic unit of society, and by its nature society has a head. Hence: "If the man is the head, the woman is the heart, and as he occupies the chief place in ruling, so she may and ought to claim for herself the chief place in love." (Pius XI, *Casti Connúbii*, §27)

From all the preceding, we can say:

> **PRINCIPLE 47: Marriage is the lifelong union of one man and one woman, primarily for the purpose of begetting and educating children, and secondarily for the mutual support of the spouses.**

Matrimony As A Sacrament

6.6 – The Church maintains that the sacraments were instituted by Jesus Christ as part of the New Covenant between God and Men. The Church has solemnly affirmed that Matrimony absolutely belongs among the sacraments. St. Paul said this clearly: "For this is a great sacrament; but I speak in Christ and the Church." (Eph 5:32) The Church reaffirmed this throughout the ages, from a short missive written by Pope Leo the Great to the sweeping and definitive *Casti Connúbii* of Pius XI; from the council of the Lateran to the council of Trent. The Tridentine fathers wanted to be abundantly clear, and bring together the teaching of the Church as received in the deposit of faith by the Apostles, to combat the raging heresies of the day, which, sadly, we are still fighting now. They wrote:

> Since, therefore, matrimony in the evangelical law, by grace through Christ, excels the ancient marriages, our holy Fathers, the Councils, and the tradition of the universal Church have with good reason always taught that it is to be classed among the sacraments of the New Law... (Dz 970 – Council of Trent, Session 24)

Followed shortly by Canon 1 of the same Session 24 of the Council:

CANON 1 – If any one saith that matrimony is not truly and properly one of the seven sacraments of the evangelic law, [a sacrament] instituted by Christ the Lord; but that it has been invented by men in the Church; and that it does not confer grace: let him be anathema. (Dz 971)

In addition it is critical to note that the Sacrament of Matrimony cannot be separated, in any way, from the contract that exists between the husband and wife in a Christian Marriage. As Leo XIII points out in *Arcánum Divínae Sapiéntiae*, §23:

> Let no one, then, be deceived by the distinction which some civil jurists have so strongly insisted upon – the distinction, namely, by virtue of which they sever the matrimonial contract from the sacrament, with intent to hand over the contract to the power and will of the rulers of the State, while reserving questions concerning the sacrament to the Church. A distinction, or rather severance, of this kind cannot be approved; for certain it is that in Christian marriage the contract is inseparable from the sacrament, and that, for this reason, the contract cannot be true and legitimate without being a sacrament as well. For Christ our Lord added to marriage the dignity of a sacrament; but marriage is the contract itself, whenever that contract is lawfully concluded.

Thus, the marriage contract and the Sacrament of Matrimony are one and the same among Christians, and cannot be separated by any power, civil or religious. In addition, the contract still exists among non-Christians, though without the sacrament:

> ...Our predecessor, Pius VI of happy memory, writing to the Bishop of Agria, most wisely said: "Hence it is clear that marriage even in the state of nature, and certainly long before it was raised to the dignity of a sacrament, was divinely instituted in such a way that it should carry with it a perpetual and indissoluble bond which cannot therefore be dissolved by any civil law. Therefore although the sacramental element may be absent from a marriage, as is the case among unbelievers, still in such a marriage, inasmuch as it is a true marriage, there must remain and indeed there does remain that perpetual bond which by divine right is so bound up with matrimony from its first institution that it is not subject to any civil power." (Pius XI, *Casti Connúbii*, §34; Dz 2235)

Education Of Children

6.7 – God created marriage, as we have seen above, primarily for the procreation of children. In justice, parents owe their children some formation, so these children may grow into adults and fulfill the role God chooses for them. Hence education:

> ...denotes the sum of all those cares and activities by which the life and growth of the child's body are safeguarded and promoted, and the due development of all his faculties, physical, mental and moral, is secured. The work of education, therefore, begins at the child's birth, and is fully completed only when he has reached the mature age at which he can fully take care of himself.[134]

---

134 Fr. E. Cahill, *The Framework of a Christian State*, p. 352

According to Pius XI, education "...aims at securing the Supreme Good, that is God, for the souls of those who are being educated, and the maximum of temporal well-being for human society." (*Divíni Illíus Magístri*, §8)

Thus we see education must be:

1. Aimed at the formation of souls for God.

2. Aimed at the temporal well being of society.

Canon 1381 of the 1917 "Old Code" of Canon Law states:

> The religious education of the children in all schools whatsoever is subject to the authority and inspection of the Church. The Ordinaries have the right and the duty to take care that nothing contrary to faith or morals be taught, or any unlawful custom or conduct tolerated in any school within their diocese. The teaching of religious knowledge and the books used are also subject to their approval. Furthermore, for the purpose of safeguarding religion and morals, they have the power to demand the removal of any teacher from the school, or to forbid the use of any book.[135]

6.8 – However, it is important to understand the role of parents in education and the interaction between the Church and parents in the education of children.
Canon 1113 (1917 Code) states:

> Parents are under a grave obligation to see to the religious and moral education of their children, as well as to their physical and civil training as far as they can, and, moreover, to provide for their temporal well-being.

6.9 – In addition to the rights of parents and the right of the Church to educate children, we must see how this plays out with the second society, namely the State. This interaction between the family, the Church and the State is most clearly spelled out in the encyclical *Rappresentanti in Terra*, by Pius XI in 1929.

> ...[S]ince education consists essentially in preparing man for what he must be and for what he must do here below, in order to attain the sublime end for which he was created, it is clear that there can be no true education which is not wholly directed to man's last end, and that in the present order of Providence, since God has revealed Himself to us in the Person of His Only Begotten Son, who alone is "the way, the truth and the life", there can be no ideally perfect education which is not Christian education. (§7)

> In general then it is the right and duty of the State [rulers] to protect, according to the rules of right reason and Faith, the moral and religious education of youth, by removing public impediments that stand in the way. In the first place it pertains to the State [authority],

---

135 Cf. 1983 Code, can. 804; also see above 4.18

in view of the common good, to promote in various ways the education and instruction of youth. It should begin by encouraging and assisting, of its own accord, the initiative and activity of the Church and the family, whose successes in this field have been clearly demonstrated by history and experience. It should moreover supplement their work whenever this falls short of what is necessary, even by means of its own schools and institutions. For the State more than any other society is provided with the means put at its disposal for the needs of all, and it is only right that it use these means to the advantage of those who have contributed them. (§46)

Over and above this, the State [authorities] can exact and take measures to secure that all its citizens have the necessary knowledge of their civic and political duties, and a certain degree of physical, intellectual and moral culture, which, considering the conditions of our times, is really necessary for the common good. (§47)

Now the education of youth is precisely one of those matters that belong both to the Church and to the State, "though in different ways", as explained above. Therefore, continues Leo XIII, between the two powers there must reign a well-ordered harmony. Not without reason may this mutual agreement be compared to the union of body and soul in man. Its nature and extent can only be determined by considering, as we have said, the nature of each of the two powers, and in particular the excellence and nobility of the respective ends. To one is committed directly and specifically the charge of what is helpful in worldly matters; while the other is to concern itself with the things that pertain to heaven and eternity. Everything therefore in human affairs that is in any way sacred, or has reference to the salvation of souls and the worship of God, whether by its nature or by its end, is subject to the jurisdiction and discipline of the Church. Whatever else is comprised in the civil and political order, rightly comes under the authority of the State; for Christ commanded us to give to Caesar the things that are Caesar's, and to God the things that are God's. (§52)

6.10 – In summary, the primary right of education belongs to the parents in all things natural, while the primary right in all things spiritual and moral belongs to the Church. The Church oversees the natural education of her children with a view toward their supernatural end. State authority should aid these efforts as needed and reasonable.

> **PRINCIPLE 48: The role of rulers of the State in education is to supplement the work of the parents and the Church. In addition, the State has the responsibility to educate its citizens on their specific civic and political duties.**

Right Of The Church To Govern Marriage

6.11 – For brevity and clarity, the Council of Trent document, from Session 24, gives the following:

> Since, therefore, matrimony in the evangelical law, by grace through Christ, excels the ancient marriages, our holy Fathers, the Councils, and the tradition of the universal Church have with good reason always taught that it is to be classed among the sacraments of the New Law; and since impious men of this age, madly raging against this teaching, have not only formed false judgments concerning this venerable sacrament, but according to their custom, introducing under the pretext of the Gospel a carnal liberty, have in writing and in word asserted many things foreign to the mind of the Catholic Church and to the general opinion approved from the time of the apostles, not without great loss of the faithful of Christ, this holy and general Synod, wishing to block their temerity, has decided, lest their pernicious contagion attract more, that the more prominent heresies and errors of the aforesaid schismatics are to be destroyed, decreeing anathemas against these heretics and their errors.

This is followed by 12 canons, the most relevant to the rights of the Church to regulate marriage being:

> CANON 3 – If any one says that those degrees only of consanguinity and affinity, which are set down in Leviticus (18:6f), can hinder matrimony from being contracted, and dissolve it when contracted; and that the Church cannot dispense in some of those degrees, or establish that others may hinder and dissolve it: let him be anathema. (Dz 973)
>
> CANON 4 – If any one says that the Church could not establish impediments dissolving marriage (cf. Mat. 16:19); or that she has erred in establishing them: let him be anathema. (Dz 974)
>
> CANON 5 – If any one says that the bond of matrimony may be dissolved because of heresy, or grievous cohabitation, or voluntary absence from a spouse: let him be anathema. (Dz 975)
>
> CANON 6 – If any one says that matrimony contracted, but not consummated, is not dissolved by a solemn profession of religion by either one of the married persons: let him be anathema. (Dz 976)
>
> CANON 7 – If any one says that the Church errs, in that she has taught, and still teaches, in accordance with the evangelical and apostolic doctrine [Mat. 19:1; 1Cor. 7:10f], that the bond of matrimony cannot be dissolved on account of the adultery of one of the married parties; and that both, or even the innocent one who gave not occasion to the adultery, cannot contract another marriage during the life-time of the other; and, that he is guilty of adultery,

who, having put away the adulteress, shall take another wife, as also she, who, having put away the adulterer, shall take another husband: let him be anathema. (Dz 977)

CANON 8 – If any one says that the Church errs, in that she declares that, for many causes, a separation may take place between husband and wife, in regard of bed, or in regard of cohabitation, for a determinate or for an indeterminate period: let him be anathema. (Dz 978)

CANON 11 – If any one says that prohibition of the solemnization of marriages at certain times of the year is a tyrannical superstition, derived from the superstition of the heathen, or condemns the benedictions and other ceremonies which the Church makes use of in them: let him be anathema. (Dz 981)

CANON 12 – If any one says that matrimonial causes do not belong to ecclesiastical judges; let him be anathema. (Dz 982)

From these it is clear that the Church defines the laws concerning marriage. Further, Pius VI clarifies Canon 12 concerning the judicial setting appropriate to marriage in the letter *Deessémus Nobis*, to the Bishop of Motula, in 1788:

> It is not unknown to us that there are some, who, attributing too much to the authority of the secular princes, and captiously interpreting the words of this canon [12, above], have undertaken to defend this: that, since the Tridentine Fathers did not make use of this form of speaking, "to the ecclesiastical judges *alone*", or, "*all* matrimonial cases", they (the Tridentine Fathers) have left to lay judges the power of at least investigating matrimonial cases which are of pure fact. But we know that even this sophism and this false kind of quibbling are devoid of all foundation. For the words of the canon are so general that they embrace and comprise all cases. Moreover, the spirit or purpose of the law extends so widely that it leaves no place for exception or limitation. For if these cases pertain to the tribunal of the Church alone for no other reason than because the marriage contract is truly and properly one of the seven sacraments of the evangelical law, then, just as this notion of the sacrament is common to all matrimonial cases, so all these cases ought to pertain to the ecclesiastical judges alone. (Dz 1500a)

The Role Of State Government Concerning Marriage

6.12 – As the Church has the right to regulate and judge in matters of marriage, the State has a duty to cooperate, and support the Church and her laws. The State does not have the right to establish laws or practices contrary to the laws of the Church, nor to set up tribunals or courts to make determinations on the validity of marriage, as we see in *Acerbíssimum Vobíscum*, of Pius IX:

We say nothing about that other decree in which, after completely despising the mystery, dignity, and sanctity of the sacrament of matrimony; after utterly ignoring and distorting its institution and nature, and after completely spurning the power of the Church over the same sacrament, it was proposed, according to the already condemned errors of heretics, and against the teaching of the Catholic Church, that marriage should be considered as a civil contract only, and that divorce, strictly speaking, should be sanctioned in various cases; and that all matrimonial cases should be deferred to lay tribunals and be judged by them; because no Catholic is ignorant or cannot know that matrimony is truly and properly one of the seven sacraments of the evangelical law, instituted by Christ the Lord, and that for that reason, there can be no marriage between the faithful without there being at one and the same time a sacrament, and that, therefore, any other union of man and woman among Christians, except the sacramental union, even if contracted under the power of any civil law, is nothing else than a disgraceful and death-bringing concubinage very frequently condemned by the Church, and, hence, that the sacrament can never be separated from the conjugal agreement, and that it pertains absolutely to the power of the Church to discern those things which can pertain in any way to the same matrimony. (Dz 1640)

Thus, in consequence of Principle 36:

PRINCIPLE 49: State authority should make laws to safeguard marriage, to protect the parties of marriage, to facilitate the ends of marriage, (both primary and secondary), and when necessary to enforce the rights of the parties. In addition, consonant with Church law, the State can regulate and define the civil consequences of marriage, including but not limited to taxes, inheritance, and the property of the parties.[136]

PRINCIPLE 50: State rulers do not have the authority to dissolve marriages, Christian or non-Christian.

As for Christians, the State authority does not have the right to set up a Civil or Common Law Marriage, which would be more akin to bound concubinage, and not valid for them, as it would not be following the laws of the rightful authority, the Church. Further, the State cannot change the nature of marriage any more than it can change a dog into a cat. The State must simply acknowledge the limits of its authority given it from God and admit that these things are beyond that authority.

---

136 In light of this principle, and the following one, when the State promulgates and enforces laws and practices which are actively contrary to these principles, such as when civil divorce is made easy, or even encouraged through financial or other incentives to husband or wife, when the authority of the father is denied or unduly restricted, when education of children is largely given over to the State, etc., it may be wise to put in place against these usurpations what safeguards to true marriage seem possible and prudent. These could include otherwise abnormal or questionable practices, such as the use of prenuptial contracts, or neglecting to record a marriage with the civil authorities. State control over spousal property is limited by other Principles (e.g. in Chapter 8).

6.13 – As a final note, the State authority, in conjunction with the Church, must protect marriage from several pernicious errors and practices. State leaders are morally bound, where possible, to:

1. Prohibit artificial birth control. Note that some drugs have a salutary life-saving benefit to the patient while at the same time possessing the side effect of preventing conception. For grave and sufficient reason a doctor may prescribe life-saving medicines that render a patient sterile. However the sterilization of the patient can *never* morally and licitly be the desired outcome.

2. Prevent abortion, even in cases of rape or incest. Life begins at conception, and no man can prioritize the life of the mother over the life of the child, even one whose existence can be seen as an invasion by a foreign party. The parents of an unborn child, even one from rape or incest, cannot prioritize their well-being over that of the new life. The government should however facilitate care and adoption services, making access to them easy and affordable.

3. Outlaw the practice of sodomy, homosexuality, or other practices contrary to nature. More so, the State should never condone so called "same-sex marriage" as a legitimate form of marriage. The Church does not condemn or hate persons with homosexual tendencies or desires. The Church abhors the offense given to the Creator in committing unnatural acts, or in desiring them, and the misery these persons live in (whether they admit to it or not), because of their radical opposition to Natural Law. (cf. 2.3)

Summary

6.14 – God is the Author and Creator of marriage. He created marriage to be a lifelong union between one man and one woman. In the New Law, founded by Jesus Christ, marriage is elevated to the dignity of a sacrament. The customs of men cannot change the nature of marriage, nor can they separate the sacrament from the contract of marriage in Christian marriage.

The natural purpose of marriage is the procreation and education of children. The parents have the natural right to the education of their children. The Church has the supernatural right to the education of her children and rightfully oversees the natural education with a view to the supernatural end of her children. The civil authority meanwhile should support parents and the Church in their mission to educate children as the surest means to forming superb citizens.

The Church has the right and duty to regulate marriage. She can determine impediments to marriage, appropriate times for marriage to be contracted, etc. Further, only the Church has the right to determine the validity of a particular marriage.

Finally, State rulers have the responsibility to uphold the institution of marriage, and to legislate the purely civil matters pertaining to marriage with an eye on the common good.

CHAPTER 7

GENDER EQUALITY AND INEQUALITY

Introduction

7.1 – *The world must be a society where everyone is equal.* Such is the guiding principle of revolution in the modern age. Beginning with the French Revolution's elimination of the nobility and clergy as separate classes, the principle of equality has moved to bring equality between not only classes, but also the male and female sexes. This has gone to such a level that society is beginning to reject even the basic biological differences between men and women in order to force equality on them. While they are the same human species and are equal insofar as they are both human beings, the fact remains that male and female are different, and from these differences arise natural inequalities of talents, and separate rights and duties.

Modern society so emphasizes the complete equality between men and women that we might be tempted to react in a way that makes the two sexes different by fundamental nature. Men and women, however, are both of the same *human* nature; that is, they are both rational animals. Therefore, in discussing the equality and inequality between men and women, we must begin with what makes them equal: their common human nature. Afterwards comes a comparison of the individuated natures of male and female with the necessary rights, duties, and inequality arising from the different sexes. Being a male or female changes which role a person has within a family as well as in society, so these complementary characteristics will be explained. Throughout this investigation into gender equality and inequality, various current errors will also be addressed.

Human Nature Of Male And Female

7.2 – In the book of Genesis we see that God created mankind as men and women: "Let us make man to our image and likeness...And God created man to his own image: to the image of God he created him: male and female he created them..." (Gen. 1:26-27) Also, from this first book of the Bible it is clear that God created man from the slime of the earth, and woman he created from the rib of the first man. Yet, both are of the same human nature and created in the image and likeness of God. They both have an immortal soul and have the obligation to live virtuous lives, and they have the same end; to be in heaven forever. So whatever is common among all persons having human nature is the same between the two genders.

> **PRINCIPLE 51: Both men and women possess the full dignity of human nature, and are equal insofar as they share this same human nature.**

Individuated Human Nature : The Two Sexes

7.3 – Though men and women are essentially identical in human nature, they are unique insofar as they are male or female individual persons. Women and men possess, fully and completely, human nature from their creation in the "image of God", and therefore enjoy complete equality in moral value and position before God. But when God creates a human soul in the matter it animates, He creates a specific mode of being for that individual person. This is the individuated nature of that person, which is either male or female.

With regard to the differences, there are indisputable anatomical, physiological and psychological differences between men and women, which make certain that a feminine personality assumes the complete human nature in a different manner than the masculine. As will be shown below, the argument cannot be made that doctors can provide an operation, or drug therapies, to physically change the genders. According to God's plan, the manifestations of individuated human nature, with regard to social interests and vocational callings, are distinctive. While these distinctions can be diminished or enhanced by education and custom, they can never be eradicated.

REAL SCIENCE PROVES TWO GENDERS

7.4 – There are hundreds of absolutely indisputable, real, and scientifically measurable physical differences between males and females. So far, 6,500 genes have been discovered that express differently in men compared to women.[137] Research on this has only recently begun. No doubt many more differences will be discovered.

Structural Body Differences

1. The average man has heavier bones, which are less susceptible to injury and have greater stress capacity.

2. Men generally have larger muscles, and are thus stronger.

3. Men have a 20 to 25% larger heart, larger lungs, and a higher concentration of hemoglobin in the blood. This means an average 11% higher blood oxygen capacity, leading to more endurance.

4. Men tend to have more fast-twitch muscles than women, thus men generally can move faster, with more explosive power.

5. Women have 5 to 10% more body fat on average, meaning a less favorable muscle to weight ratio when it comes to doing strenuous physical tasks.

6. Women have wider hips than men. This means men have a more straight-ahead stride, which is more efficient in walking, and especially running.

---

137 https://bmcbiol.biomedcentral.com/articles/10.1186/s12915-017-0352-z Gershoni, Pietrokovski, 2017 (accessed 2 Nov. 2025).

7. Male skin is thicker than female skin. Thicker skin is less easily damaged by sunlight, physical injury, and mechanical stress.

These are well-established scientific facts which no one disputes, but most of them do not even need scientific verification, as they are evident to simple observation by the senses.

Systemic Body Differences

7.5 – These are too numerous to list, but the most important are probably the differences between men and women in levels of the hormones testosterone and estrogen. Men have on average 600 ng/dl of testosterone, while women have 40 ng/dl.[138] In women, the level of estradiol (the most important type of estrogen) varies during the menstrual cycle, from about 2 ng/dl to as much as 40 ng/dl. Men however normally maintain a steady state of about 2.75 ng/dl.[139]

These hormones have extensive effects on the body, and subsequently on behavior. We are concerned here with behavior, and specifically behavior so far as it impacts social life.

1. Testosterone is known to be a cause of aggressive and risk-taking behavior.[140] Estrogen promotes the production of serotonin in the brain, which is a chemical that helps to balance moods in women, while estrogen acts differently in the male brain compared to the female brain; more of it in the male brain does *not* necessarily equate with a more balanced mood.

2. Levels of testosterone and estrogen in men remain relatively stable from puberty out to about the age of 30. This means men are less affected by the physical or emotional changes caused by variations in hormone levels.

3. On the other hand, the menstrual cycle of women by nature involves cyclic changes in estrogen and progesterone levels. These changes are known to affect mood from puberty, and during a woman's entire fertile life. The most common symptoms are depression and anxiety. When severe, they are called Premenstrual Syndrome. Additionally, a period of depression experienced after giving birth is a common experience. In up to 10% of cases, this can be severe. The time leading into menopause, called perimenopause, lasting four years on average, typically produces hot flashes, cold flashes, and/or other symptoms, and often also concentration and minor memory problems. Physical and mood challenges can continue through menopause, which lasts four to five years on average. Mood changes are by definition emotional instability, and as all of us experience, emotions can easily affect decision making.[141]

---

138 ng/dl means nanograms per deciliter.
139 https://upload.wikimedia.org/wikipedia/commons/c/cb/
     Blood_values_sorted_by_mass_and_molar_concentration.png (accessed 2 Nov. 2025).
140 Studies in the United States and around the world universally find that boys are more likely to engage in physically risky activities than girls.
141 menstrual-matters.com/blog/depression-anxiety/ (accessed Jan. 2019–see WaybackMachine). There are thirteen studies referenced. The author of this blog is clearly "feminist", but a discerning reader

In recent years there has been much talk about the so-called "male menopause". However, the term hardly corresponds to any reality. The facts are that, indeed, men as they age experience a reduction in testosterone level, but this reduction is nothing as drastic as the hormonal changes experienced in a true – that is, female – menopause. For most men, there is a steady decline of about 1% per year beginning at age 30 or so. There are certainly some men who experience more severe drop-off, and this can produce similar effects on mood as does true menopause, but this is usually a result of some medical condition, such as diabetes.[142]

Differences Between Male And Female Brains

7.6 – Between six and seven weeks after conception, the expression of a gene in the Y chromosome results in the development of the testes in males. At about the ninth week, they receive a boost in testosterone levels, and this leads to *permanent* masculinization not only sexually, but in many other ways, including differences in brain structure and operation.

It is now known that male and female mammalian brains are permanently dissimilar, such that, among other things, they do not even respond in the same way to sex hormone replacement therapies.[143]

Scientists generally study four primary areas of difference in male and female brains: processing, chemistry, structure, and activity.[144]

    1. Processing

Male brains utilize nearly seven times more gray matter for activity while female brains utilize nearly ten times more white matter. Gray-matter areas of the brain are localized. They are information and action processing centers in specific areas of the brain. This can translate to a kind of tunnel vision when males are doing something. Once they are deeply engaged in a task or game, they may not demonstrate much sensitivity to other people or their surroundings.

White matter is the networking grid that connects the brain's gray matter and other processing centers with one another. The gray vs. white matter difference may explain why, in adulthood, females are great multi-taskers, while men excel in highly task-focussed projects.

    2. Chemistry

Male and female brains process the same neurochemicals, but to different degrees, and in different ways, and through gender-specific body-brain connections. Some dominant neurochemicals are serotonin, which, among other things, helps us sit still; testosterone, our sex and aggression chemical; estrogen, a female growth and reproductive chemical; and oxytocin, a bonding-relationship chemical.

---

    can distinguish the tendentious interpretation of the science from the scientific facts themselves.
142 https://www.mayoclinic.org/healthy-lifestyle/mens-health/in-depth/male-menopause/art-20048056 (accessed 2 Nov. 2025). There are ten studies referenced.
143 https://www.ncbi.nlm.nih.gov/pmc/articles/PMC2879914/. (accessed 2 Nov. 2025). A multitude of studies are referenced.
144 https://www.psychologytoday.com/us/blog/hope-relationships/201402/brain-differences-between-genders. (accessed 2 Nov. 2025). Our information is taken from this source. Original source: Gregory L. Jantz, Ph.D, *Raising Boys By Design*, Waterbrook, 2013.

In part because of differences in processing these chemicals, males on average tend to be less inclined to sit still for as long as females, and tend to be more physically impulsive and aggressive. Additionally, males process less of the bonding chemical oxytocin than females.

3. Structural Differences

A number of structural elements in the human brain differ between males and females. "Structural" refers to actual parts of the brain and the way they are built, including their size and/or mass.

Females often have a larger hippocampus (our human memory center). Females also often have a higher density of neural connections into the hippocampus. As a result, girls and women tend to input or absorb more sensorial and emotive information than males do. By "sensorial" we mean information to and from all five senses. If one notes observations over time of boys and girls and men and women, one finds that females tend to sense a lot more of what is going on around them throughout the day, and they retain that sensorial information more than men do.

Additionally, *before boys or girls are born*, their brains develop with different hemispheric divisions of labor. For instance, females tend to have verbal centers on both sides of the brain, while males tend to have verbal centers on only the left hemisphere. This is a significant difference. Females tend to use more words when discussing or describing incidents, stories, persons, objects, feelings, or places. Males not only have fewer verbal centers in general but also, often, have less connectivity between their word centers and their memories or feelings. When it comes to discussing feelings and emotions and senses together, females tend to have an advantage, and they tend to have more interest in talking about these things.

4. Blood Flow And Brain Activity

While on the subject of emotional processing, another difference worth looking at closely is the activity-emphasis-comparison of male and female brains. The female brain, in part thanks to far more natural blood flow throughout the brain at any given moment (more white matter processing), and because of a higher degree of blood flow in a concentration part of the brain called the *cingulate gyrus*, will often ruminate on and revisit emotional memories more than the male brain.

Males, in general, are designed differently. After reflecting more briefly on an emotive memory, they tend to analyze it somewhat, then move on to the next task. During this process, they may also choose to change course and do something active and unrelated to feelings, rather than analyze their feelings at all. Thus, observers may mistakenly believe that males avoid feelings in comparison to females, or move to problem-solving too quickly. It is not a matter of deliberate avoidance, but of natural tendency.

These four natural design differences listed above are just a sample of how males and females think differently. Scientists have discovered approximately 100 gender differences in the brain.[145] Nevertheless, we find today a great resistance in some

---

145 Some argue that these findings, while true, fail to account for the "plastic" nature of the brain. They claim that male/female brain characteristics are acquired through repeated behavior, not given genetically. But while it is well known that the brain can indeed "rewire" itself in rather dramatic ways, the argument fails entirely due to the equally certain fact that the brain differences mentioned *are* given genetically; they are *already in place before birth*.

quarters to these scientific facts, notwithstanding that they fit the common-sense consensus of all history.

The New "Gender Theory"

As against the above realities, some today are proposing what they call "Gender Theory".

WHAT IS GENDER THEORY?

7.7 – This so-called "Gender Theory" is actually several schools of thought, but they are not substantially different, and so, to include them all under one umbrella term is legitimate. "Gender Theory" incorporates the following base tenets:

1. Gender is not equivalent to biological sex, but is the *expression* of sexuality.

2. Gender, as the expression of sexuality, is a construct of the interactions of an individual with the social environment.

3. Therefore, genders are not given by nature, but are learned.

In the earlier days of "Gender Theory" biological sex was considered to be both real and "binary" (male or female). Gender was distinguished from sex in that, regardless of one's given biological sex, gender was the choice and/or *expression* of the sex (as if it is possible to choose one's biology, or "express" it differently than what it is!). Also, since gender supposedly did not depend upon one's physical sexual reality, and was a social construct, one could be socially formed, and/or choose, to be not only either male or female, but also asexual or bisexual (androgynous).

In the last two decades or so, things have been taken by some people to new extremes of reality denial, so some "gender theorists" have added another fundamental tenet:

4. Biological sex does not exist. (Yes, you are reading that correctly. See 7.9 below, concerning Judith Butler)

Assuming biological sex does not exist, it would naturally follow that both sex and gender are pure voluntary and imaginary constructs, so that any number of "genders" can simply be invented out of thin air – and this is precisely what the latest crop of "gender theorists" actually do. There are already many, many imaginary genders they have pretended to discover, and more are being added all the time.

This has to be called out for what it is: willful disconnect from reality. This is the insanity to which the ever-increasing slavery to sin has led modern man.

HISTORICAL BACKGROUND OF GENDER THEORY

7.8 – It may be useful to give a brief exposition of how we got here. The focus is on England, but the stages of development were not much different in continental Europe, or in the United States.

Already in the 1700s the revolutionary ideals of Liberty, Equality and Fraternity began to be considered in respect of "freeing" women, and making them equal to men, at least in regard to property rights and certain other things.

The "feminist" movement in the 1800s, first in England and then spreading elsewhere, succeeded in passing some laws in this respect.[146]

1869 – Women are allowed to vote in local elections, and are allowed to legally keep their own earnings against the will of their husbands.

1877 – The Malthusian League was founded, to promote birth control.

1880 – The first women are awarded degrees from a British university.

1882 – Women are allowed to own property separate from their husbands'.

1892-1899 – The first female dentist, architect and electrical engineer.

The original feminists agitated only for such things as the above, perhaps not considering that a woman could not do some of them without taking on masculine traits.

Simultaneously with the beginning of the feminist movement were the first rumblings of the sexual revolution. The death penalty for sodomy was abolished in the 1860s in England, and prostitution and pornography had already begun to flourish.

By the end of the 1800's, the New Woman had made her appearance; one who rejected traditional female roles, including child bearing, and wanted to usurp male roles. She was the counterpart of the Decadent; the dandified, effeminate man, who was sometimes also a homosexual (e.g. Oscar Wilde). These names came from an influential essay *The Decadent And The New Woman*, written by Linda Dowling, who described these types as "the twin apostles of the social apocalypse"; that is, the harbingers of the end of society. That prophecy is being fulfilled now.

In the 1900s were seen:

1908 – The first woman mayor.

1913 – The first woman magistrate.

1914 – The first policewoman.

1917 – The Women's Royal Naval Service is formed.

1918 – Women over 30 are allowed to vote nationally if they fulfill property qualifications.

1919 – A law opens other previously male-only professions to women. The first woman is elected as parliamentary minister.

In the Roaring Twenties, sexual promiscuity became common.

1928 – All persons of either sex are allowed to vote if over 21.

1929 – The first woman cabinet minister.

1950s – In the U.S., Planned Parenthood aids in the development of birth control pills, which begin to be used in the 1960s.

---

146 We place "feminist" in quotes because in strict reality "feminism" is exactly the opposite of what it pretends to be. This movement has always had as its goal (conscious or not) to *masculinize* women; to therefore crush true femininity out of existence. Initially, this was not in the physical or even spiritual domains, but only the socio-political domain. However, because the socio-political domain by nature has always belonged to men, and will always do so, the only way that women can compete with men in that domain is to acquire their physical and spiritual traits. The term 'feminism' for this movement is then not merely a lie, but the *opposite* of the truth. And to add the other half of this perspective, we can say that the movement against so-called "toxic masculinity", insofar as it implies a battle against the natural leadership role that men have, is in reality a movement advocating toxic *effeminacy* in men. Ironically, real toxic masculinity is simply the masculinism which is today called "feminism". See the Glossary entry *Feminism*.

1955 – The first woman TV newsreader (Britain).

1973 – Women are allowed to join the stock exchange (Britain). In the U.S., abortion is legalized.

1975 – Sex Discrimination Act makes "discrimination" illegal in employment, education and training.

1976 – The first female firefighter.

1979 – Margaret Thatcher is the first female prime minister of England.

Ca. 1980 up to the present – The moral neutrality of homosexual or other deviant sexuality has been exponentially more promoted.

In the above timeline, the average reader probably would, and should, be struck by the fact that we have moved from the traditional "binary" male and female conception of gender and its consequent distinction of roles in society – which goes back to the dawn of time – to a near total destruction of any idea of gender at all – and that within a span of a mere 150 years. Further, we see that the corruption of gender roles clearly goes hand in hand with the corruption of sexual behavior. With contraception and abortion treated as normal, the act of sex is therefore also considered as normally purely recreational and inconsequential, or at best as an expression of "love" (which is in truth of a disordered, sensual and selfish sort).

MAIN PROPONENTS OF "GENDER THEORY"

7.9 – This survey finishes by giving a list of what we view as the three most important persons who influenced the genesis and progress of "gender theory", with the most basic facts regarding their persons, work and ideas.[147]

Simone de Beauvoir (1908-1986) – Born of a devout Catholic mother and a pagan father, she lost her faith in her teens and remained atheist thereafter. She was the ninth woman to receive a degree from the Sorbonne. All her intellectual influences from higher education were Modernist. She was an Existentialist "philosopher", "feminist", and promiscuous bisexual, who seduced at least two of her female students. Along with Michel Foucault and other radicals, she signed a petition in 1977 to abolish the age of consent in France. She was the first to separate gender from biological sex; famous among gender theorists for the saying: "One is not born but becomes a woman". She complained that men stereotyped women as "Other", considered them imperfect men, and used this as an excuse to organize a "patriarchal" society. Until late in life, she refused to be part of the "women's movement", because she thought women were, or should be, the same as men, and therefore the specifically female should not be exalted.[148]

Michel Foucault (1926-1984) – He was born into a conservative, but not devout, Catholic family. He characterized himself in his early years as a "juvenile delinquent". His education was varied; three years at a Jesuit college; later, studies under a Hegelian and Marxist professor. Still later he also studied Kant, Husserl, Heidegger, and the Marxist philosopher Althusser. He later rejected many Marxist ideas, but was always a Leftist, and a political activist for leftist causes. He was strongly influenced

---

[147] Information about their personal lives is not given as an *ad hominem* argument against their theories, for these are easily refuted on their own terms, but to further show that belief in gender theory, like belief in anything else, usually reduces to practice, and gender theory leads to a practice that is corrupt.

[148] In a classic display of Liberal blindness, she failed to see that her desire to be thought the same as a man was the deepest possible slavery to the "patriarchal" society she condemned.

by Nietzsche. He studied and taught modern psychology, in which he was influenced by Freud and other moderns. At some point in his life he became an atheist. He was a promiscuous sado-masochistic homosexual who attempted suicide several times, took drugs, and was the first public person in France to die of AIDS-related causes. Coworkers described him as a dandy. An amoralist, he viewed society as an expanded version of Bentham's panopticon, a prison where the inmates knew they could be watched from all sides, at any time, and punished for infractions, and therefore they regulated their own behavior. Society, he claimed, is a panopticon, where people behave as they are expected because others in society watch them and punish them with disapproval if they do not conform to accepted norms. The norms themselves are entirely arbitrary. They are merely an expression of brute power; a "disciplinary regime". Therefore sexual norms also are an arbitrary social construct.[149]

Judith Butler (1956-) – Born in the U.S.; a lesbian, "married" to another woman. She confessed herself to be rebellious as a child. Her main influences are all anti-Christian; Freud and Foucault at the top of the list. Main ideas: Agrees with Simone de Beauvoir that "a woman is not born, she is made", but also literally denies that biological differences of sex exist. In Gender Trouble, 1990, she quotes Monique Wittig's claim that even the naming of the body parts creates a fiction and constructs the bodily features themselves, fragmenting what was really once whole. Language (she says), repeated over time, "produces reality-effects that are eventually misperceived as 'facts'." Butler adds that gender is one's perception of one's sexuality; a result of "performative" actions; that is, role-playing in imitation of those around you, the parameters of whose gender expression have been established by the traditional binary male/female culture (Foucault's "disciplinary regime"). This regime is a self-perpetuating, restrictive, and deceptive system. However, the bonds of the system, once known, can be cast off. This, and her idea of a free-floating, self-created sex and gender, are foundational elements of Queer Theory.[150]

As the reader can see from the foregoing paragraphs, the modern world is moving far from a correct understanding of what it means to be a man or a woman. God created mankind as men and women. When used in its true meaning, 'gender' is 'sex', and sex is "binary"; male or female. Governments should recognize only two genders: male and female. The assignment of gender to a person must never be a matter of personal choice, but of biological reality manifested before birth.[151]

---

149 We should notice that Foucault is coming from a profoundly anti-social mindset. Social norms, as all norms, only exist as aids toward a goal; they are rules by which each individual is guided to his happiness, which happiness is the *same* among all individuals, since they share the same human nature. No one therefore should be exempted from social norms. Logically, by thus exempting individuals from these norms, Foucault denies that we have a common human nature. By extension then, he also denies that we should have any society with each other.

150 For an article that really drags all the abstruse, pseudo-intellectual, pitch-black gnostic thinking of modern "gender theory" out into the bright light of common sense, see this:
https://www.ncregister.com/blog/5-fatal-flaws-of-gender-theory (accessed 2 Nov. 2025).
Further reading: *Prenatal Sex Differences In The Human Brain*, B. Reinius & E. Jazin, 2009 (https://www.nature.com/articles/mp200979 – accessed 2 Nov. 2025) Also: *Exploring the Biological Contributions to Human Health: Does Sex Matter?*: Biological facts of sex dimorphism at all ages from birth to old age (2001). For an excerpt, see https://www.ncbi.nlm.nih.gov/books/NBK222286/ (accessed 2 Nov. 2025) which shows, among other things, that it has been known for four decades that a testis-determining locus, *TDF* (testis-determining factor), resides on the Y chromosome. Since then our knowledge has been advancing rapidly. For some time now, there has been no excuse for not knowing that sex is gender, and that it is physically determined before birth.

151 We are aware that there are cases where determining biological or birth gender is difficult. About 0.2% of persons are born with some sort of DSD (Disorder of Sexual Development). Although these

PRINCIPLE 52: There are two distinct genders found in human nature: male and female. This individuated human nature is manifested in a person's body and soul, making man and woman different yet complementary individuals.

Male And Female Aptitudes : Consequences For Societal Roles

7.10 – In this section we will first return to our exposition of the physical differences between men and women as established by empirical science, and see how they result in different roles for the two sexes in society in general. We will limit ourselves to aptitudes directly derived from the physical differences only. This is not to deny that there are other differences, at least as valid, established by other sciences, but we choose here to stay on the common ground of facts that all rational persons must accept. We will be referring back to sections 7.4 (Structural Body Differences); 7.5 (Systemic Body Differences); and 7.6 (Differences Between Male And Female Brains).

Next we will add considerations of Church teaching, first on the roles of men and women in the larger society, then on the roles of husband and wife in the first level of society in particular; that is, in the family.

PHYSICAL DIFFERENCES BETWEEN MEN AND WOMEN : THEIR ROLES IN SOCIETY IN GENERAL

7.11 – Men are more apt, by body and brain design, for:

1. Heavy manual labor, and working outdoors. (see 7.4, all points)

2. All physically demanding sports, especially contact sports. (7.4, all points; 7.5, point 1)

3. All tasks potentially demanding great physical efforts, endurance, fortitude, or stability of mind: Police, firefighting, military service, others. (7.4, all points; 7.5, all points)

4. All tasks requiring linear, logical, focussed thinking, or stability of mind: Philosophy, government, the methodical sciences, and the teaching of these disciplines, especially to other males. (7.5, point 2; 7.6, points 1, 3, 4)

7.12 – Women are better designed, physically and mentally, for:

1. Physical tasks requiring precision, sensitivity, delicacy, or multi-tasking: Medical work, musical performance, child care, others. (7.4, all points; 7.6, points 1, 2, 3)

---

people must be treated with great tact and compassion, their number is so small that a specific discussion on this issue is not in the scope of our work. Nor should such atypical cases enter into or shape the broad social policy. It should further be noted that those suffering from a DSD are the only people who are "born that way", in the sense of being gender confused or ambivalent at birth.

2. All mental tasks requiring verbal skills, multi-tasking, wholistic or sensual-experiential-emotive approaches: Education of infants and small children of both sexes, trial-and-error sciences (quasi-sciences) such as natural medicine, the arts in general, and the teaching of these disciplines, especially to other females. (7.6, all points)

3. Any task, mental or physical, that requires patience or long-term application, or social grace. (7.5, point 1; 7.6, point 2)

7.13 – After examining this breakdown, it will surely be noted that in some particulars it does not seem to correspond to what we have seen throughout history.

For example, it may be said that most surgeons have been men, while women would seem to have greater natural aptitude for such delicate work. The glib response would be that women, until recent years, have been traditionally excluded from this profession. This would be true, but there is another reason, and that is that the surgical profession cannot be carried on without a background of knowledge in the methodical science of medicine. In other words, surgery is *per se* a physical task, but no one can do it without a mental education that requires disciplined logical application. Then too, nearly all doctors, surgeons included, are required to give diagnoses, and good diagnosis demands logical and dispassionate thinking skills.

Again, it may be said that, in spite of the fact that women seem to have better verbal and artistic skills than men, it is the latter who have most often become famous artists, even in the literary domain. Once more, we can admit that this has been partially, even largely, a result of societal barriers. But in regard to literary pursuits in particular, we can note that a deep command of language requires much more than just a large vocabulary, or a readiness to speak. A firm grasp of the methodical science of grammar is most helpful. Additionally, deep literary or artistic inspiration can only be drawn from knowledge and understanding that penetrates into the intellectual bedrock. Because of their natural tendency to concentrated linear thought, men generally drill deeper therein. Men probably work much harder to find a good manner of artistic expression, but when they do, it may often be more profound.

Further, we can note a huge contributing factor to these apparent discrepancies: The vast majority of women throughout history have given birth to one or more children. The natural result of this is that they have spent a great deal of their time raising them; much more time than the fathers have. And given the natural aptitude of women for training small children (not to mention the biological fact that they alone can breastfeed), this is how it should be. Men in contrast, even fathers of families, not only have more time for the pursuits in which they have historically excelled, but often make their very living in them, which adds a motivational factor.

And finally, there is a very important caveat that both helps to explain the discrepancies, and should be taken into account when considering how these natural aptitudes apply to the formulation of rules for male and female societal roles: natural aptitudes can be modified by training. For instance, with practice, women can learn to think more logically and linearly, and men can become better at verbal or social skills, or multi-tasking. In fact, it has been said that the ideal human being would be one who, in the mental/spiritual domain, would, while retaining his or her natural mental talents, also learn to acquire the advantages of the mental talents of the opposite sex.

Still, when all is said and done, it remains true that males and females in general do have the aforesaid natural talents and inclinations. It will never be possible for men in general to perfectly master the mental or physical skills that women have, nor vice versa. Nor is this even desirable, for these talents are given by God exactly because He has created the two sexes for different, and complementary, roles. It is therefore a violation of nature for a woman to want to acquire naturally male mental or physical talents in *preference* to her own, or vice versa for men. Fighting against nature is not only a battle doomed to defeat beforehand, but even if "victory" would be possible, the spoils of that war would only be misery. Happiness, even of the natural sort, consists precisely in perfecting nature, not destroying it.

> **PRINCIPLE 53: Because God made humans as men and women, the State must recognize that the wholesome complementary relationship between the sexes is part of the Divine Plan. Thus, State laws must discourage the confusing of the roles of men and women, and the State ought to encourage men and women to pursue tasks that are in accord with their masculine or feminine natures, respectively.**

CHURCH TEACHING : ROLES OF HUSBAND AND WIFE IN THE FAMILY

7.14 – The foundation of the larger society is necessarily not the individual, but the living union of man and woman, ideally in the home; a union wherein the different characteristics of the sexes cooperate in a division of labor, but not apart from each other, for the purposes of raising children, and the spouses' mutual support, in that order of priority. It is a partnership of their complementary characters.

> Who shall find a valiant woman? Far and from the uttermost coasts is the price of her. The heart of her husband trusteth in her, and he shall have no need of spoils. She will render him good, and not evil, all the days of her life. She hath sought wool and flax, and hath wrought by the counsel of her hands... She hath put out her hands to strong things, and her fingers have taken hold of the spindle. She hath opened her hands to the needy, and stretched out her hands to the poor. She shall not fear for her house in the cold of snow: for all her domestics are clothed in double garments. She hath made for herself clothing of tapestry: fine linen, and purple is her covering. Her husband is honorable in the gates, and when he sitteth among the senators of the land... Strength and beauty are her clothing, and she shall laugh in the latter day. She hath opened her mouth to wisdom, and the law of clemency is on her tongue. She hath looked well to the paths of her house, and hath not eaten her bread idle. Her children rose up, and called her blessed: her husband, and he praised her. Many daughters have gathered together riches: thou hast surpassed them all. Favor is deceitful, and beauty is vain: the

woman who fears the Lord, she shall be praised. Give her the fruit of her hands: and let her works praise her in the gates. (Prov. 31:10-31)

Let women be subject to their husbands, as to the Lord: Because the husband is the head of the wife, as Christ is the head of the Church. He is the savior of His Body. Therefore as the Church is subject to Christ, so also let the wives be to their husbands in all things. Husbands, love your wives, as Christ also loved the Church, and delivered himself up for it...let every one of you in particular love his wife as himself: and let the wife fear her husband. (Eph. 5:22-25)

In like manner also let wives be subject to their husbands: that if any believe not the Word, they may be won without the Word, by the conversation of the wives. (I Peter 3:1)

Furthermore, this doctrine, which has always been held by the Church, was emphasized by Leo XIII in the encyclical *Arcánum*, February 10, 1880, wherein he declares:

> The husband is the chief of the family and the head of the wife. The woman, because she is flesh of his flesh, and bone of his bone, must be subject to her husband and obey him; not, indeed, as a servant, but as a companion, so that her obedience shall be wanting in neither honor nor dignity. Since the husband represents Christ, and since the wife represents the Church, let there always be, both in him who commands and in her who obeys, a heaven-born love guiding both in their respective duties. (§11)

7.15 – The characteristics of Christian Marriage, as detailed in Chapter 6, bear repeating. The five-fold characteristics of Christian Marriage, as revealed to us by God Himself are:

1. Perfect Unity: One man and one woman, joined for the propagation and education of children.

2. Perpetual Stability: The union, properly formed and consummated, may not be broken by any earthly power.

3. Perfect And Permanent Fidelity: Both parties have sworn the use of their body to the other for the ends of marriage. They may not lawfully give themselves to another while the contract of marriage is still in place.

4. Equality In Primary Rights: Both the man and the woman are equally persons, each possessing an immortal soul, each destined for heaven. Both have equal rights on the other's body, as St. Paul declares to the Corinthians.

5. Inequality Tempered With Love In The Ruling Of The Family: Although equal in dignity and essential rights, the husband and wife form a basic unit of society and by its nature society has a head. Hence: "...if the man

is the head, the woman is the heart, and as he occupies the chief place in ruling, so she may and ought to claim for herself the chief place in love."[152]

God perfectly paired the differences in natural endowments to make perfect the indissoluble marital union between one man and one woman. Man becomes father, with consequent rights and duties that include support and protection. Woman becomes mother, with corresponding maternal rights and duties. The mother is the embodiment of the completely developed feminine person, which is in total conformity with the ends of marriage.[153]

7.16 – Given these characteristics, the notion of total equality of the sexes within the context of marriage is an impossibility. Consequently, the State is without authority to legislate in matters of equality that trespass on the rights and duties of the marital union. The State should uphold these and the following truths:

> The same false teachers who try to dim the luster of conjugal faith and purity do not scruple to do away with the honorable and trusting obedience which the woman owes to the man. Many of them even go further and assert that such a subjection of one party to the other is unworthy of human dignity, that the rights of husband and wife are equal; wherefore, they boldly proclaim the emancipation of women has been or ought to be effected. This emancipation in their ideas must be threefold, in the ruling of the domestic society, in the administration of family affairs and in the rearing of the children. It must be social, economic, physiological. Physiological; that is to say, the woman is to be freed at her own good pleasure from the burdensome duties properly belonging to a wife as companion and mother – (We have already said that this is not an emancipation but a crime). Social; inasmuch as the wife being freed from the cares of children and family, should, to the neglect of these, be able to follow her own bent and devote herself to business and even public affairs. Finally economic; whereby the woman, even without the knowledge and against the wish of her husband, may be at liberty to conduct and administer her own affairs, giving her attention chiefly to these rather than to children, husband and family.
>
> This, however, is not the true emancipation of woman, nor that rational and exalted liberty which belongs to the noble office of a Christian woman and wife; it is rather the debasing of the womanly character and the dignity of motherhood, and indeed of the whole family, as a result of which the husband suffers the loss of his wife, the children of their mother, and the home and the whole family of an ever watchful guardian. More than this, this false liberty and unnatural equality with the husband is to the detriment of the

---

152 Pius XI, *Casti Connúbii*, §27
153 We are speaking in the natural plane here; this is not to say that the life of marriage and childbirth is superior to that of virginity consecrated to God, for a religious nun or sister becomes a mother on the higher supernatural plane.

woman herself, for if the woman descends from her truly regal throne to which she has been raised within the walls of the home by means of the Gospel, she will soon be reduced to the old state of slavery (if not in appearance, certainly in reality) and become, as amongst the pagans, the mere instrument of man.

This equality of rights which is so much exaggerated and distorted, must indeed be recognized in those rights which belong to the dignity of the human soul and which are proper to the marriage contract and inseparably bound up with wedlock. In such things undoubtedly both parties enjoy the same rights and are bound by the same obligations; in other things there must be a certain inequality and due accommodation, which is demanded by the good of the family and the right ordering and unity and stability of home life.[154]

PRINCIPLE 54: Having distinct rights and duties as men and women, the two sexes have different roles within the family. The man is the head of the family and the woman is the heart.

7.17 – The State is without authority to legislate in matters of equality that trespass on the rights and duties of the marital union, which is between one man and one woman.

PRINCIPLE 55: The State, recognizing the decisive importance of wholesome child-rearing for the health of society, should shape its policies and direct its incentives to encouraging women to devote themselves to raising children within the context of life-long marriage.

Specifically, economic conditions should foster the ability of families to live on the husband's income.

CHURCH TEACHING : ROLES OF MEN AND WOMEN IN THE LARGER SOCIETY

7.18 – For all the above reasons, Man gets authoritative "pre-eminence" in society, and this is not of his own accord, but from the structure of nature. And nature itself is because of God's plan, as revealed to us by His Church: "The man...is the image and glory of God, but the woman is the glory of the man." (I Corinthians 11:7) The Apostle Paul, in this reference to the creation of the first man and woman, presupposes the image of God in the woman. But because this image manifests itself more specifically in a man's supremacy over creation (Genesis 1:26), and since man as the born leader of the family first exercised this supremacy, he is called directly "God's image" in God's capacity as ruler. Woman takes part in this supremacy only indirectly under the guidance of the man and as his complement or helpmate. We cannot restrict St. Paul's statement as applying to the family alone, for he clearly

---

154 Pius XI, *Casti Connúbii* §§ 74 – 76 (Dz 2247 & 2248).

inferred from the Genesis account the social status of woman in the larger community. Therefore, woman's natural position in the family translates to every form of society that develops from the primordial society of the family.[155] St. Paul underlines this in the following:

> But I suffer not a woman to teach, nor to use authority over the man, but to be in silence. For Adam was first formed, then Eve. And Adam was not seduced, but the woman being seduced, was in the transgression. Yet she shall be saved through childbearing, if she continue in faith, and love, and sanctification, with sobriety. (I Tim. 2:12-15)

Sacred Scripture also portrays women being in charge of a country as a result of men defaulting on their responsibilities: "Woe to the wicked unto evil: for the reward of his hands shall be given him. As for my people, their oppressors have stripped them, and women have ruled over them." (Isaias 3:11-12) And as St. Thomas Aquinas explains, women are naturally subject to man, because in man the discretion of reason predominates. (cf. 2.21, and Principle 16).

Revolutionary thought over the last 200 years has encouraged women to seek "emancipation" from the leadership of men, whether this be in the family or in society at large. The Church has been clear that "emancipation" with regard to the duties of wife and mother is basically not freedom, but a fraud. Being a fraud, it results not in emancipation, but as Pope Pius XI puts it, a "wretched crime", which actually leads to the unhappiness of both women and society. Today we find women in the workplace and men in the home, each fulfilling the traditional roles of the opposite sex. From this we see that men and women *can* go against the natural tendencies of their genders. Normally, however, they will and should do the things fitting for their status as man or woman. A generation or more of gender-bending may make role reversals habitual, and thus seem normal, but they are not. People may even feel happy in these reversals, but they are not; they have simply never experienced what real happiness is.

7.19 – It may be that modern times require some adjustments, at least transitional and temporary, until traditional roles of men and women in the larger society can be reestablished. As Pius XI details:

> Nevertheless, wherever the social and economic conditions of the married woman, because of changed ways and practices of human society, need to be changed in some manner, it belongs to public authority to adapt the civil rights of woman to the necessities and needs of this time, with due consideration of what the different natural dispositions of the feminine sex, good morality, and the common good of the family demand; provided, also, that the essential order of domestic society remains intact, which is founded on an authority and wisdom higher than human, that is, divine, and cannot be changed by public laws and the pleasure of individuals.[156]

However, in §95 of the same encyclical, he quotes Leo XIII:

---

155 Described by St. Thomas in the *Summa Theol.*, I, Q.92, a1, ad 2. See 2.21.
156 Pope Pius XI, Encyclical *Casti Connúbii*, §77 (quoted from Dz 2248)

> From the beginning of the world, indeed, it was divinely ordained that things instituted by God and by nature should be proved by us to be the more profitable and salutary the more they remain unchanged in their full integrity. For God, the Maker of all things, well knowing what was good for the institution and preservation of each of His creatures, so ordered them by His will and mind that each might adequately attain the end for which it was made. If the rashness or the wickedness of human agency venture to change or disturb that order of things which has been constituted with fullest foresight, then the designs of infinite wisdom and usefulness begin either to be hurtful or cease to be profitable, partly because through the change undergone they have lost their power of benefitting, and partly because God chooses to inflict punishment on the pride and audacity of man. (*Arcánum*, §25)

And so it is plain that the State must strive that these adjustments occur along natural lines.

> **PRINCIPLE 56: Whatever economic and social roles women may fill, women should be discouraged from emulating specifically masculine traits. Similarly, the State must discourage public displays of effeminacy by men.**

> **PRINCIPLE 57: The State should take measures to ensure that women workers are paid justly and are treated with due consideration for women's modesty and dignity.**

PREPARATORY NOTE FOR FOLLOWING CHAPTERS

The various conclusions we present as we progress through this work are not equally certain. We are proceeding from the most certain to the least certain. Everything we are presenting is based on Revelation, Nature and Reason, with the auxiliary support of history. However, Chapter 1 is most firmly rooted in infallible Revelation, which always supports, and is supported by, Nature, Reason and history. As we move through succeeding chapters, we progressively have to rely more on the latter three sources of knowledge. Moreover, the issues become more multi-faceted, and details become more important and numerous. For these reasons, we do not pretend that the reader should grant equal weight to all the Principles we have presented or will present.

For example, Chapter 7 treated the question of gender equality. This chapter is tightly connected to Chapter 2, which referenced Scripture and Tradition to show that a husband has authority over his wife and family (see 2.21). Revelation is so clear on this point that it must be considered infallible dogma. Thus it is absolutely certain that man and woman are *not* equal in respect of authority, at least. In Chapter 7 we delved into other ways that man and woman are unequal; that is, we explored their mental and physical differences, and we found that these synced with and helped explain what was said in Chapter 2. Here, our conclusions depended more on simple observations of Nature, as it has shown up throughout history, with quite a bit of scientific data added on top of that, and all considered with reason. One would have to be crazy to deny our conclusions, but they are not mainly rooted in Revelation.

The question of private property, to be investigated in Chapter 8, similarly lies at a transition point between Revelation and Nature-combined-with-Reason. Although, as we will show, Scripture and Tradition have something to say on the matter, the right to private property is not a *dogma* of the Church. Whether or not man should possess private property is firstly a question related to his nature. We will also have to remember that *both* Revelation and Reason tell us that man's nature is *fallen.* It can only be known whether private property is suitable to man or not after it is known what man's *fallen* nature is.

The question of economic equality and inequality, to be dealt with in Chapter 9, then considers whether men should possess unequal amounts of property or not, and it does so using the same emphases on method as did Chapter 8.

The conclusions of both Chapter 8 and Chapter 9 will, of course, impact man's economic relations with his neighbor – and that impact will be dramatic; it will condition all economic questions.

God willing, a future volume will then take up the question of Catholic Economics *per se,* and in some detail.

CHAPTER 8

PRIVATE PROPERTY AND THE STATE

Definitions And Distinctions

8.1 – As usual, in order to prevent misunderstandings, we must clarify and distinguish important terms. In the first place, what do we mean by 'property'? Then too, what is the difference between 'private' property as compared to 'public', 'common', 'communal' or 'corporate' property?

> *Property is a thing possessed by someone, and in his control, so that he can freely dispose of it.*

Now of course, this "someone" can be either a physical and thus individual person, or it can be a moral person (e.g. a legal entity). A moral person would be some group of persons, specifically a society, no matter how small (see again 2.11). This society acts as a single person, in virtue of the fact that all its members have a common, mutually beneficial goal.

As a practical matter, it is frequently useful also to make other distinctions as to the various entities capable of possessing property, as follows:

Private Property
This is property belonging to individuals, but also to corporations or other social groups, so long as these groups do not pertain to any level of civil government.
Examples: 1) A house or a business owned by John Doe. 2) A publicly traded corporation. Although shares are constantly changing hands, nevertheless, at every given moment, all shares are owned mostly by non-governmental persons or entities, and thus the corporation remains privately owned.

Common or Communal Property
This is property belonging to corporations or other social groups, but not individuals. It sometimes pertains to government.
If not belonging to government, this communal property is also private, because it is under the control of a non-governmental social entity; only members of that entity can make use of its property. Example: A privately held corporation, or a cooperative. Such a company is owned by a number of persons, each having a more or less great share in it. These shares are not traded, and the individuals owning them govern the cooperative for their common interests.
If pertaining to government, common or communal property is specified by being called *public* property. Often, it is considered as owned by the people as communal property, but is simply managed by the government. It normally may be used by the general public; that is, by any citizen without distinction, provided the rules set by government for its use are followed. Examples: city parks, state or national parks or forests, or wilderness areas.

Government Property

Government property may be communal (public), as stated above, but normally the term *government property* means property that belongs to a government entity, *and* is restricted to governmental use. Depending on the level of government owning this property, it may be specified by being called *city, municipal, county, state* (e.g. Florida), or *State* (i.e. federal) property. Depending on the country in question, names for these levels of government may be different; e.g. in Canada there are no *states*. The governmental equivalent of a *state* in Canada would be a *province,* so Canadians would speak of *provincial* property, not *state* property. Examples: military installations or training facilities, court or police buildings, the land or other property connected with these, etc.

Private Property : Arguments From Reason

ARGUMENT FROM THE NATURE OF MAN

8.2 – Man, as a creature who is made up of a spiritual soul and material body (cf. 1.5 – 1.7), exercises control over the part of the world that is placed before him. The basis for man's possession of what is *outside* of himself is grounded in his ability to first possess *himself*, through his *knowledge* of himself, and his free actions. Such a self-reflective and unified moral being as man is can naturally act within the world and order it so as to attain the intellectual and physical good for both himself and others. Creatures which cannot, through self-reflection, possess themselves and their ends, cannot exercise real control or possession over any part of the world, because they neither possess freely their own being nor can they direct anything toward the achievement of freely chosen, rational ends.

Briefly, to possess something, in the sense of having personal property, cannot be done except by beings that know *what* personal property *is*; a being has personal property only when, and because, it *is* a person, and thus perceives a long-term rational purpose in the thing it possesses. Every person then is by nature capable of possessing private property.[157]

8.3 – Further implications:

1. Man's intellectual nature leads to intellectual private property.

   Simply because man is aware of his own thoughts, and they originate with him, they belong to him. But the products of his thought, therefore, also originate with him and belong to him. If anybody could make whatever use he wanted (especially a monetarily profitable use) of another man's thought, manifold injustices would be done on a daily basis, and motivation for productive thought would be gravely undercut. Thus by nature there is a thing called intellectual private property; thus by nature we have copyright laws, patents, trademarks, laws against plagiarism, etc.

2. Man's material nature leads to material private property.

---

[157] See *Summa Theol.* II-II Q.66, a1

By nature man's body requires certain material goods: food, clothing, shelter, etc. Thus, since by nature man owns his own body, and is obliged to care for it, he has both the right and the duty to obtain and own what is necessary to that care. It is by nature impossible, even in theory, that a man could share the food that actually goes into his own mouth or the clothes he presently wears. It is by nature more or less impossible also in practice that man share even other less urgent physical necessities: shelter, means of transportation, tools, real estate, etc.

Still, in some Catholic monasteries at any rate, community property is a very workable principle, even to the extent that clothing and personal items, while reserved by the superiors to the use of individuals, do not in fact belong to them, and could be assigned to others if the common good required it. Even food is common property, at least until actually consumed. Moreover, intellectual property of individuals also belongs to the monastery community.

So the question arises: While an individual *can* possess private property, *should* he? Is not living with all things in common more congenial? Does it not tend better to the common good? Did not the first Christians do so? Should not all men then live with all property in common?

ARGUMENT OF ST. THOMAS AQUINAS

8.4 – St. Thomas answers in the negative:

> [Man has] the power of procuring and dispensing [exterior things]. Because of this, it is permitted that a man possess properties. And it is even necessary for human life, on account of three things: Firstly, of course, because everyone is more solicitous to take care of something that belongs to him alone than something which is the common property of all or many; for everyone, shirking labor, leaves to another that which pertains to the community... In another way, because human affairs are handled in a more orderly way if to each person there impends a proper duty of taking care of some thing; for there would be confusion if, without distinction, whatever person would care for whatever thing. Thirdly, because in this way the state of men is kept more peaceful, where everyone is content with his own. For we see that, among those who possess an indivisible thing commonly, quarrels more frequently arise.[158]

We must notice here that St. Thomas' reasons do not proceed solely from the integral nature of man; that is, from man as created by God, before original sin. His argumentation includes human nature, of course, but mainly accounts for the *fallen condition* of that nature, which condition is itself not from nature.

St. Thomas therefore is saying that private property is permitted by Nature, and is thus a natural right (because "man has the [natural] *power* of procuring and dispensing exterior things"). But he is saying more. He is saying also that, for men in general, tainted as they are with original sin, it is a *necessity*. For instance, the "shirking labor" he speaks of is a clear reference to the capital sin of sloth, which is one of the tendencies of original sin in humankind. Again, the "quarrels" he says will

---

158 *Summa Theol.* II-II Q.66, a2, resp.

arise when property is held in common are a result of the capital sins of avarice and envy, also arising from original sin.[159] More recent authors adduce a fourth reason: that man will not learn the needed virtue of personal responsibility if his needs are always taken care of by the community. This reason, however, is also based on the capital sin of sloth, and so is implicitly covered by St. Thomas already.

8.5 – Realization of the reality of original sin is a key point, for its perverse inclinations, in practice, can be more or less healed *only* in *some* men, by more or less arduous application to the acquisition of virtue, especially with the aid of the grace of Christ, through His Church. The consequences are two:

1. Communities where all property is held in common *can* be formed, provided the members thereof are sufficiently virtuous to make them work. However, *it is not the community property principle that makes them work, but the virtue of the community that makes the principle work.* (cf. 5.14)

2. *Large scale* human societies can *not* hold all property in common, for original sin assures that there will never be a large enough percentage of persons possessed of enough virtue and selflessness to make it work.

PRIVATE PROPERTY IS MANDATED BY THE LAW OF NATIONS

8.6 – And this is why St. Thomas also says that private property is a *command* of the Law of Nations.[160] That is, in larger societies at least, private property *must* be allowed, for the common experience and consensus of nations throughout time have shown that this is necessary for peace and order.

ALL HUMAN HISTORY SUPPORTS THE RIGHT TO PRIVATE PROPERTY

8.7 – History fully supports that there is a natural right to private property, and also that this right is part of the Law of Nations. Examples could be given *ad infinitum*. We restrict ourselves to a few.

Trigonometry was first developed in ancient Egypt to enable the re-surveying of land each year after the Nile's flood receded, to apportion land to individual farmers according to previous boundaries. The importance of land borders strongly implies property rights. Almost half of the Code of Hammurabi, an ancient Babylonian body of law, is devoted to property and contract law, again implying the existence and importance of private property ownership and private enterprise. The Chinese Communists had eliminated private property in China by 1958, but only twenty years later, a reformer, Deng Hsiao-Ping, took power and began to modify, and eventually dismantle, the large farming communes. By 1992 a flourishing real estate market in rural and urban properties had been established. These pro-private-property reforms, begun in 1978, resulted in rapid economic growth and prosperity for China.

---

159 Cf. 2.15 & 2.16, concerning original sin and the capital sins.
160 See *Summa Theol.* II-II Q.57, a3, and Cahill, *The Framework of a Christian State*, p. 39.

Private Property : Arguments From Authority

SCRIPTURE AND THE CHURCH TEACH THAT PRIVATE PROPERTY IS OF THE NATURAL LAW

Scripture

8.8 – The Seventh and Tenth Commandments are of the Natural Law, but are meaningless if private property is not a human right. It cannot be a sin to steal or covet another's property if that other person does not have a right to possess it.

The Church

8.9 – Pope Leo XIII said in 1891:

> The right to possess private property as one's own is granted man by **nature**... Nor is there any reason why the providence of the State should be introduced; for man is older than the State, and therefore he should have had by nature, before any State had come into existence, the right to care for life and body... Now, when a man applies the activity of his mind and the strength of his body to procuring the goods of nature, by this very act he attaches to himself that part of corporeal nature which he has cultivated, on which he leaves impressed a kind of form as it were, of his personality; so that it should by all means be right for him to possess this part as his own; and by no means should anyone be permitted to violate this right of his. (*Rerum Novárum,* §§6-9, quoted from Dz 1938a)

Also, Pope Pius XI, in *Quadragésimo Anno*, reaffirmed the right to own private property asserted by Pope Leo XIII, saying:

> For the **natural** right of possessing private property and of transmitting goods by inheritance should always remain intact and unviolated. (*QA* §49, quoted from Dz 2256)

SCRIPTURE AND THE CHURCH TEACH THAT PRIVATE PROPERTY IS OF THE DIVINE LAW

Scripture

8.10 – The Seventh and Tenth Commandments are of the Natural Law, but are also of that part of Supernatural Law called Divine Law, because they are revealed in Scripture.

Various other passages in Scripture support private property. Ecclesiasticus counsels a man to retain control of his estate until he is near death, and then to distribute it to his heirs:

> Give not to son or wife, brother or friend, power over thee while thou livest; and give not thine estate to another, lest thou repent, and thou entreatest for the same. As long as thou livest, and hast breath

in thee, let no man change thee. For it is better that thy children should ask of thee, than that thou look toward the hands of thy children. In all thy works keep the pre-eminence. Let no stain sully thy glory. In the time when thou shalt end the days of thy life, and in the time of thy decease, distribute thine inheritance. (Ecclus.[Sirach] 33:20-24)

This passage strongly implies that ownership and control over property are fitting for a man to have, as is the power to give property to heirs.

Sacred Scripture does not explicitly direct rulers to foster the ownership of private property among their subjects, but in many places it strongly implies that rulers should do so, through negative injunctions against expropriating such property. An example is the expropriation of Naboth's vineyard by the wicked ruling couple, Achab and Jezebel. Immediately after they had seized Naboth's vineyard for their own selfish purposes, a prophet arrived at court to predict that Achab would die and his blood would be lapped up by dogs. This prophecy came to pass. (1 Kg. 21:1ff)

A Catholic civil ruler recognizes that Scripture's moral injunctions apply to himself and to those who wield power under him. The Commandment "Thou shalt not steal" is therefore binding upon the State, and upon all its officers.

Leviticus 19:35-36 tells us: "Do not any unjust thing in judgment, in rule, in weight, or in measure. Let the balance be just and the weights equal, the bushel just, and the sextary equal."

Leviticus 19:15 tells rulers: "Thou shalt not do that which is unjust, nor judge unjustly. Respect not the person of the poor, nor honor the countenance of the mighty. But judge thy neighbor according to justice."

These admonitions clearly show that another person's right to his property is not to be violated.

Our Lord Jesus Christ Himself many times acknowledged the right to private property. One example occurs in the parable of the workers in the vineyard. Some of the hired workers complain to the vineyard owner that the recent hires received as much pay as themselves. The owner replies: "Friend, I do thee no wrong. Didst thou not agree with me for a penny? Take what is thine and go thy way: I will also give to this last even as to thee. Or is it not lawful for me to do what I will?" (Mt. 20:10-15)

The Church

8.11 – While the Church has always condemned usury, it has never condemned the making of profit *per se*, nor the ownership of private property, nor private enterprise. In the following passage from a letter to the Archbishop of Geneva, by Pope Alexander II, ca. A.D. 1160, the legitimacy of private ownership and trade is assumed, while only usury is condemned:

> In your city you say that it often happens that when certain people are purchasing pepper or cinnamon or other wares which at that time are not the value of more than five pounds, they also promise to those from whom they receive these wares that they will pay six pounds at a stated time. However, although a contract of this kind according to such a form cannot be considered under the name of

usury, yet nevertheless the sellers incur sin, unless there be a doubt that the wares would be of more or less value at the time of payment. And so your citizens would look well to their own interests, if they would cease from such a contract, since the thoughts of men cannot be hidden from Almighty God.

Additionally, Pius XI tells us that productive use of unclaimed property traditionally gives to him who works the land title to it:

> Moreover, not only the tradition of all times but also the doctrine of our predecessor, Leo, clearly testify that ownership in the first place is acquired by the occupation of a thing that belongs to no one, and by industry, or specification, as it is called. For no injury is done anyone, whatever some may say to the contrary, when property is occupied which rests unclaimed and belongs to no one; but the industry which is exercised by man in his own name, and by the aid of which a new kind, or an increase is added to his property, is the only industry that gives a laborer a title to its fruits.[161]

8.12 – In the end we can, with full confidence, make the following observations: Any law *imposing* the practice of community property on a large scale is evidently contrary to the Natural Law, the Supernatural Law, and the Law of Nations. Since the consequences of practicing large-scale community property are gravely harmful, all the members of such a community would be free to disobey any Human Law imposing it, for such a "law" would be totally null and void. (See Principle 20 and its footnote). State rulers are also prohibited from expropriating the private property of citizens for their personal advantage and that of other State officials, or for the enrichment of friends and allies of the ruler or such officials.

This doctrine would also seem to put a limit on the tendency of governments in the 20th and 21st centuries to claim vast areas of uninhabited land as exclusively their own.

> **PRINCIPLE 58: Man as a self-reflective and intellectual creature has the right to own, control and possess property so as to achieve his ends as a rational being. In the case of individuals as well as families, rulers must safeguard the right of property owners to pass on property of all kinds to their designated heirs.**

> **PRINCIPLE 59: Governments, respecting the principle of subsidiarity, must strive to peacefully bring about the widest possible private ownership of land, productive assets, homes, and other property.**

Private Property Can Also Be Communal

8.13 – So far we have considered only private property owned by an individual or a family. But because man is a social creature, many of his activities will require cooperation with a group larger than one family. These larger groups will often have

---
161 *Quadragésimo Anno,* §52 (quoted from Dz 2258)

need to manage property in order to accomplish their goals. There is therefore such a thing as community ownership; a community or social body constitutes a moral person, which is capable of ownership. Individual members of that social body can use the common property in accordance with rules established by the authority in charge of that body.

Thus, rulers must recognize and protect another type of private property: communal property. With this type of ownership, a collective larger than a family owns and controls property, but this type of ownership is not governmental ownership. Here are some types of private groups which need to own property to carry out their essential functions:

Firstly, religious communities, each of whose members has taken a vow of poverty, may still own considerable property in common. For example, a convent may own land, buildings, equipment, books, animals, clothing, food; in short, all the necessities for the material and spiritual life of its members.

Secondly, a village may own land, water, fencing, or other resources which allow the villagers to make a living. An example is the communal grazing grounds enjoyed by English villagers before the Enclosure Movement destroyed rural agricultural life in the 18th and 19th centuries in England, and drove the people into urban factory life. Such communal grazing grounds or other resources may or may not have formal deeds or other documents, but should nonetheless be honored and protected by the authorities, to foster small-scale agriculture and enterprise.

Thirdly, voluntary associations, such as the medieval guilds were, may own buildings and other assets to further their purpose in unifying and regulating the practice of a specific trade within a town. Encouragement and preservation of such associations or guilds by the civil authority was once, and could be in the future, a way to practice subsidiarity, to promote self-reliance and useful productivity among the populace.

Fourthly, modern self-help collectives such as local water-sharing groups or more formal irrigation districts or small-scale electrical cooperatives, are all examples of socially useful private communal property ownership.

Given the errors of Communism and Socialism in the 20th and 21st centuries A.D., it is important to distinguish between forced collectivization (or government-controlled ownership), which is against Catholic doctrine, and voluntary private communal ownership, which is consistent with Catholic doctrine, especially when the communal group's purposes are in some way an expression of their love for the true God. Principle 26, that of subsidiarity, helps us to understand the distinction between unjust and just communal ownership.

> **PRINCIPLE 60: The State must, for the happiness and prosperity of its citizens, strongly defend and preserve the right to own private property by individuals, families, and voluntary collectives.**

The Right To Private Property Is Not Absolute

8.14 – According to the exposition of 2.27 and following, above, and with a little thought, we can discern that the right to own private property, whether individual or communal, is, like most other rights, subject to certain limitations. These limitations are the duties arising from the fact that man is a social creature, and from the fact that the common good is higher than an individual's good. In the case of private property, free exercise of this right is conditioned by two things.

Firstly, it depends on the owners – whether individual, family, or collective – at least abstaining from using the property to do serious and persistent harm to their neighbors, the region or the nation. A higher authority, preferably local but if necessary national, may with justice prevent the owner(s) from using the property to do serious harm to others. Examples of such abuse of property could be: the setting of fires which spread to neighboring properties, or that release gravely toxic substances into the atmosphere; kidnapping of persons and keeping them imprisoned on the property; shooting weapons from the property at people without grave reasons of self-preservation; or poisoning a lake, river or other waterway bordering a property in such a way that the lives and well-being of others are threatened. However, it must be noted that the authorities should not terminate the owner's possession of the property which has been employed for abusive purposes. Even in the extreme case of the imprisonment or even execution of the owner, ownership should still be preserved, and the heirs of the owner still have rights to own and control the property, with the same limitations on its use as discussed herein.

> **PRINCIPLE 61: In the interests of preserving peace and tranquility in society, the State may limit the use of private property by the owner or owners, to prevent such property from being used to harm or endanger the health or safety or well-being of other citizens.**

8.15 – Secondly, a certain amount of private property may be expropriated by governments insofar as needed to fulfill their mandate to provide for the temporal common good within the domains detailed in 4.25. This is normally the only legitimate reason for governments to take private property, and includes the indispensable action necessary for the existence of every State: taxation. Three major considerations bear on whether the taking of private property for this motive is just or unjust:

1. The amount taken

   As of 2016, total government spending in the United States (federal, state and local) was between 36% and 42% of the total gross domestic product, depending on the economists calculating the figures. This is too high a percentage for a Catholic ruler to accede to; a just figure would probably be less than 15%.

2. The sector of society from which it is taken

   The way taxes are collected would be the subject for an entire future Chapter.

3. Whether the projects carried out with those taxes truly promote the common good or not.

The taking of private property by State government is just if and only if those resources are employed in ways that do not violate any of these rules, or any Principles given elsewhere in this work. Specifically, use of taxes must not tend to weaken the Catholic Church or the Faith of the people, or weaken traditional family structure, or violate the principles of subsidiarity and solidarity. Taxes should also not be used to violate Catholic principles of just war by pursuing unjust military actions outside the homeland, killing or impoverishing people without a compelling reason of self-defense.

> **PRINCIPLE 62:** In order for government, which exercises the sovereignty of the nation and has care for the common temporal good, to fulfill its functions and achieve its ends, it must have property sufficient for it to attain those proper ends. State government must not, however, seek to concentrate ownership of land or other property in its own hands or in the hands of any lower level of government.

> **PRINCIPLE 63:** Government must not seek to institute, or preserve where it is already instituted, mandatory State ownership of land, farms, industrial buildings or equipment, homes, or other property, when that State ownership results from unjust confiscation of private property.

CHAPTER 9

ECONOMIC EQUALITY AND INEQUALITY

Introduction

Before going on to economics *per se*, it seems appropriate to examine in some detail the question of economic equality vs. inequality. In modern times, this has been a burning question, to the point that real or perceived injustices in this area have led to extremely hard feelings and even several violent political revolutions.

The Catholic Attitude Toward Economic Equality And Inequality

9.1 – We have already seen that private property is a human right, as discussed in Chapter 8. But what is the justification for anyone to possess *greater* riches than others?

A first consideration is that willing acceptance of at least some suffering in society, after the example of Christ, will always be necessary: "For the poor you have always with you..." (Mk 14:7) Utopian expectation of a perfect life in this world implies a denial of original sin, and only leads to more strife, as this expectation will inevitably be frustrated. Even if a material utopia were possible, it would actually be a grievous curse on the human race. No one can even acquire basic natural virtues (e.g. fortitude, temperance, patience), let alone merit true, supernatural happiness, without some suffering. As the Scripture says: "For whom the Lord loveth he chastiseth: and he scourgeth every son whom he receiveth." (Heb. 12:6, implicitly citing Prov. 3 and Ecclus.[Sirach] 30)

Acquisition of wealth is certainly not presented in Scripture as the highest good. Generosity, voluntary poverty, and giving up one's goods in order to serve God are among the highest virtues, both according to the Old Testament and the New. But just as the three evangelical virtues of poverty, chastity and obedience are not required to save our souls, but heroic steps toward perfection, giving away all one's goods is not a *sine qua non* for salvation. In fact, striving to obtain sufficient property to provide sustenance and education for one's progeny is a necessary part of fulfilling the duty imposed on those in the married state of life.

As the Catholic Church has traditionally taught, holy poverty is associated with Our Lord Himself, with John the Baptist, with prophets such as Elias, and with the Apostles. Also, the vow of poverty has been an essential element of religious orders and congregations in the Catholic Church, and we should keep in mind that religious life has been specifically designed for the pursuit of Christian perfection. Our Lord has taught that, if one wishes to be perfect, it is necessary to sell (at least the superfluous) goods one has, and follow Him, and that the rich man will enter into heaven only with difficulty. (Matt. 19:21ff) Nevertheless, prosperous property owners, including those with numerous servants, have been counted among those favored by God: Abraham, Isaac, Jacob, Job, David, and Lazarus the brother of Mary and Martha. So, contrary to certain utopian opinions, and the egalitarian belief systems of the present time, ownership of private property, even a great deal of private property, is not inconsistent with Catholic faith or with salvation. While the practice of both justice and charity can and should work to minimize *extremes* of both poverty and riches in society (as we have today), there neither can nor should be equality in this matter, as we will demonstrate.

JUSTIFICATION FOR THE EXISTENCE OF ECONOMIC INEQUALITY

Arguments From Reason For Economic Inequality

9.2 – As Chapter 7 showed, men and women, notwithstanding their equal potential in moral dignity, have significant physical and psycho-spiritual differences. It is also easy to see that, even within one gender or the other, individuals also possess varying physical and psycho-spiritual qualities, talents, aptitudes and virtues, outside of the more profound ones that distinguish the two sexes in general. Among men, for instance, though all are inclined by nature to logical and analytical thought, some are much more so than others. These differences among individuals inescapably result in differing success in the acquisition of material goods. This is as it should be. God clearly wants variety, since the Nature He created does not clone humans, but produces each person from a gene selection process that is so vastly complex as to guarantee that no individual will be repeatable. We can of course add to this physical uniqueness of each person the further changes, both physical and spiritual, brought about by that person's environment, life experiences, and personal choices. The Catholic Church has always recognized and honored God's will for inequalities of this sort. Variety is truly the spice of life.

There are further reasons for the inevitability of the existence of economic inequality. If the foundation of private claims to property is the working and developing of land and other resources, as well as inheritance, then it is plainly obvious that not all individuals will have earned, by their skill and efforts, title to equal amounts of land and other resources, nor will have inherited the same amount of property.

Reason also leads us to see that a large productive process, such as, for example, the construction of a privately-held dam across a river, requires many elements obtainable only from a variety of people with diverging interests and capacities. Some want only to work a set number of hours in a week, receive their pay, and go home with no sense of responsibility, outside of working hours, for any matters connected with the dam; such workers need to be supervised and coordinated by those with a managerial bent. Others have accumulated capital and can purchase gravel, concrete, steel, pipes and other materials as an investment in future revenue accruing to the dam. Others have the inclination and the training to draw up blueprints and make calculations to ensure the soundness of the structure, while still others supply the use of their machines to aid in construction. And directing all these people toward a common end must be a person with authority, who must be obeyed during the entire project, or else chaos and disintegration will prevent the project from reaching a successful conclusion.

Arguments From Scripture For Economic Inequality

9.3 – In Sacred Scripture, Psalm 127 begins: "Blessed are all they that fear the Lord: that walk in his ways. For thou shalt eat the labors of thy hands: blessed art thou, and it shall be well with thee."

Here, virtue (fearing God) is linked to the possession of goods resulting from a man's own efforts, to which he is clearly entitled.

In Deuteronomy 15:11 we are told: "There will not be wanting poor in the land of thy habitation."

And Truth Himself has said in Mark 14:7: "For the poor you have always with you."

Arguments From The Church For Economic Inequality

9.4 – Pope Leo XIII wrote in *Rerum Novárum*, §8:

> For God has granted the earth to mankind in general, not in the sense that all without distinction can deal with it as they like, but rather that no part of it was assigned to any one in particular, and that the limits of private possession have been left to be fixed by man's own industry, and the laws of individual races.

Here, Pope Leo clearly implies that the greater and more productive a man's own industry, the greater the claim he will have to the fruits thereof, subject to the laws of that place.

In §9, Pope Leo states:

> Truly, that which is required for the preservation of life, and for life's well-being, is produced in great abundance from the soil, but not until man has brought it into cultivation and expended upon it his solicitude and skill. Now, when man thus turns the activity of his mind and the strength of his body toward procuring the fruits of nature, by such act he makes his own that portion of nature's field which he cultivates – that portion on which he leaves, as it were, the impress of his personality; and it cannot but be just that he should possess that portion as his very own, and have a right to hold it without anyone being justified in violating that right.

Here, we are told that not only labor, but "activity of his mind" and "skill", are investments which entitle a man to the products that they engender.

Again, §10 of *Rerum Novárum* says:

> Is it just that the fruit of a man's own sweat and labor should be possessed and enjoyed by anyone else? As effects follow their cause, so is it just and right that the results of labor should belong to those who have bestowed their labor.

And Leo notes in §15:

> ...that ideal equality about which they [socialists] entertain pleasant dreams would be in reality the leveling down of all to a like condition of misery and degradation.

And continues in §17:

> Socialists may in that intent [to reduce society to one dead level] do their utmost, but all striving against nature is in vain. There naturally exist among mankind manifold differences of the most important kind; people differ in capacity, skill, health, strength; and unequal fortune is a necessary result of unequal condition. Such inequality is far from being disadvantageous either to individuals or to the community. Social and public life can only be maintained by means of various kinds of capacity for business and the playing of many parts; and each man, as a rule, chooses the part which suits his own particular domestic condition...

Pope Pius XI, 40 years later in *Quadragésimo Anno* (1931), quoted with approval Pope Leo's words in §8 given above. He also asserts, in his own section 79, that:

> ...[I]t is gravely wrong to take from individuals what they can accomplish by their own initiative and industry and give it to the community...

This also strongly implies that a person's initiative and industry entitle him to the property which is produced or enriched by such industry, even if by this he holds greater wealth than others.

Both Popes Leo XIII and Pius XI state that a person's initiative and industry entitle him to property and riches created by such activity. This inevitably leads to inequality in material wealth, since different individuals have different talents, energy and motivation. Due to these differences, different individuals bring into being differing amounts of marketable goods. As Pius XI put it in *Quadragésimo Anno*:

> That ownership is originally acquired both by occupancy of a thing not owned by anyone, and by labor, or as is said, by specification, the tradition of all ages as well as the teaching of Our Predecessor Leo clearly testifies. For, whatever some idly say to the contrary, only that labor which a man performs in his own name and by virtue of which a new form or increase has been given to a thing grants him title to these fruits. (*QA* §52)

If a man has title to the fruits of "labor which a man performs in his own name", it follows that it is unjust for anyone to confiscate those fruits and to bestow them on others who have been less industrious or less productive.

Leo XIII had earlier stated in *Rerum Novárum* that: "Each needs the other: capital cannot do without labor, nor labor without capital." (§19)

These statements of Pius XI and Leo XIII taken together sharply contradict statements by proponents of Socialism that those with capital unjustly exploit workers by the mere act of hiring and employing them to create wealth. Thus it is against Catholic social teaching to use coercion to eliminate differences in wealth among individuals, provided that such wealth is a result of "labor which a man performs in his own name".[162]

> **PRINCIPLE 64:** Economic inequality, *per se*, is both just and inevitable.

Ways Of Acquiring Wealth

9.5 – As said above, "ownership is originally acquired both by occupancy of a thing not already owned by anyone, and by labor". But at any given time in history, of course, there will also be property owners who have done little or nothing to develop and earn their property, because they inherited the property from a more or less distant ancestor who earned the right to own the property. This situation is inevitable and must be tolerated if the right to pass on property to heirs is to be honored.

Other bases on which an individual, family, or even a State, could claim ownership to property, other than the "merit criterion" and subsequent inheritance, are *conquest* and *donation*.

By conquest is meant the taking of land or other property by force, such as in war. Much of the land ownership in the world can be traced back to conquest, often centuries in the past. When such ownership is of long-standing, and a stable social structure has grown up around it which a Catholic State can gradually transform into a just social order, it may be best to allow the ownership patterns to continue, implementing incremental change if needed. If the conquest is recent or if glaring injustices and social dysfunction stemming from that conquest threaten the society with serious instability, authorities in a Catholic State may have to study the historical and social situation in depth, and work toward a re-allocation of property ownership while seeking to preserve as much justice and social peace as possible.

By donation is meant the distribution of property to various individuals and groups by some authority. This may range in scope from the private gift of one owner to another, to the mass distribution of unused lands to settlers.

Once a Catholic government is established in a nation, of course, it should not permit the transfer of property by unjust conquest or fraud to occur. The Catholic State may itself engage in donation in the case of unoccupied lands or other property, or in the case that the State seizes properties whose owners obtained them by crime or fraud.

> **PRINCIPLE 65:** Wealth that a person has brought into being through his own efforts, and in his own name, should be his to own, use, and control, and to pass on to his progeny.

---

[162] We are assuming here, of course, that the man in question has been fulfilling the duties associated with the possession of his property, which we have spoken of in 8.14, and will say considerably more of in 9.6 through 9.15.

Economic Justice And Charity In A Catholic Society

9.6 – Although economic inequality in society is *in itself* just and inevitable (Principle 64), in particular societal situations there assuredly can be and are inequalities caused by *in*justices. These not only can but must be eliminated. There are also ways that even the inevitable inequalities can be reduced to a minimum.

SOCIAL JUSTICE

9.7 – When discussing the question of social justice we must recall what justice *is*. It is to give to someone what is his due (cf. 2.27).

This is usually thought of as an obligation from one individual to another, as when an employer is obligated to give a just wage to a worker, while the worker is obligated to give to the employer sufficient productive effort in exchange for that wage.

However, we have seen that *A society is a stable union of a number of persons in fellowship and cooperation for a common purpose of benefit to all* (2.11). And we have seen that a society is a moral person (cf. 8.1).

Therefore, since the 'someone' to or from which something is due is always a person, justice concerns not only debts between individual persons, but also between any combination of societal/moral persons and individual persons. Hence individual persons have obligations to society, and the moral person called 'society' has obligations to individuals.

However, it is safe to say that in our time most people, when thinking of "social justice", consider mainly (or even only) what society owes to them as individuals. The cry of "social justice" is most often used as a guilt-bludgeon by individuals, or special interest groups within the larger society, to browbeat that larger society into giving them something. As often as not, what they are demanding is some sort of handout or privilege, rather than a legitimate service or right.

This kind of thinking completely ignores one half of the equation. Let us take a closer look at our definition of society in order to see why.

The Individual's Debt To Society, And Society's Debt To The Individual

9.8 – Why are the individual persons in a society united in fellowship and cooperation in the first place? For a common purpose of **benefit** to **all**. That means that each individual person gets something of value from the society in which he lives. Most people do not even think of what they actually already get from society, but they think plenty about what society is *not* giving them at present, and which they think it *should* be giving them. Here again original sin rears its ugly head.

But what are some of these benefits that we as individuals receive from the society in which we live? Here are just a few:

1. Division of labor. This means that some persons specialize in certain tasks. They are therefore able to do them better and more productively than other people. Specialists trade their goods and services for those that others produce, who are also specialists in their own fields. The results are that:

a) Each one of us is relieved from the massive burden of having to learn, and become expert in, every single temporal endeavor that is necessary to us. Just a moment's consideration shows that this benefit is huge. What would our lives be like if each one of us had to farm all of his own fruits, nuts, grains, vegetables and other produce; keep, raise, and butcher his own livestock and poultry; be his own real estate agent and build his own house from the ground up (and maintain it); build and maintain his own vehicles, plus produce the fuel for them? These things are only the basics, and not even a comprehensive list at that. Without division of labor we would all instantly be thrown back into a Stone-Age, Hunter-Gatherer lifestyle.

b) Being relieved of the said burden of having to be a jack-of-all-trades, we each have a great deal of leisure or recreational time that otherwise would not exist.

2. This leisure time allows for the development of philosophy, theology, and all advanced culture, including education, sciences and the arts. And all this is nothing less than time to do those things which concern man's very reasons for existing.

We could add much more, but the point should be made: each individual owes a literally immeasurable debt to society simply for being allowed to live within it.[163]

To this perspective on the fact that man is a social animal by nature must be added another fact: that Nature prefers the good of the species to that of the individuals within it. Thus all social beings by nature, man included, must prefer the good of society to their own individual good.

9.9 – Thus a true idea of social justice must consider two things:

- What society owes to each individual within it.

- What each individual owes to society.

It is a two-way street: society owes to the individual his true rights, and aid in grave need,[164] and the individual owes to society a return of some portion of goods and/or services, as needed by society; a portion to be taken from that increased temporal well-being that merely living in society allows him to enjoy.

The Definition Of Social Justice

9.10 – From this we can form a true definition of that virtue called 'social justice'...but before we do so, we must consider: Society is a moral person, not a real

---

163 Note well: "immeasurable" is said only of the supernatural good of eternal life which correct philosophy and theology lead to. In a religiously pluralistic society, or any other founded on false philosophy or theology, the benefits it confers on individuals are at best only material, and thus very definitely limited.

164 This aid would be analogous to that which the human body as a whole is obliged to provide to the individual parts of the body; the body as a whole cannot maintain health or life unless it supplies its members with the blood that infuses life and health into them: nutrition, oxygen, disease-fighting agents, etc.

person, and therefore cannot be possessed of any virtues. And so to include what society owes to individuals in our definition will present a problem. To resolve this, we must simply consider society not in its moral personhood, but simply as the collective of *individuals* comprising it. And so we will say:

> **Social justice is the virtue that inclines one to render to society what one owes to it, and to strive that society render to its members what it owes to them.**[165]

Here we may note what Pope Pius XI says: "...it is of social justice to require from each person what is necessary to the common good."[166]

And we can observe that our definition is substantially the same; we have only clarified that "what is necessary to the common good" includes working toward political processes or policies that will guard individual rights, and will aid individuals in their legitimate needs.

This of course means that individuals must engage in political action that will lead to this. (cf. Principle 30)

The essential take-away from what we have presented so far is this: *In respect of social justice, "society" is not some nebulous abstraction, or some government or corporate body which owes things to us. It is all the* **real** *and concrete individuals that are mutually benefiting each other, and who therefore owe things to each other.*

Considerations On Achieving Social Justice

9.11 – Even if thus correctly understood, social justice involves several practical considerations or inconveniences in its realization:

Firstly, the duty of individuals to return service for the common good of society is graver according as it is more immediate. Thus family comes first, then the local community, the region, the State and the world, in that order.

Secondly, individuals differ in their means and ability to render their debt to society for the benefits they receive from it. This means they correspondingly differ in obligation.

Thirdly, as this duty extends to wider circles of society, it becomes not only less grave, but less clear and hence less enforceable. There comes a point where, unless there is only *one* person who can possibly remedy the situation, the duty to do so does not clearly fall on any particular person's shoulders, and in any case it is rarely evident what *degree* of aid is required of anyone. Therefore, Human Law is needed to specify and enforce this obligation – but at the same time, it is perhaps impossible to write law that will justly account for all the changeable circumstantial details.

Fourthly, even if the Human Law is enacted and enforced, compliance entails effort and expense by government.

Fifthly, in order to maintain justice to all those who must give aid, including the wealthy – for justice is due to them no less than to the needy – only the *minimum* can

---

[165] We have refrained here from discussing the classic technical distinctions of *commutative, legal,* and *distributive* justice, or that of *contributive* justice (suggested by Fr. Heinrich Pesch), or other distinctions, such as *participative* justice. While valid subdistinctions, these are mainly of interest and use only to specialists.

[166] *Divíni Redemptóris,* §51. Most English translations are gravely incorrect here, saying "...to require **for** each person..." This is nearly the opposite meaning of the original Latin: "...**ab** síngulis exígere...". If Pius XI had meant to say *"for each person"*, he would have written **ad** *síngulos exígere,* or simply *síngulis exígere.*

be demanded of them. Otherwise, government will on its part be guilty of the injustice of theft.

Sixthly, and most importantly from the supernatural standpoint – or even from the standpoint of mere natural human dignity – when giving of one's surplus is enforced by law, such giving is less likely to be willingly done. No virtue or nobility is to be found in forced compliance.

SOCIAL CHARITY

9.12 – The Supernatural Law of Christian charity goes much farther than the Natural Law of justice. If widely put in practice, it not only resolves all these difficulties, so that the minimum aid to neighbor will be provided, but it goes beyond the minimum, and tends toward true sufficiency. How?

A full explanation is already implied merely in the real meaning of the word 'charity'.

> *Charity is the virtue that inclines us to love God above all things, for His own sake, and our neighbor as ourselves, for the love of God.*

Drawing from this, we can define that type of charity called social charity:

> *Social charity is the virtue that inclines us to love our neighbors as ourselves, for the love of God.*

Social charity is no different than charity itself. The adjective 'social' simply puts a focus on the social aspect of charity which is already in the definition of charity.

Therefore:

Firstly, those possessed of true charity, because they love their neighbors *as themselves*, will do *more* than the minimum for their neighbors, for who wishes the minimum for himself?

Secondly and accordingly, to the extent that charity actually exists in society, Human Law and enforcement become simply unnecessary; people will do what is needed *voluntarily*.

Thirdly and most importantly, those who give from charity give freely, thus meritoriously. In this way the givers earn a supernatural and eternal reward as well as the natural honor of nobility and virtue.

Fourthly and not so obviously, if one has *true* charity (according to the Catholic definition given above), one will ultimately be acting for the love of God. This overarching motivation obviates certain disorders that can and will otherwise arise. It will prevent us from serving our neighbor out of vainglory; out of what is in reality a love of *ourselves* above all things. It will also prevent us from being motivated above all things by a worship of our neighbor; that is, worship of mankind itself, as a moral, but not real and personal being; a sort of chimerical, abstract deity. Both of these are forms of idolatry. Vainglory would also cause resentment by the recipients of such "charity"; they would begrudge the condescension of a giver who pretends to possess some moral superiority which they sense to be false. Treating mankind as an idol would lead to an excess indulgence on the part of the givers, who will consider *all* the less well off as being equally worthy of aid, simply because of their human nature. They would then strive for an absolute secular-humanistic and communistic economic equality among all, without regard to individual ontological or moral differences. Thus individuals will be treated unjustly.

WHO IS MY NEIGHBOR?

9.13 – Speaking of individual ontological persons as compared to collective moral persons, a question arises: Society being a moral person...it is an abstraction of sorts; there is no *real* person called "society". How then can we speak of the "rights" of society?

As hinted above, we must admit that, strictly speaking, we cannot do so. In the same breath, however, we must add that the question is really irrelevant. For what we really mean when we speak of the "rights of society" is not in fact the rights of society as a moral and abstract person; we are actually speaking of the rights of each and every individual concrete person within the society of which we are a part. Therefore, by the expression "rights of society", we really mean the rights of our *neighbors*; the rights of the real individual countrymen who surround us.

Now those of an individualist bend of mind may say: "Well then, I have the duty of rendering aid to those in need with whom I have immediate contact, but no others. I don't really owe anything to someone I've never actually associated with."

This assertion is false.

As we have explained, each individual person *is* in reality associated to a number of societies all at the same time. In order of proximity, these are the family, the town or local community, the region (e.g. county), the larger region if any (e.g. federated state), the State, and the world. Again, each individual person *benefits* from every other person in society, the more so, of course, as he has immediate dealings with them, *but individuals also benefit, in one way or another, from all other persons in the wider societies*, provided those persons are doing any useful work in the world. For instance, all residents of the United States benefit from a Montana wheat farmer, for by his special expertise and diligence, he provides a type of quality food which he makes available at a good price to all. Even residents from other countries (say Japan) may be beneficiaries of his work. In turn, the farmer is indebted to an auto worker in Detroit or elsewhere, who helps build the trucks he needs to use on his farm.

Each individual person therefore has obligations to all persons in these societal circles, although it must indeed be acknowledged and restated that these obligations are graver in the degree of the proximity one has to the society in question, so that familial obligations rank highest, and others progressively less so.

From a supernatural standpoint, we must even say that each of us owes both justice and charity even to our enemies. (Mt. 5:43f)

These things add weight to our statement that while the State must defend the rights of individuals to own private property and to profit from the use thereof, such rights are not absolute and do not override the considerations of the common good of all citizens or of all mankind (cf. 8.14). Popes Leo XIII and Pius XI both emphasized the fact that there is both a private and a social aspect to property ownership. (*Rerum Novárum* §22, *Quadragésimo Anno* §§45-51)

BOTH INDIVIDUALS AND SOCIETY HAVE A GRAVE OBLIGATION IN JUSTICE AND CHARITY TO AID THOSE IN GRAVE NEED

The Obligation Of Individuals To Give Alms

9.14 – It is said that charity begins at home (Gal. 6:10). Therefore it is best to look at the closest obligations first. Each of us, under the Fifth Commandment (which, as we have seen in 2.8, is both Divine and Natural Law), is required to render aid to our neighbor under certain conditions. What are the conditions?

St. Thomas Aquinas summed up the constant teaching of the Church since earliest times, by giving the circumstances under which almsgiving is obligatory, as follows:[167]

1. One has goods above one's own grave life necessities and those for whom one has a more direct responsibility to care (e.g. family).

2. The one requiring assistance is in urgent need of grave life necessities.

"Grave life necessities" here means food, clothing, shelter, and anything else needed to maintain physical life and reasonable health.

As with any moral question, the obligation of course varies according to the given concrete situation. It is graver in the measure that one has the means to provide aid. If one already only has enough for life's necessities plus a little more, one is much less obligated than a truly wealthy man, who has goods well above even those merely needed to maintain his security and proper social position.

Even when one's neighbor is not in the grave need mentioned, but is still pressed by poverty, almsgiving is highly to be commended, for it increases the spirit of fraternity and generosity in society. (Lk 12:33; Eph. 4:28; Acts 10:2ff; Acts 10:31; I Peter 4:8f; *Summa Theol.* II-II Q.32, a6).

Should Government Ever Be Involved In Material Charities?

9.15 – We have to recognize that, since the State is made up of individuals, it shares in human nature. It therefore has the same essential moral obligations as any individual person. The degree of these obligations, and the means for fulfilling them are, of course (just as they are for individuals), modified by circumstances. What these circumstances are can be summed up in that the State authority has the ultimate responsibility in society for matters concerning the temporal common good, while on the other hand, micro-management by the highest authority of very personal matters, such as the distribution of alms, works badly in practice.

We can resort to the principles of subsidiarity and solidarity to resolve this issue. By subsidiarity, corporal works of mercy should be done at the lowest possible level of society, and at higher levels only as necessary. By this means, these works will be done more efficiently, and solidarity in charity and common effort will be promoted all around, for at the local level, members of the immediate community will be concretely involved in it; they will feel a connection and a responsibility to their immediate community, and this will easily extend to the wider communities of state or province, and the nation, and eventually the world. But if a community has a need not addressable by its own resources, a larger region (county, province, federated

---

[167] *Summa Theol.* II-II Q.32, a5 & 6. See also II-II Q.66, a7.

state) should step in to provide some of its own, from a wider pool of contributions. If an entire province or federated state is widely affected (normally only through some catastrophe), aid from the entire State should be brought to bear.

It should be remembered that when the State is involved, or even individual states within a federation, more or less bureaucracy will also be involved, which of necessity is bound by detailed rules that do not admit of a personal touch, and cannot be adjusted to circumstances by prudence or individual on-the-spot judgments. While State assistance may be necessary in modern, intellectually fragmented and pluralistic societies, to the degree that a State is more Catholic, public assistance should become more local, and more usually handled by Catholic religious or lay organizations. In medieval times, the guilds handled almsgiving *ad intra* (taking care of their own members), and monks and nuns cared for the indigent in society at large.

Finally, and in truth most importantly, "charity" which is enforced is *not* Charity. If government collects taxes for the purpose of redistribution in order to effect "charitable" works, and does so under threat of punishment for failure to pay them (as is always the case), those who pay them are not giving freely, and so they do not do so out of Charity at all, but rather fear of punishment. Therefore they get no merit before God (or even man) for any good their taxes may do; their opportunity to merit is stolen from them. Further, neither will God smile upon the State as a whole for such enforced "charity", for the State's moral worth is merely the sum of that of its citizens.

> **PRINCIPLE 66: When one has goods above the life necessities of oneself and those one has direct responsibility to care for (e.g. family), one has an obligation to aid those who stand in need of such necessities through no fault of their own. This obligation devolves also upon society, and should be fulfilled in accordance with the principle of subsidiarity. State authority should not impede or limit, but should encourage, voluntary acts of material charity, by any citizens, toward the poor and distressed. The State ought not employ its power of taxation to provide public welfare unless no other means are available to relieve extreme distress. If it does employ such means, they should be directed toward the goal of reintroducing the recipient individuals into a productive and self-sustaining condition as soon as possible.**

No matter what form it takes, those who receive public assistance should be discouraged from looking upon such assistance as an "entitlement"; i.e. as something that they have an *absolute* right to; a right that exempts them from any duties or obligations (cf. 2.29f).

Through Sloth, A Person Forfeits His Claim On Society's Wealth

9.16 – Scripture, especially in the Proverbs, repeatedly associates laziness, or sloth, with well-deserved poverty.

"The slothful hand hath wrought poverty: but the hand of the industrious getteth riches." (Prov. 10:4) "Because of the cold the sluggard would not plough: he shall beg therefore in the summer, and it shall not be given him." (Prov. 20:4)

St. Paul clearly states in II Thessalonians chapter 3:

> Neither did we eat any man's bread for nothing, but in labor and in toil we worked night and day, lest we should be chargeable to any of you. Not as if we had not power: but that we might give ourselves a pattern unto you, to imitate us. For also when we were with you, this we declared unto you: that, if any man will not work, neither let him eat.

St. Gregory the Great enumerated seven deadly (capital) sins, among which is sloth. St. Thomas in the *Summa Theol.* (I-II Q.84, a4) gives six deadly sins, including sloth. Since a vice cannot be rewarded by a Catholic State, it follows that there should be no reward for laziness.

Pope Pius XI, while calling for a more equitable distribution of wealth between the rich and the workers, nonetheless strongly condemned idleness in §61 of *Quadragésimo Anno*:

> Therefore, with all our strength and effort we must strive that at least in the future the abundant fruits of production will accrue equitably to those who are rich and will be distributed in ample sufficiency among the workers – not that these may become remiss in work, for man is born to labor as the bird to fly – but that they may increase their property by thrift, that they may bear, by wise management of this increase in property, the burdens of family life with greater ease and security...

PRINCIPLE 67: A person who could work, and thereby contribute to the sum total of goods and services in the economy, but because of idleness does not do so, forfeits any claim in justice to the goods and services produced by the other members of society.

Of course, although a person through idleness forfeits the right to material support from society, there is nothing stopping individuals or non-governmental organizations from giving it anyway, but they should have a prudent plan for it that will not encourage the vice of sloth. And this brings us to the question of "hard cases" in works of charity.

Hard Cases

9.17 – How should society deal with those who are physically able to support their own lives, but *will* not? And we must consider also others who are indeed unviable, but through their own fault; they have made themselves that way through chronic alcohol or other substance abuse, or various other addictions. Some of these conditions become permanently disabling.

Firstly, we should remember that such souls can never lose their essential humanity, and thus cannot be abandoned. Secondly, such radical dereliction is almost always originally and in great part a result of the sins of those who were responsible for the formation of these persons; often these souls have been gravely neglected or even spiritually and/or physically abused.

A beginning of a solution must be found in the realization that the main reason people become "deadbeats" is because, by whatever influence, they have become convinced that life is either meaningless or, if still possessed of some meaning, nevertheless hopeless in that they see no possibility of actualizing that meaning, or actually finding happiness in life.

The words of St. Augustine, spoken so many centuries ago, are as valid as ever: "Our hearts are restless, Lord, until they find their rest in Thee."

A truly and widely Catholic society never lacks generous souls who are willing to seek out and come to the aid even of self-made derelicts. Now, because the problem in such people is normally in essence spiritual, so must the solution be, and therefore it would make no sense for governments to run programs attempting to help them, for State rule as such addresses only the material common good of society. When it does attempt to intervene in the aid of derelicts, the endeavor is expensive and the results negligible from the standpoint of what really counts, which is the spiritual rehabilitation of the person.

We therefore recommend that, except when public order requires it, these people be always taken care of at the local level, by independent religious and/or lay organizations.

APPENDIX 1

On Ranking The Value Of Human Goods

So far as man's reason for being is concerned – that is, his temporal and eternal happiness – human goods are valuable under three different aspects.

The First Aspect: Relative Vs. Absolute Value (Material vs. Spiritual Value) Of Human Goods

App. 1.1 – The thing that distinguishes man from beast is the immortal soul that man possesses. In this soul reside the mind and free will, possessed of a spiritual – that is, intellectual and immaterial – nature. This means that whatever knowledge or virtue a man acquires in this world will remain with him for eternity in the next, to be enjoyed by him, and shared with others, forever. From this fact alone; that is, from the aspect of *duration*, spiritual goods are seen to be infinitely more valuable than the material ones. Further, even if knowledge and virtue were to end with this earthly life, they would still immeasurably surpass material goods, which are the goods of the body only. The body alone, as such, does not even *know* the material goods or satisfactions which it enjoys; it simply possesses and enjoys them, with no intellectual appreciation.[168] Finally, knowledge and virtue are the prime means by which we acquire even these material goods.

Material goods therefore are only of relative value; they have value only so far as their possession is useful for the acquisition of spiritual goods, which have value absolutely and in themselves.

In sum: *All human goods fall into one of two categories; the material and the spiritual. Spiritual goods are of an infinitely greater value than material goods. In practice, material goods have value only insofar as they serve as aids to the acquisition of spiritual goods.*

The Second Aspect: The Degree That Material Human Goods Advance Spiritual Goods

App. 1.2 – After the material vs. spiritual distinction, human goods could be ranked according to their value within their own category; i.e. one material good vs. another, or one spiritual good vs. another.

However, material goods being nearly useless unless they aid the spiritual, they must always be ranked according to the degree of their usefulness to the spiritual, as follows:

1. The Support Of Bodily Life And Health. Though the body is material, it is the vehicle for the acquisition of most spiritual goods, and this acquisition ceases when the life of the body ceases. One can acquire

---

168 To understand this better, observe how pets, such as dogs or cats, respond to being given food, caresses, or other material satisfactions. These experiences may be highly pleasurable, even quasi-ecstatic, but animals cannot possibly *know* them *as such*. Nor can they compare them to other such pleasures, or conceive any *purpose* in them; delighting in them *as being* part of the "big picture" which is the vast aggregate of all created good, which is the universe.

knowledge and virtue only while one is physically alive. Further, poor health can make that acquisition more difficult, or even impossible.[169]

2. The Excellence Of A Spiritual Good That A Material Good Serves. For example, a material good such as a book on social principles serves the acquisition of a kind of knowledge much more helpful to attaining human happiness than does a book on model airplane building. Both kinds of knowledge, being knowledge, are spiritual goods, yet the latter, at most, only advances man's temporal purpose in life, and if so only minimally.

The Third Aspect: The Degree Of Commonality Of Human Goods

App. 1.3 – Finally, human goods can be ranked according to their degree of commonality, or shareability. Certainly, a good that is in no way limited by any connection with matter is also not limited by physical *quantity*, and thus can be distributed infinitely, and without diminishment. But a purely immaterial good is a purely spiritual good, and 'spiritual' means intellectual or moral. For this reason, the more purely intellectual and moral a good is, the more simultaneously and undiminishably shareable it is – and this is the same as saying that it is more able to be common.

However, man receives his knowledge through the physical senses (see 1.6), and communication of spiritual goods is usually bound up with material things, or connected in some way or degree to them. Normally, for example, knowledge, or good moral example and influence, come by way of physical media, by seeing written words (as you are now) or hearing the sound waves of a speaking voice or of good music. Of course, if this knowledge or moral influence penetrates to and remains in the memory, the physical communication is no longer needed (though in the case of music the physical re-rendition is always more powerful than that which the memory alone recalls). Thus the knowledge or moral influence available in audio or visual material is in practice limited in shareability to the number of people that will actually be able to obtain the material media, and imbibe and retain its content (in mental and immaterial form).

For this reason, the only intellectual and moral goods that are shareable in an unlimited degree are those that can be distributed to an unlimited number of human minds, straight from the source and without the intervention of material media. The only source that can effect this kind of distribution is God. He does this by simply placing directly in as many minds as He wants whatever knowledge or good moral movements He wishes to place there. This action of His is called actual grace. Actual grace in turn leads to sanctifying grace, which is a participation in the nature of God Himself, and is a sort of possession of God.[170]

This said, it must be understood that even these graces cannot be infinite in number, power or intensity, because they are limited by the Eternal Divine Plan, which cannot distribute an infinite amount of grace to any creature, let alone to all creatures, because the perfection of the universe requires variety in creatures, and

---

169 This latter point does not apply universally. Many saints actually used physical infirmities to *aid* themselves in the acquisition of virtues, such as patience and fortitude. It mainly refers to physiological maladies that inhibit the operations of the mind and will.
170 Hence the most efficient use of a person's time is to call down upon the human race as much of this grace as possible, through prayer, penance and good works.

this can happen only through an unequal and limited distribution of gifts.[171]

It is also perfectly clear that, the greater the commonality of a good, the more valuable it is, because, for any good of value X, that value increases in proportion with each additional person that is able to benefit from it, and to the degree that its benefit remains undiminished when thus shared. Though God and His grace are not *actually* shared in an infinite degree with creatures, the *potential* for sharing them is infinite, and nothing of them is *taken* from one person in order to make more available to another.

In sum: Only spiritual goods have absolute value, and this value is increased both by the number of persons that can share in them, and, when shared, by the undiminishability of that value.

App. 1.4 – We can then list the degrees of commonality below, from lowest to highest value:

1. **Individual Goods.** By definition, these are not common goods at all, and as such they have zero shareability value; they can be enjoyed by only one person at a time. We mention them here, however, by way of contrast with goods that *are* common, mentioned below. In the individual category are tools, machines, food, drink, clothing, or any other objects *whenever* they cannot be used *simultaneously* by two or more individuals.

2. **The Common Goods Of A Species.**[172] These are goods that can be simultaneously enjoyed by two or more beings of a species – in our case the species *homo sápiens*. These are the common goods of human societies, of whatever size, from the family to the world. After the application of the first and second aspects mentioned above, which determine the *intrinsic* values of human goods, we can consider the value that may be *added* to them by their *extension* throughout the human species, given that a good is amplified in value in the measure of the number and dignity of beings that share in it, as well as the degree to which it *retains* its absolute value as it is shared.

   As regards material common goods, it should be noted that, if possessed in some quantity, they can indeed become common goods, at least at a minimal level. For example, a person giving someone else half of his sandwich converts that sandwich into a common good, but the value of that sandwich for each person is also diminished by half in the process. In contrast, air is at the opposite extreme of material shareability value, for its value extends to the whole world, and is largely undiminishable due to its vast quantity and pervasive presence. *It follows that the degree of commonality or shareability value of material goods is a function of the availability of the supply for satisfying the demand.*

   Another example: A large shelter has greater value than a small one so far as it accommodates more people. However, any shelter's value will be affected

---

171 See *Summa Theol.* I Q.23, a5, ad3
172 There are of course very many species of creatures, but as said above, we will consider only our own species. This is not at all to suggest that non-intellectual creatures do not share in or contribute to the common good of their own species, or of the universe.

negatively so far as the necessity of sharing its amenities reduces their availability to all. A four-bedroom, one-bathroom house is of less value than the same house having two or more bathrooms.

An example of determining the commonality value of spiritual goods: Knowledge is generally of greater shareability value than the moral quality of a community, for people are generally more receptive to receiving knowledge than they are of imitating moral example.

The shareability of species-level common goods can be conveniently categorized with reference to the level of society they extend to. For instance, we can speak of familial common goods, enjoyed only by members of a family (e.g. the house they live in; family affection); we can speak of municipal common goods, which extend to an entire town (e.g. the common water supply; a public town library); also regional common goods, which extend to a county or federated state (e.g. a county or state road system; a library book-sharing network); also national common goods (e.g. a country's military resources; cultural heritage); or world common goods (e.g. well-functioning international common markets; public domain artistic and intellectual works). Of course, world common goods are at the highest shareability level, so far as they benefit the entire species and not just some group within it.

3. **All Creation As A Common Good.** As said before (2.6), all creatures, from the inanimate to the angelic, naturally find greater individual fulfillment in serving larger and higher – that is, more common – goods. However, only intellectual creatures, meaning Angels and men, actually understand and thus *consciously* enjoy those common goods.[173] Further, Angels and men are able to understand and enjoy the whole ensemble of common goods – that ensemble called the universe – to different degrees according to their differing abilities and graces.[174] While no one but God is truly omniscient, and able to perfectly know, in one prolonged simultaneous Now, the ingenious and wonderful design of every individual being in the universe, as well as the marvelously harmonious integration of each with every other in the ineffably vast and mobile work of art which is the whole of creation, man is capable, even on this earth, of rare instances of some sort of profound sense of the glory of it all. A single such moment, or a grateful memory of it, may be good enough in itself to outweigh a lifetime of prior miseries in this world. As for the next world, if we be so fortunate as to merit a destination to the celestial regions, this comprehensive view will become amplified, and permanent.[175]

---

173 Because of this, St. Thomas distinguishes the common goods that can be shared and distributed by both men and Angels as genus-level common goods. While men and Angels are different species, they both fall into the larger category, or genus, of intellectual creatures. See *Summa Contra Gentiles*, Bk. III, Ch. 24, 7 & 8. We have avoided the technical distinction of genus in favor of what we hope is an approach more simple and suitable to our purpose.
174 *Summa Contra Gentiles,* Bk. III, cap. 112, 5: "unaquaeque intellectualis substantia est quodammodo omnia, inquantum totius entis comprehensiva est suo intellectu." Each and every intellectual substance is in a certain way all things, inasmuch as, by its intellect, it is comprehensive of [able to comprehend] all being.
175 *Summa Theol.*, Suppl. Q.92, a3

4. **The Creator As Common Good.** The most shareable and excellent good in the universe is the Creator of the universe, God Himself. The mind balks at the mere thought of attempting to describe this Common Good of all common goods, but we are forced to make whatever weak attempt we can. As the source of all being, and as Being Itself, God is the ultimate common good, the source and possessor of every good, whether individual or common. The possession of God is therefore the possession of every good, in the sense that all good can be known in knowing God. Moreover, this knowing of God is entirely non-rivalrous and undiminishable. Any number of persons can possess any "amount" of God, without in the least reducing His availability to any number of others.

Social Common Goods : Setting Priorities

App. 1.5 – From the above, we can synthesize an approach by which government can prioritize its actions so as to optimize its pursuit of establishing and maintaining the commonweal at the highest possible level. We will not establish a detailed empirical scientific method. We leave the creation of such a method to specialists – if any will wish to dedicate themselves to it. For our part, we suspect that it would be of limited value, given the unpredictabilities involved in life in general and in the response of human free will to detailed plans of any kind. Hence the approach we present is simple and broad.

Consider first the philosophical axiom: *primum in intentióne est últimum in executióne* (the first priority in intention is the last in execution). That is to say, one has an ultimate goal, but that goal will be reached only by numerous steps. The first step is the least desired and least important in itself. Subsequent steps are increasingly more desired and important in themselves, and the last step is what is maximally desired in itself. But one step leads to another; you will *not* arrive at the true and ultimate goal without the intervening steps.

The ultimate goal is to maximize the number of souls that will attain to the vision of God, Who is the ultimate Common Good. But this will happen only through a process of ascent, from providing for immediate and urgent material common goods, to less urgent ones, then to material aids leading to basic spiritual common goods (education, virtues), and finally to aiding the Catholic Church in supernaturalizing these spiritual improvements by directing them to God.

From this consideration, we can form a basic To-Do list for governmental authorities. It can be found in sections 4.2 through 4.4.

APPENDIX 2

On Civil Obedience, Disobedience, Rebellion

Historical Background

PLATO

App. 2.1 – *Crito:* Plato, in the persona of Socrates, posits that the laws have to be obeyed unquestioningly. The argument is very eloquent, but it proceeds from a principle of a social contract between the individual citizen and the State authority. The citizen, simply by agreeing to remain a citizen, when he could emigrate if he wished, has agreed to be bound by the laws of the rulers.

The social contract principle is not valid, but even if it were, the argument is invalid because, firstly, any implied agreement is not by any means necessarily unconditional or universal; it does not imply that one agrees to be bound by *all* laws of the State, present or future, or that there can never be circumstances that override the duty of obeying them. More importantly, it also assumes that there is no higher authority than that of the State rulers; a higher authority that could take precedence in certain cases.

Plato's Socrates states also that it is not the laws that have sentenced him to death, but evil men (the judges). But if this is the case, then the judges have broken the law by their unjust sentence. Therefore it is they who are betraying the law, betraying the State, and breaking the social contract. Thus not only is he not obliged to accept their judgment, but if he does so he condones their rebellion, and helps to undermine that very law and State and contract he swears to uphold at the cost of his life.

It may further be contended that Socrates was not arguing a general principle, but only his free choice to sacrifice his rights in his own case, and this contention is supported by his account, in the *Apology*, as to how he abandoned a leadership position in a grand jury that was intent on committing a similar manifest injustice, where a group of admirals was being tried en masse, instead of one by one, as they ought to have been.

ARISTOTLE

App. 2.2 – *Politics*: He treats thoroughly of many political topics, but does not say anything about the moral value of rebelling against a tyrannical government. In regard to civil obedience, he does say this:

> It has been well said that 'he who has never learned to obey cannot be a good commander.' (Bk 3, ch. 4)

> In all well-tempered governments there is nothing which should be more jealously maintained than the spirit of obedience to

[constitutional] law...for transgression creeps in unperceived and at last ruins the State... (Bk 5, ch. 8)

He therefore insists that both rulers and subjects ought to have a constitution, and that *both* should religiously adhere to it. This is reinforced in his ch. 9.

CICERO

App. 2.3 – *De República*: Cicero refers to Aristotle in this work, and his treatment clearly follows Aristotle's doctrine. But he also makes a clear moral judgment as to rebelling against a tyrannical government:

> Can we call the State of Agrigentum a commonwealth, where all men are oppressed by the cruelty of a single tyrant; where there is no universal bond of right, nor social consent and fellowship, which should belong to every people, properly so named?...Thus, wherever I behold a tyrant, I know that the social constitution must be not merely vicious and corrupt,...but in strict truth no social constitution at all. (Bk. 3, XXXI)

> ...Lælius was complaining that there were no statues of Nasica erected in any public place, as a reward for his having slain the tyrant. Scipio replied..."...that divine nature ought to have, not statues fixed in lead, nor triumphs with withering laurels, but some more stable and lasting kinds of rewards." (Bk. 6, VIII)[176]

Further, in *De Officiis* Bk. 3, ch. 4, §19; 3, 6, §32, and 3, 21, §85, Cicero justifies Julius Caesar's assassins.[177]

ST. AUGUSTINE

App. 2.4 – Cicero's reasoning in Bk. 3 is approved by Augustine in *Civitas Dei*, Bk. 2, ch. 21, and Bk. 4, ch. 4. Augustine, however, does not advocate tyrannicide, or even rebellion. He does not go as far as Cicero in claiming that a tyrannical government is no government at all.[178]

THE SYNTHESIS OF ST. THOMAS AQUINAS

App. 2.5 – Overview: He was familiar with the thought of all these men. He even wrote a commentary on Aristotle's *Politics*. He represented a conservative side of the medieval spectrum of political thought on this question; that is, his ideas were not new or radical. Aquinas accepts Cicero's view that a tyrannical government is not truly a government.

---

176 This and the foregoing quote are taken from *De República*, trans. C. D. Yonge, *Cicero's Tusculan Disputations*, Harper & Brothers, New York, 1877
177 *De Officiis*, with trans. by Walter Miller, Heinemann, London, 1913. (https://archive.org/details/deofficiiswithen00ciceuoft/mode/2up – accessed 3 Nov. 2025)
178 *St. Augustine's City of God and Christian Doctrine*, trans. Marcus Dods, Christian Classics Ethereal Library. (https://ccel.org/ccel/schaff/npnf102/npnf102.i.html – accessed 3 Nov. 2025)

Note: In the following summary of St. Thomas' teaching on Civil Obedience, Disobedience and Rebellion, numbers in braces following a statement indicate that its teaching pertains to corresponding numbered box(es) in the flowchart at the end of this Appendix.

St. Thomas' teaching, in chronological order.

Commentary on the Sentences (II, D44, Q.2, a2)

1. Civil authority comes from God: "Christians are bound to obey the authorities inasmuch as they are from God; and they are not bound to obey inasmuch as the authority is not from God."{1} But a ruler who is unworthy of his office because of a defect of his person is still a legitimate authority and must still be obeyed. {4 to 7}

2. Authority becomes invalid when

    a) The authority is not real because of a defect in manner of acquisition; power was taken by violence, simony, usurpation, or other illegitimate means {1}. In this case, no obedience is owed. If someone has the ability, he can drive away the usurper. {10 to 15}. However, the usurper can become legitimate by the consent of the subjects or by recognition from a higher authority, and then he cannot be deposed. {2}

    b) The authority is being abused. {3 or 4}

       i) When there is a command to sin. In this case, we are obliged to disobey. {4 to 6}
       ii) When there is a command that is simply outside the authority's commission. In this case, we are not obliged to obey, but may do so. {4 to 9}
    (cf. *Summa Theol.* II-II Q.104, a5)

3. Cicero's justification of Julius Caesar's assassins was because Caesar took power by force and ruse, and the subjects were unwilling to accept it, and there was no recourse to a higher authority to judge the matter.

Note here that St. Thomas does not clearly condone assassination; he speaks of Cicero's opinion, not necessarily making it his own. In the response, he allows only that a usurper can be driven away (*repéllere*). In II-II Q.42, a2, ob3, he says again that those who liberate the people from tyrannical power are praised, but he does not say they are worthy of that praise. However, in II-II Q.64, a2 & a3 (see below) he makes clear that he does hold them praiseworthy, even if they must kill the tyrant, *provided* there is the sanction of a higher authority for it. {13 to 15}

Summa Theologiae **(probably the parts we give here were written before *De Regno*)**

I-II Q.96, a4, resp.

Positive human laws are either just or unjust. If just, it is because they are derived from the Eternal Law, and bind in conscience. If unjust, that is in two ways:

1. They are contrary to human good, because:

    a) They serve the private good of the ruler rather than the common good. {3}

    b) They command something outside the ruler's commission. {4}

    c) Unfair burdens are imposed, even if these be for the common good. {8}

Such laws do not bind in conscience unless on account of avoiding scandal or disturbance. {9}

2. They are contrary to the Divine good, because they command disobedience to God. Such laws it is in no way permitted to observe. {4 to 6}

II-II Q.42, a2, ad3

While sedition is always a mortal sin (because it goes against the common good), rebellion against a tyrant is not sedition, unless it causes a greater disturbance than the tyrannical regime does. Rather, rebellion helps the common good, because the tyrant is himself seditious in that he spreads discord among the people so as to control them more easily for his own gain. Thus the tyrant may be resisted, provided that, in the circumstances, more good will result than harm. {3 to 9, or 3 to 11 & possibly following, or 2 to 9, or 2 to 11 and possibly following}

II-II Q.64, a2, resp.

> If some man is a danger to the community, and is corrupting it because of some sin, he is praiseworthily and beneficiently killed, that the common good may be preserved. {15}

II-II Q.64, a3, resp.

> The care of the common good is committed to leaders having public authority, and therefore to them alone, and not to private persons, is it permitted to kill malefactors. {13 to 15}

II-II Q.64, a7, resp.

> From the act of someone defending himself there can follow a double effect: one being the conservation of his own life, but the other being the slaying of an invader. Accordingly, an act of this sort, from the fact that the conservation of one's own life is intended, does not have an aspect of illicitness, since it is natural to anything

that it conserve itself in being so far as it can. Nevertheless, an act proceeding from a good intention can be rendered illicit if it is not proportioned to the end. And therefore if someone, for defending his own life, uses greater violence than is suitable, it will be illicit...but it is not necessary that a man forego an act of moderated defense for his safety in order to avoid the slaying of another, because a man is more obliged to provide for his own life than for the life of another.

But because it is not permitted a man to *intend* to *kill* [another] man for the *common* good except by public authority...it is illicit that a man intend to kill a man in order to defend himself, except to him who has public authority, who, intending to kill a man for its defense, refers this to the public good, as appears in a soldier fighting against an enemy, and in a judge fighting against thieves – although even these sin if they are moved by private [blood] lust. {12 to 15}

II-II Q.104, a1, resp.

From the order of nature itself, divinely instituted, inferiors in natural affairs have to be subject to the motion of superiors; thus also in human affairs, from the order of Natural and Divine Law, inferiors are held to obey superiors. In fact, obedience is the most meritorious of the moral virtues (cf. a3). {7}

II-II Q.104, a5, resp.

It can happen in two ways that a subject is not held to obey his superior in all things. One is on account of a precept of a higher power. Another is if the superior commands something which is not subject to him...in things which pertain to the interior movement of the will, a man is not held to obey man, but only God. {4 to 6, or 4 to 9}

This latter means the civil power cannot punish thought "crimes" or interior bad intentions.

II-II Q.104, a6, ad3

If power is not held justly, but is rather a usurpation, or if laws are unjust, subjects are not bound to obey, unless perhaps in order to avoid scandal or danger. {3 to 9, 4 to 9, or 3 to 11}

De Regno, Bk 1, ch. 7

This treats of the conditions justifying rebellion against the government.

The question is: Do the people have to be martyred rather than remove or assassinate a king?

Three possible solutions:

1. If a given community by custom appoints a ruler, it is not unjust for the community to depose the king or restrict his power if he abuses it. {3 to 15, and 3 to 9}

2. If on the other hand, it pertains to a higher authority to appoint a king over a certain community, then the remedy for the wickedness of the tyrant is to be sought from that authority. {3 to 13}

3. If no human aid is possible against the tyrant, recourse is to be made to God, the king of all, who is the help of those in tribulation. {3 to 14}

A summary of his responses would be that the decision to remove or assassinate a ruler cannot be made by private judgment, but only by some authority.

The Greater Context Of *De Regno*:

App. 2.6 – The following quotes contain considerations that may help in making prudential judgments in particular circumstances.

> If there be not an excess of tyranny it is more expedient to tolerate the milder tyranny for a while than, by acting against the tyrant, to become involved in many perils more grievous than the tyranny itself. For it may happen that those who act against the tyrant are unable to prevail and the tyrant then will rage the more. But should one be able to prevail against the tyrant, from this fact itself very grave dissensions among the people frequently ensue: the multitude may be broken up into factions either during their revolt against the tyrant, or in process of the organization of the government after the tyrant has been overthrown. Moreover, it sometimes happens that while the multitude is driving out the tyrant by the help of some man, the latter, having received the power, thereupon seizes the tyranny. Then, fearing to suffer from another what he did to his predecessor, he oppresses his subjects with an even more grievous slavery.

> If the excess of tyranny is unbearable, some have been of the opinion that it would be an act of virtue for strong men to slay the tyrant and to expose themselves to the danger of death in order to set the multitude free…But this opinion is not in accord with apostolic teaching. For Peter admonishes us to be reverently subject to our masters, not only to the good and gentle but also the froward. (1 Pet 2:18-19)

> Should private persons attempt on their own private presumption to kill the rulers, even though tyrants, this would be dangerous for the multitude as well as for their rulers…danger to the people from the loss of a good king would be more probable than relief through the removal of a tyrant.

To proceed against the cruelty of tyrants is an action to be undertaken, not through the private presumption of a few, but rather by public authority.

If to provide itself with a king belongs to a given multitude, it is not unjust that the king be deposed or have his power restricted by that same multitude if, becoming a tyrant, he abuses the royal power. It must not be thought that such a multitude is acting unfaithfully in deposing the tyrant, even though it had previously subjected itself to him in perpetuity, because he himself has deserved that the covenant with his subjects should not be kept.

If, on the other hand, it pertains to a higher authority to provide a king for a certain multitude, a remedy against the wickedness of a tyrant is to be looked for from him.

Should no human aid whatsoever against a tyrant be forthcoming, recourse must be had to God, the King of all, Who is a helper in due time in tribulation...But to deserve to secure this benefit from God, the people must desist from sin, for it is by divine permission that wicked men receive power to rule as a punishment for sin, as the Lord says by the Prophet Hosea (13:11): "I will give you a king in my wrath", and it is said in Job (34:30) that He "makes a man that is a hypocrite to reign, for the sins of the people".

When all is said and considered, questions of civil obedience, disobedience, and especially rebellion, prove to be both extremely complex and often conditioned by circumstances, some of which are not foreseeable. Moreover, they are also often fraught with the greatest peril not only to individuals but to the entire State. For these reasons we offer the following flowchart which can be resorted to in concrete situations if they arise. Of course, it cannot guarantee correct decisions in such matters. Great prudence is still necessary in applying it, even under the rather rash assumption that it is by nature adequate to all possible cases. Nevertheless, it seems to us that it would provide at least the indispensable principles and the beginnings necessary for correct decisions.

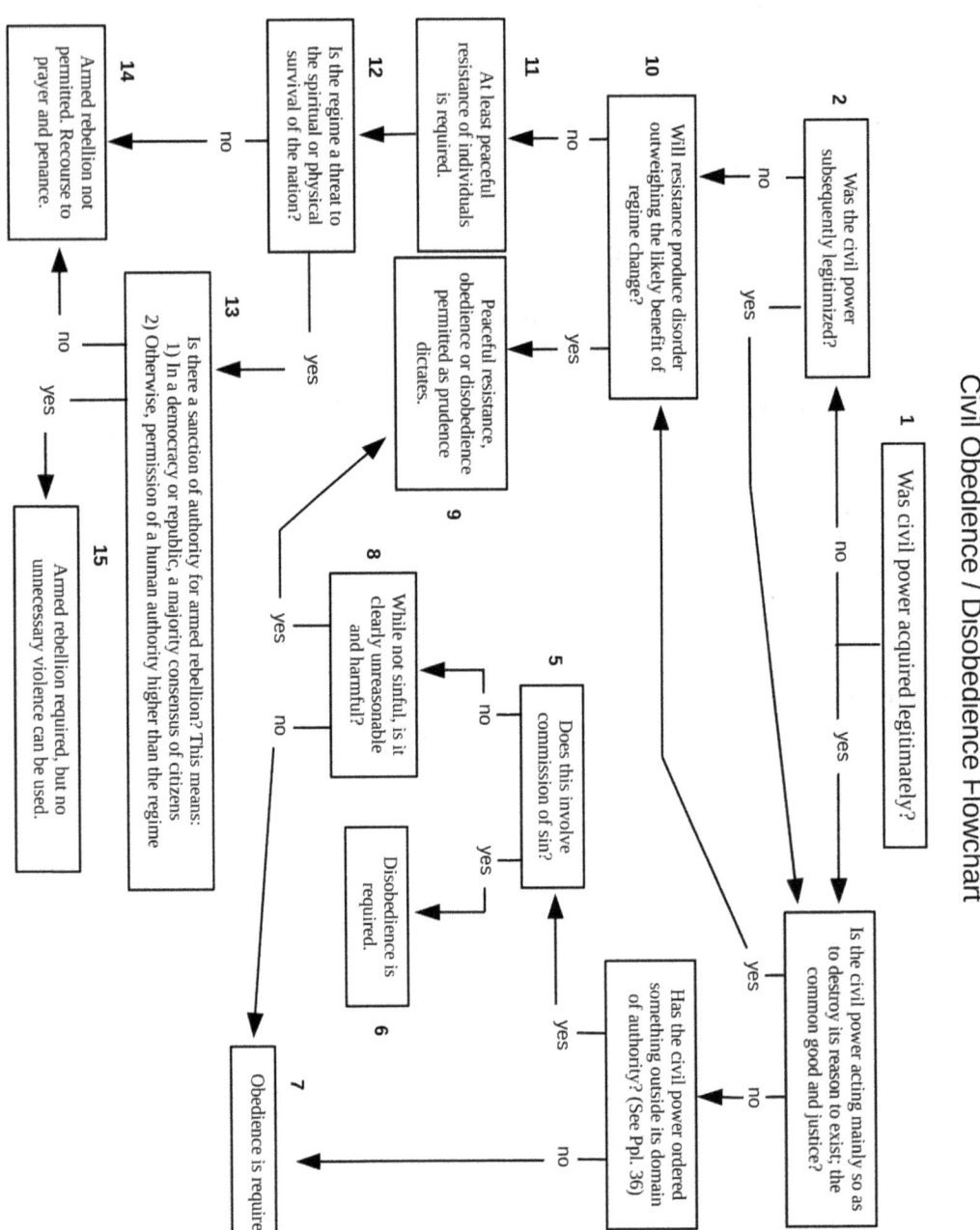

APPENDIX 3

On Moral Hazard And The Welfare State

(Further considerations on Chapter 9: Economic Equality And Inequality)

Moral Hazard

App. 3.1 – The concept of "moral hazard" is widely known in banking and insurance circles. It refers to the perverse incentives felt by a person who is fully or partially shielded from the negative consequences of his poor decisions. An example would be a teenager whose automobile insurance is provided by his parents. The teenager knows that if he wrecks the car he is driving, all costs, including medical costs for his recovery, will be borne by the insurance company. Because he himself does not pay the premiums, he may feel no constraint on his reckless driving, because the pain of future premium increases is absorbed by his parents, or is so far in the future that it means little to him.

Conservative authors such as Charles Murray in *Losing Ground* and Marvin Olasky in *The Tragedy Of American Compassion* have documented the rise of dysfunctional behaviors in mostly minority communities due to the growth of the American Welfare State between 1950 and 1980. Welfare has given men an excuse to abandon the mothers of their children, and the children themselves; it has given women incentives to be promiscuous and reckless in their decisions. The current chaotic and amoral state of black ghettos and Indian reservations in the United States is a result of the perverse incentives created by the Welfare State. The dissolution of white marriages and families, as well, is correlated with the rise of alternatives to marriage, such as government-funded health care, child care, housing subsidies, and food stamps, not to mention intrusive and coercive agencies such as child protective services.

Not only is the work ethic of the populace adversely affected by the availability of government welfare programs, but the same populace serves as a pool of political support for ever-increasing government intervention and surveillance. To citizens raised with the conviction that government should and will solve one's economic, health, family, and even emotional problems, the government assumes in their eyes the importance that God, Church, and family should have, but no longer have, for the majority of modern citizens.

Because the Catholic State strives to strengthen the family and the Church, and seeks to facilitate the spiritual as well as material well-being of its citizens, it must avoid and oppose all such perverse incentives. It should not seek to make its citizens worship Mammon, in the form of a vast, bureaucratic Welfare State.

Caveat: Coercive and redistributive measures may be justified and needed in the face of large fortunes which clearly have been obtained through fraud and deception. The question of what to do with large fortunes which consist mostly or wholly of ill-gotten gains (the billions owned by George Soros come to mind) has yet to be addressed and resolved. But here it should be stated that even if a Catholic State, coming to power on the ruins of finance capitalism, found it expedient to expropriate certain holdings acquired dishonestly and through parasitic activities, the expropriated resources should still not be used to finance any kind of Welfare State. Taking a hypothetical example, if 50,000 acres of land were expropriated, a local board should be convened to distribute that land to multiple citizens who are likely to farm, ranch, manufacture, build houses on, or otherwise productively use those assets. In all such redistribution, the perverse incentives of moral hazard should be reduced as much as possible, and the Catholic principle of subsidiarity must be observed.

The overall principle here is that, so to speak, it may be advisable to give a man a robber baron's fishing pole, but it would be wrong to put that man on the dole so that he receives his daily fish from the government.

Some Background Information On The Obligation To Aid The Needy

App. 3.2 – On aid to the poor, in Book VI, ch. 6 of the *Politics*, Aristotle says:

> Where a democracy has revenues, demagogues should not be allowed, after their manner, to distribute the surplus; the poor are always receiving, and always wanting more and more, for such help is like water poured into a leaky cask. Yet the true friend of the people should see that they be not too poor, for extreme poverty lowers the character of the democracy. Measures should therefore be taken which give them lasting prosperity, and as this is equally the interest of all classes, the proceeds of the public revenues should be accumulated and distributed among its poor, if possible, in such quantities as may enable them to purchase a little farm, or make a beginning in trade or husbandry.

As usual, Aristotle's insight is in accord with Natural Law, and thus it is not surprising to find that the Catholic attitude is in that respect the same, as has been stated over the centuries.

There are of course the Scripture accounts of distributions to the needy (Acts 11:29ff; 1 Corinthians 16:1; Galatians 2:10), balanced by St. Paul's admonition that we have already quoted; in sum: *if any man will not work, neither let him eat.*

Later, the Fathers of the Church maintained that assistance to the truly needy was a grave obligation (see *Catholic Encyclopedia*, art. Alms and Almsgiving). This was recorded as far back as A.D. 380, in the *Apostolic Constitutions* (Bk. III, c. 4), and this in a part that was taken from the *Didascalia* of the Apostles, which goes back to the 3rd century. But echoing St. Paul, those *Constitutions* also say:

> But when someone is pressed by lack of sustenance because he is a glutton, or given to drunkenness, or lazy, he does not merit assistance; nay rather he is unworthy of the Church of God. Of this sort the Scripture speaks, saying: "The slothful, hiding his hand in his bosom, will not be able to bring it to his mouth again." [Prov. 19:24] "For every drunkard and whoremonger will beg, and every-

one given to sleep will be clothed with tatters and rags." [Prov. 23:21]... For idleness is truly the mother of hunger.[179]

Today we may resort to the words of Fr. Edward Cahill: "Charity without justice is unreal. Justice without charity has too little of the 'milk of human kindness' to respond to the actual needs of men." (*The Framework of a Christian State*, p. 539)

App. 3.3 – St. Thomas' principles are the perennial teaching of the Church. Some people in modern times, even popes, have tried to go against them by appealing to certain rather radical statements of the Fathers which seem to expand or intensify the obligations of material charity. They forget that these statements were made in a context of large and unjust gaps between rich and poor brought about either by an as-yet-unChristianized society and/or widespread hardship caused by barbarian invasions or other social unrest. The claim of the Moderns is that today's civilization requires more government involvement in assistance to the poor than formerly, or they pretend to extend new "rights" to man. While the former claim has some merit, since as we have noted, modern societies are pluralistic and thus unable to achieve the necessary unity of action, the latter claim is entirely false.

Arthur McGovern, S.J., gives an overview of these developments in the *Notre Dame Journal of Law, Ethics and Public Policy*, Vol. 11, No.2, art. 3: Entitlements and Catholic Social Teachings.

He says that Leo XIII, in *Rerum Novárum*, implicitly and generally calls for government welfare programs. But an actual reading of the text reveals this to be a complete fraud. On the contrary, *RN* §30 makes perfectly clear that such things are traditionally the work of the Church, and condemns those who "would substitute in its stead a system of relief organized by the State". And in §§31-33 he affirms that the job of government consists simply in its usual duty of making just laws so as to merely enable and foster charitable activity.

McGovern also cites Pius XI's *Quadragésimo Anno* to this same effect: §25, §58, note 20. But Pius XI merely references and confirms the teachings of Leo.

The argument began to be made by John XXIII, in the encyclical *Mater Et Magístra*, 1961, §60, that modern needs are too extensive to be handled at the local level, or by the Church, or various charities, and that government assistance was in some cases necessary. Later, in *Pacem In Terris*, 1963, he spoke of various "rights" of man:

1. Rights to medical care, security in case of sickness or inability to work due to old age, widowhood, unemployment, or any other case when one is deprived of the means of subsistence through no fault of one's own, a right to a basic education, and of sharing in the benefits of culture.

2. "Rights" to bodily integrity [whatever that is], and "necessary social services" [whatever those are].

3. A "right" to technical and professional training in keeping with the stage of educational development in the country to which one belongs.

---

[179] *Apostolic Constitutions,* Bk. II, c. 4, *Patrológia Graeca, V. 1,* Migne, col. 599, 1857. Our translation from the Latin text.

The first category indeed contains rights, though it should be said that these pertain only to basic physical and mental sustenance. However, these rights are best served not by the government, but by subsidiary means.

The second category is stated so vaguely that it is essentially meaningless.

The third category contains no rights at all. No one has a right to technical and professional training, period. This is simply not necessary to living a human life.

Further, in a pluralistic State, it is a snake in the grass to assert that the State government has the duty to provide a basic education, or the right to culture, for in this case the State authority, holding to the pseudo-religion of secular humanism as it does, will end by trying to brainwash all other religions right out of existence.

To the extent that these "rights" do not concern the necessaries of life, they are sheer Liberal inventions coming from a secular materialistic view of man's purpose in life.

Apparently, having seen enough of the damage done to both the moral fiber and the finances of States which accepted such "rights" and tried to satisfy them with government programs, John Paul II in *Centésimus Annus* backpedaled quite a bit.

In any case, we maintain the perennial doctrine of the Church. That doctrine is founded on the permanent reality of human nature; it does not need to be updated, but only applied prudently in the present circumstances.

GLOSSARY

This glossary does not give a definition of every term used in this book. It is meant to serve as a convenient reference to all those that we have explicitly and clearly defined in the body text, and any others that we have not so defined, but for which we think such explicit definitions are likely to be useful in order to remove any possible doubts or confusion as to their meaning.

Agnostic adj. – Professing not to know anything beyond material phenomena. In particular, professing not to know God. From the Greek *agnostos* (ignorant, unknowing).

Anarchy n. – The absence of societal authority. From the Greek *an* (without) and *archos* (leader).

Aristocracy n. – A government of the best citizens, or those supposed as such; an upper class or nobility. From the Greek *aristos* (best), and *krateein* (to rule). Cf. *oligarchy*, and *plutocracy*.

Art n. – The correct making or doing of things. The very notion of art requires acceptance of right vs. wrong, which in turn requires acceptance of some *purpose* in the making or doing of things. Things or acts that further the purpose are right, while those that obstruct it are wrong. Good art achieves the purpose for which that art exists, while bad art does not.

Authority n. – In a societal context, the right to command or to direct affairs. In the context of disputations, the word of a trusted source in support of an argument. Ultimately from the Latin *auctor* (author, originator, creator), through its derivative *auctóritas* (authorship, authority). Clearly, the truest right to direct a thing will lie with the creator of the thing directed, and the most certain argument from authority will come from the actual creator of the thing about which one argues.

Capital n. – Accumulated wealth that can be used as a resource to produce further wealth.

Capitalism n. – Devotion to the use of capital. This devotion can be rational. In other words, it can view capital according to its true worth, in view of man's ultimate reason for being. Original sin, however, tends to steer its use to selfish purposes.

    Capitalism, Laissez-faire n. – A form of capitalism where the laws or customs of the State leave people free to indulge their selfish and materialistic goals, and use capital to maximize profit, with little concern for their own true good or that of their neighbor. From the French *laissez faire* (allow to do).

Cause n. – Anything that influences the being of a thing.

    Cause, efficient n. – That which, by its own action, produces a thing.

    Cause, final n. – That on account of which a thing is produced; the reason why a thing is made.

    Cause, formal n. – In the sense used in this book, a synonym for 'essence' (q.v.)

    Cause, material n. – The material out of which a thing is produced.

Charity n. – The love of God above all things, and our neighbor as ourselves, for the love of God. Charity can be an act (e.g. giving alms to the poor) or a virtue (i.e. a habitual disposition to do such acts). Normally, one must first have (the virtue of) charity before one can do (acts of) charity (cf. *virtue*). In modern times, the word 'charity' has largely lost its supernatural aspect, and most often incorrectly refers to a purely areligious and secular humanitarian virtue, or acts proceeding from that virtue. Metonymically (i.e. by an alteration of meaning), a 'charity' can be an institution dedicated to doing acts of charity, such as the St. Vincent de Paul Society.

>**Charity, Social** n. – The virtue that inclines us to love our neighbors as ourselves, for the love of God. Social charity is simply charity considered as love of neighbor, which includes love of all men (Lk. 10:25ff). This charity clearly ought to be stronger and more active the closer our neighbor is to us.

Church n. – An organized Christian society existing to offer worship to the God of the Old and New Testaments, to instruct its adherents in all spiritual matters, and to define doctrines of a Christian faith. The only true Church is the Catholic Church.

Code of Canon Law n. (see *Law, Canon*)

Communism n. – A social system in which class distinctions and private property are abolished, and all goods are shared in common. True Communism is an impossibility, since original sin guarantees that goods will not justly be shared in common without an authority to enforce it, but the introduction of authority introduces a class of leaders. True Communism would simply be another word for anarchy. That is why there has never been a truly Communist society, and "Communist" governments have been, and always will be, dictatorships.

Constitution n. – An established form of government; e.g. a monarchy, republic, etc. Colloquially, the written document that legally defines that form of government; i.e. the Constitutional Law (q.v. under Law).

Culture n. – The knowledge, beliefs, arts, laws, institutions, norms, customs, and social behavior habits found in a society. The various aspects of a culture can also be considered separately, so that one can speak of scientific culture, educational culture, moral culture, etc. From the Lat. *côlere, cultus* (cultivate, care for).

Democracy n. – The wielding of the State's political power by a relatively large portion of the citizens, in particular by a portion of the citizenry much larger than an aristocracy. A pure democracy is a one-man-one-vote system where each voter directly expresses his choice on political issues. A representative democracy is more accurately known as a republic (q.v.). In this case, groups of voters elect someone to represent their interest on political issues. From the Grk. *demos* (people) and *krateein* (to rule).

Democratic Socialism n. – A combination of a socialist economic system with a democratic political system of government.

Denzinger n. – The *Enchiridion Symbolorum et Definitionum* (Handbook of Creeds and Definitions) compiled by Heinrich Denzinger. This book has gone through many editions since first being published in 1854. We have used the 30th edition, translated by Roy J. Deferrari. Later editions have become more and more subject to Modernism. This work is referred to in our text by the abbreviation Dz.

Dogma n. – A truth of Catholic faith or morals, contained in the word of God (either in Scripture or Tradition), and proposed by the Church, whether by a solemn judgment or by her universal and ordinary magisterium, as having to be believed as divinely revealed (Dz 1792). A dogma then is a teaching that, because it is revealed by God Himself, is integral to the faith itself, because to deny it would be a denial of faith in God. The "solemn judgment" is an individual declaration made by a pope, or by an ecumenical council ratified by a pope. The judgment must be clear in its intention to include the teaching as divinely revealed and included in the Catholic faith in the strict sense, as well as its intention to require the faithful to hold it as such. The "universal and ordinary magisterium" means that which has been taught by the great majority of bishops throughout the world, and for at least 200 years. The word 'dogma' can be used analogously to mean any solemn teaching of any sect.

Economics n. – The science and art of managing the production, exchange and general use of temporal valuables, so as to aid man in achieving his true purposes in life. From the Greek *oikonomia*, meaning the management of temporal household affairs.

Economy n. – The sum total of goods, services and exchanged temporal valuables, which contribute to the satisfaction of material and psychological needs and wants within a civil society or between civil societies.

Essence n. – That by which a being is what it is. The essence of a thing includes all that distinguishes it from any other type of thing, but nothing that does not do so. Thus additional qualities (or 'accidents' as they are called) are not included. For example, the essence of 'man' requires only two things: a rational soul and an animal body. To require 'accidents' such as size, weight, color, etc. would exclude from mankind any persons not possessed of such arbitrarily imposed non-essentials. Hence a definition of a thing is the verbal expression of the essence, without unnecessary details.

Eternal adj. – In the strict sense, outside time; existing in the always-having-existed and everlasting Now in which there is no succession of past, present and future. Only God and his thoughts and actions are eternal. For example, the Eternal Law and the Divine Plan are eternal in this sense. In an improper but popular sense, eternal can mean everlasting; having no end. Thus we may speak of man's "eternal salvation", when we really mean his everlasting or unending salvation. It is a common and unintentional blasphemy to speak of man as having an "eternal soul", when what should be said is that he has an immortal or everlasting soul.

Family n. – A permanent union of one man and one woman, with their children.

Fascism n. – A government under one party and one principal leader that divinizes the nation, and seeks to strongly unify and subordinate both individuals and industry to the goals it sets.

Feminism n. – A habit of mind whereby one implicitly denies the essential equality between human females and males, by focussing on non-essential and merely external characteristics of the two genders. One infected with "feminism" views specifically male qualities, such as physical strength, leadership ability, scientific habits of thought, etc., as being superior to specifically female qualities, such as greater empathy, multi-tasking ability, social grace, etc. Thus "feminism" can also be defined as an irrational devotion to that which is specifically masculine, and thus, ironically, should really be called *masculinism*.

Fortitude n. – A virtue that inclines one to pursue a good in spite of obstacles or the fear of them.

Freedom n. – A state and/or conditions in which a being is able to exercise its natural powers in order to fulfill its nature, and its reason for being. Freedom therefore does not mean an ability of a being to become or do whatever it wants, for being or acting contrary to Nature is self-destructive, and hence diminishes one's being, thus putting bonds upon one's possibilities for development and fulfillment.

Good n. – That which perfects and thus satisfies the nature of a being.

    Good, Common n. – A single good which can be shared simultaneously between two or more beings.

Government n. – The exercise of authority over the actions of men in communities, societies or States; the direction and restraint exercised in the administration of public affairs, according to established constitutions, laws and usages, or by special edicts.

Guild n. – A society of artisans or businessmen and their employees, who do a similar kind of work, which society is formed for the purpose of providing aid and protection to each other, and regulating that work as well as relations to other groups and the larger society in which it operates. A proper guild practices the principles of subsidiarity and solidarity.

Happiness n. – Strictly speaking, a state of having all that one wants, knowing that one has it, and knowing that one cannot lose it. This is a synonym for beatitude, and means the everlasting possession of God in heaven. Loosely, a condition of limited contentment or satisfaction on this earth.

Humanism n. – In the modern sense, and as used in this book: A system or attitude of thought in which natural human ideals and culture take precedence over religious ones. Modern humanism therefore tends strongly to the divinization of man.

Intellect n. – A knowing power which recognizes the essences of things, (whether absolute or relative), and hence sees the relations of things among themselves, as the relation of effect to cause, of a means to an end.

Justice n. – A virtue that inclines one to render to others what is due to them.

>**Justice, Commutative** n. – The rendering of what is due between persons in trades or business transactions.
>
>**Justice, Distributive** n. – The rendering by a society of what is due to its members.
>
>**Justice, Legal** n. – The rendering by a person of what is due to society.
>
>**Justice, Social** n. – A virtue that inclines one to render to society what one owes to it, and to strive that society render to its members what it owes to them. It inclines to both distributive and legal justice.

Kindness n. – 1) A good thing given to or done for someone that is beyond what is due to him. This could be an excess reward for a good deed or a diminished or eliminated punishment for a bad deed. In the latter case it is more properly called mercy (q.v.). 2) The habit of benevolence that inclines one to be kind and to do kindnesses.

Law n. – The rule and measure of any act.

>**Law, Canon** n. – The collection of disciplinary positive laws, established by the Roman Catholic Church, for the better ordering of the life of its own members (Lat. *Codex Juris Canonici;* Code of Canon Law). It is the main and most authoritative source of Ecclesiastical Law in the Catholic Church, but not the only one, and it principally applies only to Latin Rite Catholics. Eastern Rite Catholics are governed largely by their own legal traditions.
>
>**Law, Constitutional** n. – Any set of fundamental rules for the structure and practical operation of a State.
>
>**Law, Divine** n. – A rule or rules which have been infallibly revealed through Scripture or Tradition (e.g. the Ten Commandments).
>
>**Law, Ecclesiastical** n. – Rules given by Christ's Church to all the members of His Church. (cf. *Law, Canon*)
>
>**Law, Eternal** n. – The rules and measure for the actions of all the beings which God has created or will create, by which He intends those beings to fulfill the Eternal (Divine) Plan.
>
>**Law, Human** n. – Another name for Political Law (q.v. below).
>
>**Law, Moral** n. – The rule and measure of the personal acts of individuals, whereby a person is directed to virtue and his proper perfection. The moral law contains all rules that apply to the rightness or wrongness of individual deliberate human acts, and they are taken from other types of law, such as

Natural Law (in regard to natural perfection) or Divine Law and Ecclesiastical Law (in regard to supernatural perfection). (Cf. *moral*)

Law, Natural n. – The natural (created) inclinations in creatures to do certain things and tend toward certain ends.

Law, Political n. – An ordinance of reason for the common good, promulgated by him who has charge of a community.

Law, Positive n. – Law that has been posited, that is, published or declared in some clear manner. Positive law can be either Human (e.g. traffic laws) or Divine (e.g. the Ten Commandments).

Law, Supernatural n. – Any and all laws of God or His Church that help us to attain supernatural happiness.

Law, of Nations n. – That body of law containing the universal rational customs of men, derived from Natural Law.

Liberal n. & adj. – As an adjective: tainted with Liberalism. As a noun, a person tainted with Liberalism. Liberalism itself is a habit of mind and will coming from original sin whereby one loves oneself more than the objective truth and good, and therefore prefers one's own opinions and will over the truth and the good.

Marriage n. – The lifelong union of one man and one woman, primarily for the purpose of begetting and educating children, and secondarily for the mutual support of the spouses.

Matrimony n. – A sacramental marriage; that is, a valid marriage between a baptized man and a baptized woman. (See 1917 Code of Canon Law, 1012, §§1 & 2). The terms 'marriage' and 'matrimony' are often used interchangeably, but are not exactly synonymous. A marriage can be natural; i.e. not supernaturalized by the sacrament, while a true matrimony is always sacramental, and carries with it sacramental graces, which are actual graces that help the couple to perform the duties of the married state.

Mercy n. – A refraining from punishing someone according to his due. Refusing to give what is due (whether punishment or reward) is in itself contrary to justice, but mercy will be virtuous if there is reasonable hope that a criminal will be grateful for the mercy given and will himself make amends and do the necessary justice. In this case justice is preserved. Mercy is vicious otherwise, for it condones and encourages crime. Mercy is often used as a synonym for kindness, but this is usually a confusion. See *Kindness*.

Metaphysical adj. – Concerned with being as such, whether actual or only possible, whether material (physical) or immaterial. Thus a metaphysical truth is one that will be true in any possible universe under any possible conditions, based on what *being* itself is. For example, the metaphysical principle of non-contradiction, which says that a thing cannot be *both* what it is and what it is not, is necessarily true always and everywhere, for if a thing truly *is* being what it is, it cannot simultaneously be something which is *not* being that.

Modernist n. – A person tainted with Modernism. Modernism itself is a species of Liberalism. It is a habit of mind coming from denial of the knowability of objective truth, with a blind belief in both a beneficial physical and/or spiritual evolution, and a general consensus of thought and will that this evolution will tend to bring about in society. A key element of Modernism is its definition of truth. It completely denies the classic definition: *agreement of the mind with reality*, and replaces it with "Truth is life;...it evolves with man, in him and through him". (Loisy) Thus Modernist "truth" is simply whatever man wants and thinks. (cf. *Liberal*) A person can be a Modernist in reference to secular thought or religious thought. More usually, the Modernist attitude infects both.

Monarchy n. – The concentration of the political power of a State in one person, who rules for the benefit of all the subjects of a State.

Moral adj. – 1) Having to do with what acts, virtues or vices direct a person to his proper end, or away from it, and thus also questions of which acts or inclinations are good or bad, right or wrong. Natural morality considers the proper end as temporal happiness. Supernatural morality considers it to be supernatural happiness. (cf. *Happiness*) Natural and supernatural morality are complementary, not contradictory. 2) Possessed of moral virtue or character. For example: a moral act is a good act, an immoral act is a bad act; Joe is a moral (good) man; a societal or moral person has a legal moral character. 3) Something based on a very good reason or probability; a very likely truth, but not scientifically certain (e.g. a moral certainty).

Moral Hazard n. – The risk incurred by one party who takes on the risk of another, and thus becomes dependent on the other's moral behavior. That other party, feeling shielded from the risk, may act in a selfish fashion, by not taking care to avoid what risk he reasonably can. Thus the risk to the party taking it on increases unnecessarily and unjustly.

Natiogenesis n. – The process by which a nation is born or begun. From the Lat. *nátio* (nation) and *génesis* (generation, birth).

Nothingness n. – A state wherein nothing exists. This is a purely negative concept, or rather an anti-concept, for since no thing can exist without at least a space or context to contain it, and this context is precisely the 'state' wherein nothing is supposed to exist, and this state is itself a thing, nothingness is a metaphysical (i.e. absolute) impossibility. See also *metaphysical*.

Oligarchy n. – A government of the few. From the Grk. *oligos* (few), and *archein* (to rule). Cf. *aristocracy, plutocracy,,* and *polyarchy*.

Ontological adj. – Having to do with ontology. Ontology itself is the study of being as such; a synonym of metaphysics. Thus when viewing a thing from an ontological aspect we are viewing it from the standpoint of *what* it is – whether materially or immaterially – as a being. We are not considering where it came from, its purpose, or what it does.

Order n. & v. – 1) A disposition (arrangement) of equal and unequal things, giving to each one its own place. The principle of sufficient reason requires that every thing have an adequate efficient cause. Since even physical laws, by which physical things *appear* to be blindly and accidentally arranged, have an intelligent being as their only possible efficient cause, there are in fact no accidental arrangements of things. Thus the word *order* is essentially synonymous with the word *plan* (q.v.). It simply has a wider comprehension in that it includes merely "chance" arrangements. 2) As a verb, 'order' means *to arrange* or *organize*. Cf. *plan*.

Original Sin n. – See *Sin, Original*

Person n. – An individual substance of an intellectual nature. All beings possessed of intellect are persons (e.g. God, Angels, men).

>**Person, Moral** n. – Some society considered as a single person insofar as all its members have a common, mutually beneficial goal. Because a societal group has a common goal, it acquires a moral character. (cf. *Moral, 2*) It therefore can become the subject of rights and duties, with their related laws.

Personalism n. – As used in this work, personalism is synonymous with individualism, and in this sense: *Individualism is the belief that the individual is more important than the* *group, and therefore it is proper for the group, and its activities, to be subordinated to the well being of each individual member.* This ideal is not only false and harmful, but its realization is a metaphysical impossibility, for the group *consists* of individuals. A group of individuals cannot possibly be subordinated to each individual within the group unless each individual's well being is identical in all respects, which it isn't. Even if that were the case, either each individual caters to every other individual with exact equality – in which case there is no subordination – or each individual enjoys priority, but by equal turns, and not simultaneously, which in the long run again means that the group is not subordinate. (For more information on "personalism" see the works referenced in footnote 19).

Plan n. – An intentional (purposeful) arrangement of things. This is essentially a synonym of *order*, although the word *plan* more directly implies the necessity of a planner, and does not directly imply a need that the things arranged be "equal and unequal".

Pluralism n. – A social condition or ideology favoring the tolerance and/or intermingling of disparate religious, ethnic, racial or cultural groups. In this book we sometimes specify particular kinds of pluralism, by using the terms *religious pluralism, cultural pluralism*, etc.

Plutocracy n. – A government or State ruled by plutocrats (q.v.)

Plutocrat n. – A person who has authoritative power in a society mainly because of his wealth. From the Grk. *ploutos* (wealth) and *krateein* (to rule).

Politics n. – The science and practical art of administrating and managing government or public affairs. From the Grk. *polis* (city).

Polyamory n. – The practice of sexual intercourse with two or more persons, of either or both sexes, with a presumed longer-term friendship (simulating marriage) among all. A euphemism for sexual promiscuity. From the Grk. *poly* (many) and the Lat. *amor* (love).

Polyandry n. – The practice of a woman having two or more husbands at the same time. From the Grk. *poly* (many) and *andros* (man).

Polyarchy n. – A State in which there are many rulers. From the Grk. *poly* (many) and *archein* (to rule).

Polygamy n. – The practice of having two or more spouses. From the Grk. *poly* (many) and *gamos* (marriage).

Polygyny n. – The practice of a man having two or more wives. From the Grk. *poly* (many) and *gyne* (women).

Positivism, legal n. – The theory that societal authority (i.e. man himself) is alone the author of all the laws that govern man, and that a law merely needs to be posited by that authority in order to be valid, outside of any reference to any other authority whether of Nature or of God, or even of rational morality.

Potency n. – In the passive sense (as almost exclusively used in this work): 1) A capacity of perfection or of becoming something; a passive aptitude that can be rendered actual by outside influence. Example: obediential potency (see 1.8). 2) In the active sense: A power of doing something; a faculty or ability. Example: The intellect is a potency of knowing. From the Lat. *potens* (potent, powerful).

Potential n. & adj. – A more commonly used synonym of *potency* (q.v.). As an adjective: Not actual, but having the possibility to become actual.

Preternatural adj. – Outside the nature of man, but not nature (creation) as such. Thus an Angel is a natural creature, but relative to man an Angel is preternatural. From the Lat. *praeter* (beside) and *natúra* (nature). The preternatural gifts given to Adam and Eve were four: Infused knowledge (knowledge given directly by God into the intellect, without previous experience or study); Immortality of the body; Impassibility (freedom from injury and suffering); Integrity (subjection of the passions to reason). These gifts were lost to our first parents, and to all their progeny, due to Adam's first sin. The preternatural gifts then are not part of the fallen nature of mankind since.

Privilege n. – A stable concession to a person to do or have something beneficial to himself, granted through kindness (q.v.). Many privileges are earned in some degree by the merit of the persons to whom they are conceded, but they are never earned in strict justice, while rights are always due in strict justice. From the Lat. *priváta* (private) and *lex, legis* (law).

Property n. – A thing possessed by a person, and in his control, so that he can freely dispose of it.

> **Property, communal** – Property belonging to corporations or other social groups (moral persons), but not individuals. It may belong to government or not.
>
> **Property, government** – Property that belongs to a government entity, and is normally restricted to governmental use.
>
> **Property, private** – Property belonging to individuals, but also to corporations or other social/communal groups (moral persons), so long as these groups do not pertain to any level of civil government.
>
> **Property, public** – Communal property that normally may be used by the general public. Usually this is government property, but considered as owned by the people, and held in trust and managed by government.

Providence, Divine n. – The foresight of God. From the Lat. *pro* (before) and *vidére* (to see). The notion includes God's active intervention in creation, to help guide things to a good end.

Prudence n. – A virtue that inclines one to decide the best means of attaining a goal.

Pseudo-Religion n. – Any comprehensive system of beliefs that purports to give explanations of man's ultimate purpose and highest ideals, including moral values, but which does not acknowledge the existence of any God or gods, and/or pretends to make man himself a god.

Rational adj. – 1) Possessing the power to reason; able to deduce a new truth through previously known truths. 2) That which is characterized by, or a result of, a process of reasoning; reasonable.

Religion n. – Any comprehensive and organized system of beliefs, and/or a corresponding society that practices that system, centered on man's ultimate purpose, including his relationship to God or gods, and including the practice of some kind of worship of God or gods.

Republic n. – The wielding of the State's political power by a relatively large portion of the citizens, in particular by a portion of the citizenry much larger than an aristocracy, but through elected representatives, whom the people invest with the power of speaking and acting for them. From the Lat. *res* (thing, affair, business) and *publicum* (public).

Right n. – In the legal sense, a law commanding that what is owed to a person be allowed or given to him.

> **Right, absolute** n. – A law commanding that what is owed to a person be allowed or given to him, when this is necessary to fulfill his reason to exist.
>
> **Right, contingent** n. – A law commanding that what is owed to a person be allowed or given to him, when he has fulfilled on his part the associated duties.

Right, Divine n. – A law commanding that what is owed to an individual or moral person be allowed or given to him or it, this law either being conceded by God (e.g. to His Church), or possessed by God Himself.

Right, Human n. – A law commanding that what is owed to a human being be allowed or given to him, provided that he has fulfilled on his part any associated duties.

Science n. – 1) Certain knowledge through causes. 2) In the modern and falsely restricted sense, empirical knowledge; i.e. knowledge coming through sense data alone.

Secular adj. – Of or pertaining to this world or the present life; temporal; not concerned with religious values. From the Lat. *saeculum* (a generation or an age).

Sin n. – A deliberate deviation from Natural Law, Divine Law or Ecclesiastical Law (q.v.). All men having the use of reason are held to obey the Natural Law. All are held to accept and obey the Divine Law as soon as it sufficiently known, and the same is true for Ecclesiastical Law.

Sin, actual n. – The definition of actual sin is the same as that above.

Sin, capital n. – A kind of actual sin which is considered the head or source of other sins, or a category of sins. There are seven capital sins: sloth, lust, anger, pride, avarice, gluttony, and envy.

Sin, original n. – Not strictly speaking a sin, but an inclination to sin, inhering in every human being; a tendency to love oneself inordinately, in preference to God, the common good, and one's own true good, and thus to commit actual sins. This tendency is inherent in human nature as a result of the loss by our original parent, Adam, of an opposed inclination to justice which was gifted to him by God. (*Summa Theol.* I-II Q.77, a4; I-II Q.82, a1 & 3; Q.109, a3). This inclination in all humans to sin is not only a belief of Faith, but an empirically observable fact. One may call it 'flawed human nature', or anything else, but the reality will be the same as the Catholic dogma which we have expressed in this definition.

Social Charity n. – See *Charity*.

Social Justice n. – See *Justice*.

Socialism n. – Government ownership and control of the means of production, and control of the distribution of products.

Society n. – A stable union of a number of persons in fellowship and cooperation for a common purpose of benefit to all.

Solidarity n. – A will to work for the common and social good. The word is largely synonymous with social charity (q.v.), but emphasizes supporting unity of purpose and action, with individuals or smaller groups being willing to subordinate their interests to the larger society whenever possible.

Spirit n. – 1) A being having intellect and will, but no body; i.e. God or an Angel. 2) The human soul, which is the spiritual part of man's nature. 3) An attitude or intention residing in a spiritual being (e.g a "fighting spirit").

Spiritual adj. – 1) Having to do with the intellect and will. 2) In a looser sense, having to do with religion.

State n. – As used in this book, and when capitalized: A sovereign, independent nation. When not capitalized, a region having its own government, but more or less subject to a sovereign State. For example, the United States is a State containing fifty states. The word State may be taken to mean the social body living within it; that is, the people or the nation, or it may refer to the authority that rules this social body; that is, the government. Occasionally it may also mean both at the same time. An example of the latter case is our title for Chapter 3: Man And The State. This chapter deals with the relations of men with each other within the nation, *and* with the role of authority within these relations. We normally use the word 'State', by itself, only when both senses of the word are intended, unless context makes clear that we are using it in only one sense. When referring only to the people in the State, we will generally use the words 'people', 'nation', 'citizens', etc. When referring to government, we will generally use the words 'government', 'ruler(s)', 'authorities', etc., either alone or in apposition with the word 'State' (e.g. not just "State", but "State government").

Subsidiarity n. – An actionable principle of good government, which can be stated thus: A social body of a higher order should not exercise its authority in the affairs of a lower order of society, whether public or private, if that lower level is competent to deal with those affairs so as to achieve the common good.

Supernatural adj. – Above nature. Since nature includes all created things, 'supernatural' really means uncreated. Only God Himself, and things or actions directly connected to Him, are uncreated, and hence supernatural.

Theocracy n. – A form of government in which God Himself is recognized as the head. From the Grk. *theos* (God) and *krateein* (to rule).

Temperance n. – A virtue that inclines one to subordinate to reason the attraction to sense pleasure.

Totalitarian adj. – Characterized by total control, usually in reference to governments.

Tyranny n. – A one-man rule where the ruler seeks his own supposed good rather than that of those over whom he rules. By extension, any government, no matter the number of rulers, which seeks the supposed good of the rulers rather than of the ruled.

Vice n. – A habit of doing or being evil.

Virtue n. – A habit of doing or being good.

Wealth n. – In the sense normally used in this book, any temporal good possessed of exchange value.

INDEX

A
Agnostic...40, **157**
Amerio, Romano...................................24
Anabaptist............................39, 40, 61, 65
Anarchy............39, 61, 62, 65, 66, 73, **157**
Angel....................2, 3, 7, 9, 142, 163, 165
Apostolic Constitutions.......................154
Aquinas, St. Thomas....3, 4, 7-9, 14, 18-23, 28, 37, 55, 56, 59, 60, 68-70, 72, 76, 112, 116-118, 135, 137, 146-151, 155
Aristocracy...............58, 59, 69, 70, 83, **157**
Aristotle....15, 17, 35, 55-57, 60, 68, 77-79, 81, 145, 146, 154
Art.................ii, 20, 29, 107, 131, 142, **157**
Asset..121, 154
Athanasius, St..2
Augustine, St......7, 29, 33, 39, 52, 77, 138, 146
Authority..i, 13, 18, 20, 21, 27, 65-67, 145, 147, **157**

B
Bayle, Pierre..40
Bellarmine, St. Robert....33, 57, 58, 65, 67, 68, 77, 78, 83
Bentham, Jeremy.................................105
Bittle, Celestine, O.F.M. Cap..................13
Bonaparte, Napoleon........................57, 82
Boniface VIII, Pope............................32, 52
Butler, Judith..105

C
Cahill, Fr. Edward, S.J.........63, 89, 118, 155
Capital..............................62, 126, 128, **157**
Capital punishment.........12, 44, 46, 74, 86
Capitalism......................................153, **157**
Capitalism, Laissez-faire...................30, **157**
Catholic Encyclopedia, 1914......13, 46, 56, 65, 67, 69, 82, 86, 154
Cause..**157**
Cause, efficient..................12, 22, **157**, 162
Cause, final......................8, 12, 18, 76, **157**
Cause, formal..**157**
Cause, material.....................................**157**
Charity.................44, 51, 126, 133-136, **157**
Charity, social.. 31, 133, 135, 136, 154, 155, **158,** 165
Charlemagne, Emperor..........................56
Church...36, **158**
Church, domains of authority of. 34, 42-45, 48, 53
Cicero, Marcus Tullius..27, 29, 67, 72, 146, 147
Communism......36, 60-63, 65, 66, 122, **158**
Confucius...27
Connell, Francis J., C.Ss.R....................34
Constantine, Emperor...........................56
Constitution.27, 69, 73, 77, 79-81, 146, **158**
Contract, Social........................21, 67, 145
Culture.......ii, 15, 20, 21, 87, 131, 155, **158**

D
De Beauvoir, Simone.....................104, 105
De Koninck, Charles..............................14
De Vattel, Emer......................................76
De Vitoria, Francisco..............................76
Democracy...58, 59, 64, 66, 69-71, 154, **158**
Democratic Socialism.....................63, **158**
Denzinger..........................4, 20, 43, **158**
Didascalia..154
Digger movement..................................61
Dogma............................46, 50, 114, **158**
Dollfus, Englebert..................................57
Dowling, Linda....................................103
Draco of Athens.....................................81

E
Economics........................ii, 3, 125, **159**

167

Economy..................................iii, **159**

Edmunds, Sterling.......................74

Education.....14, 19, 20, 29, 44, 87, **89**, 90, 91, 94, 95, 98, 107, 131, 143, 155, 156

Edward the Confessor, King of England. 56

Eppstein, John............................76

Equality, economic....................125

Equality, gender...............88, 97, 98, 111

Essence.......................1, 3, 4, 64, **159**

Eternal......................................**159**

F

Family..18, 20, 21, 23, 28, 90, 108-112, 132, 134, **159**

Family, as fundamental unit of society....28

Fascism..............................64, 65, **159**

Feminism...........................103, **159**

Feral children............................17

Fortitude...............22, 106, 125, 140, **159**

Foucault, Michel....................104, 105

Franco, Francisco....................57, 65

Frederick II, Emperor..................57

Freedom............3, 9, 11, 60, 68, 112, **159**

G

Gender Theory.....................102-105

Good, Common...10, 13-17, 21, 22, 28-31, 33, 34, 44, 51, 54, 55, 58, 59, 61, 67, 69, 71, 74, 91, 112, 117, 123, 124, 132, 134, 135, 138, 140-143, 148, 149, **159**

Good, nature and kinds of......1-4, 8-10, 15-17, 32, 71, 125, 139-143, **159**

Government, best form of..............68-70

Government, forms of....................55-66

Government, functions of......28-30, 35, 36

Government, is of the natural order...65-67

Government, meaning of................27, **159**

Government, source of authority of......32, 33, 68

Government, stability necessary to..72, 73, 75, 77, 79

Government, who chooses form of....67-69

Government, worst form of...............71, 72

Gredt, Josephus, OSB.........................7, 8

Gregory XVI, Pope..............33, 39, 50, 51

Grotius, Hugo......................................76

Guild..............................122, 136, **160**

H

Hammurabi........................80, 85, 118

Happiness....1, 2, 4, 5, 7-14, 17, 24, 35, 36, 41, 53, 62, 105, 108, 112, 122, 125, 138, 140, **160,** 162

Henry II, Emperor.............................56

Henry VIII, King of England..................57

Hitler, Adolph.............................57, 58

Hobbes, Thomas...........................21, 67

Humanism..................36, 40, 50, 156, **160**

Hussites...61

I

Inequality, economic....................125-129

Inequality, economic: arguments from authority.................................127, 128

Inequality, economic: arguments from reason...126

Infallibility.........................13, 22, 46, 114

Intellect....3, 9, 10, 13, 15-17, 25, 116, 142, **160,** 163, 165

Irenaeus, St...................................32

Islam...37, 56

J

James I, King of England.....................58

Jantz, Gregory L.............................100

John Paul II, Pope............15, 19, 20, 30, 156

John XXIII, Pope..............................155

Justice.....iii, 22-24, 29, 35, 49, 65, 66, 120, 134, 155, **160,** 165

Justice, commutative....................132, **160**

Justice, distributive................132, 154, **160**

Justice, legal............................132, **160**

Justice, social....................31, 130-132, **160**

Justice, vs. mercy............................24, 161

Justinian, Emperor........................56, 81

K

Kindness................................24, 155, **160**

L

Law......5, 7, 8, 12, 25, 38-40, 42-46, 57, 77, 78, **160**

Law, Canon............................13, 90, **160**

Law, Constitutional...77-81, 145, 146, 158, **160**

Law, Divine....11, 12, 21, 22, 24, 44, 47-49, 51, 67, 70, 74, 119, 135, 149, **160**, 161, 165

Law, Ecclesiastical........12, 21, 22, 42, **160**, 161, 165

Law, Eternal....1, 2, 5, 7, 8, 11, 24, 25, 148, 159, **160**

Law, fundamental and immutable necessary to government...................72, 73

Law, Human.......20, 22, 24, 25, 35, 47, 73, 121, 132, 133, 145, 148, **160**

Law, Human: doubt of conformity to Church law...46

Law, International............................74-76

Law, Moral....20, 38, 39, 43, 46, 49, 90, 91, 120, 135, **160**

Law, Natural...ii, 8, 9, 11, 12, 14, 16-18, 20-24, 48-51, 61, 63, 66, 68, 74, 75, 87, 95, 119, 121, 133, 135, 149, 154, **161**, 165

Law, of Church above that of State...42-45, 93, 94

Law, of Nations.....68, 73-76, 87, 118, 121, **161**

Law, Political....................17, 21, 22, 76, **161**

Law, Positive.............22, 74, 148, 160, **161**

Law, Supernatural...10, 12, 14, 19-21, 119, 121, 133, **161**

Lenin (Ulyanov), Vladimir................58, 62

Leo XIII, Pope..17, 30-34, 39, 41-44, 47-50, 52, 59, 60, 62, 69, 84, 89, 91, 109, 112, 119, 121, 127, 128, 134, 155

Liberal. 25, 50, 51, 67, 79, 84, 104, 156, **161**

Lisska, Anthony..23

Locke, John..40

Louis IX, King of France........................56

Luther, Martin...39

M

Maritain, Jacques....................................22

Marriage. 20, 23, 27, 28, 50, 60, 76, 88, 95, 110, 111, 153, **161**, 163

Marriage, and education of children...89-91

Marriage, arguments of reason for..........87

Marriage, characteristics of........87, 88, 109

Marriage, equality in.....................110, 111

Marriage, history of.........................85-87

Marriage, origin of..................................85

Marriage, right of the Church to govern 44, 92-94

Marriage, role of the State in.............93-95

Marriage, sacramental nature of.......88, 89

Marx, Karl............................61, 62, 64, 104

Matrimony...................88, 89, 92, 93, **161**

McGovern, Arthur, S.J...........................155

McHugh, J. & Callan, C...........................23

Mercy..24, 161

Metaphysical..**161**

Modernist.............................20, 104, **161**

Monarchy..56-58, 64, 67, 69-72, 79, 82, **162**

Moral......iii, 4, 9, 12, 13, 15, 16, 19-22, 29, 31, 34, 36-39, 42, 44, 46, 65, 89, 90, 95, 98, 104, 115, 126, 133-135, 140, 142, 145, 149, 156, 160, **162**, 164

Moral Hazard........................153, 154, **162**

Moreno, Gabriel Garcia-.........................57

Moses................................1, 66, 70, 77, 80

Mussolini, Benito...............................57, 58

N

Natiogenesis...................................21, **162**

Nothingness......................................1, **162**

169

O

Obedience/Disobedience, civil.......145-152

Oligarchy..58, **162**

Ontological.................................13, 134, **162**

Order...2-4, 7, 8, 12, 13, 15, 17, 18, 22, 29, 30, 46, 47, 53, 66, 67, 70, 77, 112, 149, **162**

P

Paul, St....11, 19, 20, 53, 88, 111, 112, 125, 137, 154

Person...**162**

Person, Moral........115, 122, 130, 131, 133-136, **162**, 164, 165

Personalism.....................................14, **162**

Peter, St............................20, 109, 135, 150

Pius IX, Pope........33, 38, 39, 41, 42, 51, 93

Pius X, Pope..............................32, 34, 39

Pius XI, Pope.. iii, 19, 28, 30, 31, 39, 43, 54, 62-64, 88-90, 110-112, 119, 121, 128, 132, 134, 137, 155

Plan..................2, 7-11, 108, 111, 140, **163**

Plato..55, 145

Pluralism.................131, 136, 155, 156, **163**

Plutocracy.....................58, 62, 71, 72, **163**

Plutocrat..**163**

Politics......................................ii, 34, 48, **163**

Polyamory.......................................87, **163**

Polyandry.....................................86, 87, **163**

Polyarchy..71, **163**

Polygamy..86, **163**

Polygyny.....................................86, 87, **163**

Positivism, legal............................75, **163**

Potency...**163**

Potency, obediential...........................3, 4

Potential.........................17, 126, 141, **163**

Preternatural..............................4, 10, **163**

Privilege.................25, 34, 59, 76, 130, **164**

Property.......61, 63, 94, 103, 114-117, 121, 124, 125, 128, 129, 137, **164**

Property, communal.....115, 117, 118, 121, 122, **164**

Property, government............116, 124, **164**

Property, private....61, 63, 65, 76, 114-116, 126, **164**

Property, private: arguments for....116-121

Property, private: right to is not absolute
....122-124

Property, public............................115, **164**

Providence, Divine......................1, 90, **164**

Prudence........19, 22, 42, 53, 136, 151, **164**

Pseudo-Religion........36, 37, 40, 50, 51, 73, 156, **164**

R

Rational.....3, 10, 14, 16-18, 20, 22, 74, 75, 97, 110, 116, 121, 157, 159, 163, **164**

Religion.....ii, 21, 29, 34, 36-39, 43, 73, 90, **164**

Religion, freedom of..........................51-53

Religion, separation from State..........37-40

Religion, union with State...........39, 41, 42

Republic..............................55, 59, 82, **164**

Right........23-25, 28, 32, 46, 49, 60, 90, 94, 134, **164**

Right, absolute..........................20, 24, **164**

Right, contingent....20, 24, 47-51, 58, 122, 123, 134, 136, 137, **164**

Right, Divine. .24, 41, 43-45, 47, 58, 75, 89-93, 95, **165**

Right, Human......20, 23-25, 30, 44, 53, 61, 63, 65, 76, 87, 88, 91, 95, 97, 109-111, 117, 119, 121, 122, 131, 155, 156, **165**

Rights, of society................................134

Roe vs. Wade...38

Rousseau, Jean-Jacques...............13, 21, 67

S

Salazar, Antonio....................................57

Science....................98, 106, 107, 131, **165**

Scott, James Brown...............................76

Secular..**165**

Senior, John...24

Sin........5, 18, 25, 42, 52, 119, 147, 151, **165**

Sin, actual........23, 25, 42, 49, 51, 102, 121, 137, 148, 149, 151, **165**

Sin, capital................16, 117, 118, 137, **165**

Sin, original.....iii, 4, 16, 17, 21, 55, 61, 62, 65, 72, 87, 117, 118, 125, 130, 157, 158, 161, 164, **165**

Slave, slavery...........................53, 102, 111

Socialism....................62, 63, 122, 128, **165**

Society.. ii, 13, 14, 18, 22, 28, 30-32, 35, 36, 40, 62, 65, 75, 90, 97, 105, 115, 130, 132, 134, **165**

Society, as a moral person......115, 132, 134

Society, benefits of to persons. 15, 16, 130, 131, 134

Society, duties of persons to.......31, 34, 72, 132, 135-137

Society, duties of to persons....66, 91, 129, 135, 136

Society, first level of.....18, 20, 28, 88, 108, 142

Society, human law in............13, 18, 20, 21

Society, male and female roles in. .97, 103, 104, 106-113

Society, mutual duties of members in. .130-132, 134-136

Society, Natural Law in...............17, 23, 24

Society, necessity of authority in.....13, 18, 20, 21, 27, 48, 61, 67, 79, 88, 158

Society, necessity of common goal in....13, 31, 37, 39, 49-51, 60, 75

Society, origin of................................17, 18

Society, purpose of...........................14, 16

Society, second level of. .20, 21, 27, 28, 35, 90, 142

Society, third level of............31, 32, 35, 53

Socrates..145

Solidarity......31, 42, 53, 124, 135, 160, **165**

Solon of Athens......................................81

Speech, freedom of.................40, 45, 49-51

Speech, importance of.................13, 14, 18

Spirit...**165**

Spiritual.. 1-3, 15, 28, 32, 36, 42, 43, 45, 51, 91, 116, 122, 126, 137-143, 153, 161, **165**

State..**165**

State, domains of authority of......47-49, 53

Stirling-Taylor, G.R................................63

Suárez, Francisco, S.J..................68, 76, 81

Subsidiarity....30, 31, 42, 53, 60, 121, 122, 124, 135, 136, 154, 160, **166**

Supernatural......4, 5, 10-13, 16, 17, 29, 36, 91, 95, 131, 133, 143, 158, 161, 162, **166**

T

Taparelli, Aloysius, S.J............................21

Taxes..........................49, 94, 123, 124, 136

Temperance............................22, 125, **166**

Theocracy.....................37, 55, 56, 82, **166**

Theodosius II, Emperor..........................81

Theodosius, Emperor.............................56

Totalitarian.........................15, 60, 64, **166**

Trent, Council of.........................88, 92, 93

Tyranny........57-59, 63, 71, 72, 145-150, **166**

Tytler, Alexander Fraser.........................64

V

Vice................................17, 137, 162, **166**

Vincent of Lerins, St...............................46

Virtue....17, 22, 29, 35, 42, 58, 68, 70, 118, 125-127, 132, 133, 139, 143, 149, 157, 158, 160, 162, **166**

Voltaire...40

Voting...............25, 34, 59, 63, 70, 103, 158

W

Waldstein, Edmund, O. Cist...................14

Wealth......63, 125, 128, 129, 136, 137, 157, **166**

Welfare State................................153, 154

Z

Zandiks..61

NOTES

NOTES

www.ingramcontent.com/pod-product-compliance
Lightning Source LLC
Chambersburg PA
CBHW080518030426
42337CB00023B/4561